THE SCHILLER FILE

Kupferne hohle Halbkugel an der Wand [copper hollow hemisphere on the wall]

Elektrische Flammercheinung [appearance of an electric flame]

[flat triangle]
flaches Dreieck

Antimon [antimony]

nach aufwärts gebogene Spitze aus radiumhaltig erz stoff
[upward curved spike consisting of radium ore material]

Halbkugel
[hemisphere]

Glasröhren-spirale [glass tubes - spiral]

[Cu]

[Cu]

Nickel
Hohlkugel
[nickel
hollow sphere]

Antimon
halbkugel
[antimony
hemisphere]

Dünne
Blättchen
[thin
leaves]

noch
unbekanntes
Metall
[as yet
unknown
metal]

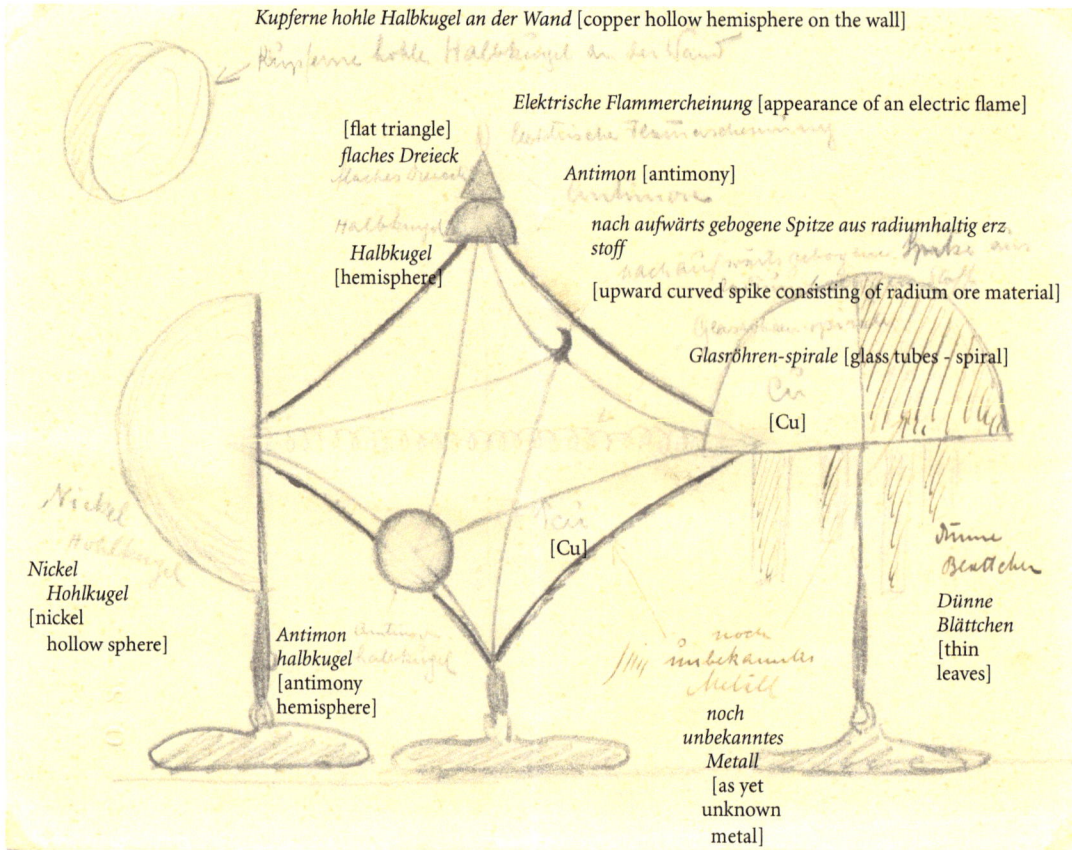

Cover diagram: Sketch of the Strader apparatus by Dr. Oskar Schmiedel, Munich circa 1912.

THE SCHILLER FILE

Paul Eugen Schiller

SUPPLEMENTS TO

THE COLLECTED WORKS OF RUDOLF STEINER

SCIENTIFIC RESEARCH SUGGESTED BY DR. RUDOLF STEINER ON

ELECTRICITY · TERRESTRIAL MAGNETISM · RADIO · CONDUCTION OF HEAT ·
SOUND-SENSITIVE FLAMES · ETHERIC FORMATIVE FORCES ·THE FOUR ETHERS ·
RESONANT OSCILLATION · REFINEMENT OF PEAT FIBRES · AND MORE

Translated by Henry Goulden

2010
SteinerBooks

2010

Published by SteinerBooks

610 Main Street, Great Barrington, MA 01230

www.steinerbooks.org

First published in German under the title *Beiträge zur Rudolf Steiner Gesamtausgabe Veröffentlichungen aus dem Archiv der Rudolf Steiner-Nachlassverwaltung* in Dornach, Switzerland. Issue Nr. 122, Summer 2000. First English edition published in 2007 by Henry Goulden Books, The Chapel, Delabole, Cornwall, U.K..

English translation © 2007 Henry Goulden Books

Library of Congress Cataloging-in-Publication data is available.

ISBN 978-88010-720-4

Printed in the United States

Contents

Preface

It has been a satisfying, although sometimes arduous task, to present the so-called 'Schiller File' in English. I am grateful for the financial help received from various quarters towards the production of the British edition of the Schiller File. Other acknowledgements are due as follows: special thanks for the expertise and professionalism provided by Dr. Desmond J. Cumberland and to Joffa Applegate for assistance in the initial setting up of the text of the Schiller File.

Concerning the work itself, I believe, no further comment is necessary: the introductions by Walter Kugler and Johannes Kühl which follow are fully adequate for this edition.

The editor of the Beiträge [Supplements] Nr. 122 originally intended to include an article by Christoph Podak entitled '*Zur Geschichte und Soziologie der anthroposophischen Forschungsinstitute in den 20er Jahren* [Towards a History and Sociology of the Anthroposophical Research Institutes in the 1920s],' but it was not included. Instead, this article first appeared in the July/August 1999 issue of the monthly journal '*Der Europäer* [The European].' It was subsequently translated into English and published in the September 1999 issue of '*Archetype*.' As this article complements the contents of the 'Schiller File' it seems appropriate that it should now be included in this edition and hence it is reprinted in the Appendix courtesy of its editor Dr. David J. Heaf.

The time is certainly ripe for fresh, imaginative research into physics, biology, geology, astronomy, and so forth. The seeds are to be found in the pages that follow—may they germinate and flourish through the work of those who study the 'Schiller File.'

Henry Goulden
2007

"*Die Sinne trügen nicht, aber das Urteil trügt.*

[The senses do not lie; it is the judgement that deceives.]"*

From: '*Sprüche in Prosa* [Amphorisms in Prose],' S. 349 in J. W. Goethe, '*Naturwissenschaftliche Schriften* [Natural Scientific Writings], GA 1e, Fünfter Band [Volume 5] (1897) (Zweite Abteilung des vierten Bandes [Part Two of the Fourth Volume]), Rudolf Steiner Verlag, Dornach/Schweiz [Switzerland], 3. Auflage [3rd Edition] Dornach 1975; 4. Auflage (Sonderausgabe) [4th edition (special edition)] Dornach 1982.

"If Anthroposophy were fanatical, if Anthroposophy were ascetic and austere, there would naturally follow a thundering against electricity. That would obviously be nonsense, for only a worldview that did not reckon with reality would speak in this way. They could say: Oh, that is Ahrimanic! Keep away from it!—One can actually only do that in the abstract. For when one has arranged just such a sectarian gathering and bargained for protection against Ahriman, then one still goes down the stairs and gets into an electric tram. So that this entire ranting against Ahriman, however holy it may sound, is—forgive the trivial expression—absolute rubbish. One therefore cannot close one's eyes to the fact that one must live with Ahriman. Only one must live with him in the right way; one must not allow oneself to be overcome by him."

RUDOLF STEINER

Lecture XII of January 28, 1923,* Dornach,
in cycle of 12 lectures entitled: '*Lebendiges Naturerkennen. Intellektueller Sündenfall und spirituelle Sündenerhebung* [A Living Knowledge of Nature. The Intellectual Fall of the Human Being into Sin and its Overcoming by the Spirit]'
GA** 220, 1982, S.*** 192f

---

* An Extract from this lecture entitled 'Concerning Electricity' is available as typescript translation Index No. N.S.L. 236 Copy B from: The Library, Rudolf Steiner House, London. See page 4 of typescript; The full lecture is available as typescript translation Index No. N.S.L. 236 Copy C. See pages 11-12 of typescript.

** Note: Rudolf Steiner's collected edition [*Gesamtausgabe* (GA)] are referred to by the GA numbers under which they were published by Rudolf Steiner Verlag, Dornach, Switzerland.

*** Where S. for *Seite(n)* [page(s)] is shown after a reference it indicates that the item is published only in German. Whereas where p. or pp. for page(s) is shown after a reference it indicates that the item is published in English.

About This Issue

"*Ever forwards!*," cried Rudolf Steiner to the students at the close of his lecture to the *Technischen Hochschule* [Technical High School] in Stuttgart on the 17th of June 1920 (GA 73a, 2005, S. 393), adopting the words he himself had heard from a Viennese professor in his student days. The word "*forwards*" is the result of a sentiment which Rudolf Steiner quotes as follows: "*Fellow students, I close with this, that those who sincerely feel for the development of mankind, and for what shall arise out of science and technology, can only say: ever forwards!*" (see also *Beiträge* [Supplements] No. 107, Michaeli [Michaelmas] 1991.)

A close connection with Natural Science permeates the entire life of Rudolf Steiner. For all that he never had any illusions about the results, but always remained a keen and sensitive observer and interpreter, as can be seen for example in the lecture cycle '*Lebendiges Naturerkennen. Intellektueller Sündenfall und spirituelle Sündenerhebung* [A Living Knowledge of Nature. The Intellectual Fall of the Human Being into Sin and its Overcoming by the Spirit]' (GA 220, 1982). And there, towards the end (Lecture XI), he provides the basis for an '*Anthroposophical realism.*' *

The descriptions in this issue lead towards starting points of a research impulse that have set a great deal in motion, although today much is already forgotten. At the beginning of the 1920s, there was much talk of new departures and the times seemed favourable for the research instigated by Rudolf Steiner: "*If our work continues in the way as it has done up to now in our research institute, then we will perhaps in 50 or 75 years come to that which actually must happen: that many details unite in a whole.*" And in the same breath he added the words spoken at 'The Christmas Conference' of 1923: "*If we were in the situation of creating the necessary institutions with the proper apparatus and co-workers…we should achieve in five or ten years what would perhaps take 50 or 75 years. We would need nothing else for this work than some 50 to 75 million [Swiss] francs.*" (GA 260, 1990, pp. 208-209.)

The processing of the tasks and suggestions of Rudolf Steiner for natural scientific research began many years ago in the Archives of the *Rudolf Steiner-Nachlassverwaltung* [Administration of the Estate of Rudolf Steiner]. The first results concerning 'bending of the colour spectrum' as well as the 'Strader Apparatus' were published in the *Beiträge* [Supplements] Nos. 95/96 (double issue), Ostern [Easter] 1987 and 107, Michaeli [Michaelmas] 1991 respectively. The work for this issue took the form of numerous inquiries into the established research institute of Rudolf Steiner's lifetime. Here, Christoph Podak of Basel has carried out pioneering work. In the course of this work it became ever clearer that the *history* of this institute required a still more fundamental approach than this issue can give, on account of the quantity of the material and the even greater number of questions arising. Nevertheless, may he be heartily thanked for his great contribution, as well as all those who took part in the issue: the late Dr. Georg Unger, for many years leader of the Mathematical-Astronomical Section at the Goetheanum, then Johannes Kühl, leader

---

* English translation of this lecture by Dr. Rudolf Steiner, held at Dornach on the 27th January, 1923 entitled 'Realism and Nominalism,' GA 220, Anthroposophic News Sheet, Dornach, Switzerland, 2nd Year, Supplement No. 3, (1934), pp. 11-14. See page 13. Typescript translation Index No. N.S.L. 134 in The Library, Rudolf Steiner House, London.

of the Natural Science Section, and above all Stephan Clerc, until recently a scientist at the *Paul Scherrer-Institut der Eidgenössische Technische Hochschule Zürich (ETH-Zürich)* [Paul Scherrer Institute of the Swiss Federal Institute of Technology Zürich], who made the attempt to provide explanations for this issue with the appropriate documents.

Walter Kugler

The Publishing of 'The Schiller File'

Anthroposophy has manifold roots in Natural Science: Rudolf Steiner never tired of stating that the development of the scientific consciousness had given men the possibility of freedom: that the way to recognition of the spiritual world rests on the natural scientific attitude and that the certainty of this knowledge is comparable to the certainty found in mathematics and Natural Science. Indeed he described at the end of his life how definite results of spiritual-scientific research, as for example in *An Outline of Esoteric Science* (GA 13, 1997),* where the evolution of Earth and the human being is described, which had been arrived at by a penetrating treatment of the results of Natural Science: *"So today Natural Science is in fact the basis for perceiving and beholding."* (01.13.1924, GA 233a, 1996, p. 340.)

On the other hand there are numerous suggestions for Natural Science coming out of Anthroposophy. These begin with the description of the scientific way of knowledge implied in Goethe's natural scientific methods, then developed in the work on a theory of the senses and in many indications scattered in lectures and books, and finally in the years after the Great War, the various trends would culminate in the three natural scientific courses, which dealt with concrete scientific branches, then the courses and the work for doctors, finally in the Agricultural Course. It goes for all these descriptions that the Natural Science impulses arising from Anthroposophy can be made fruitful for certain professions. In conclusion there is a whole series of lecture cycles more to do with technique, in which the path of anthroposophical schooling based on Natural Science is described.

Rudolf Steiner was greatly concerned that new experiments should also be made on account of the new viewpoints and educational possibilities arising from these courses. For this reason in 1920 a special institute was founded with departments for physics and biology in Stuttgart, and financed from the scanty means of the joint-stock company of *Der Kommende Tag* [The Coming Day]. The tasks of this institute were described *inter alia* by Rudolf Steiner on the 16th of January 1921, as follows: *"What we lack is not the empirical material, but the gathering together of the possibilities, that are at the same time possibilities of explaining the one phenomenon through the other phenomenon. Therefore, in our research institute we shall not be doing experiments in the sense of the old experimental methods anymore. For there really is an excess of empirical material available…"* (GA 323, Lecture XVI.) From various remarks to the co-workers at that time (such as Ernst Lehrs and Lilly Kolisko), it can be clearly seen how important this work was to him. Through the increasingly difficult financial situation brought about by inflation, the institute had to be closed. In 1926, on the initiative of Guenther Wachsmuth, the leader of the Natural Science Section at the Goetheanum, the major part of the material was brought by Paul Eugen Schiller to Dornach. There he set up a simple Physics Laboratory in the *Heizhaus* [boiler house]. Dr. Schiller worked there for the next few years above all on Rudolf Steiner's indications about the 'sensitive flame.' Other suggestions were also taken up but the experiments mostly did not produce the expected results.

---

* This book is available for download in pdf format from:
http://steinerbooks.org/research/archive/outline_of_esoteric_science/outline_of_esoteric_science.pdf.

In this issue as far as they could be obtained, the records of the conversations which participating scientists had with Rudolf Steiner are published for the first time. Dr. P. E. Schiller himself had worked in the Stuttgart laboratory as a young man and could later carry on in Dornach, and in the 1950s wrote about the co-workers he had known, and collected all the accessible notes containing the suggestions of Rudolf Steiner. In this way, 'The Schiller File' came into existence.

As personal notes the texts are very aphoristic. Often it is not clear what Rudolf Steiner had meant. Evidently the working scientists at the institute were also not clear. Therefore, it would be dishonest to attribute apparent absurdities to Rudolf Steiner. It must be left to the judgment of the individual which suggestions he finds meaningful, in order perhaps to work further on them.

It was because of this difficult situation with regards to the texts that for a long time publication was not considered. Neither the authors nor Dr. Schiller were prepared to do that. Copies of the file were originally given to interested anthroposophically working scientists, and today its publication as an historical document would seem to be appropriate.

Stephan Clerc is to be thanked that he has taken so much trouble in preparing the text in association with the work of Rudolf Steiner, adding further documents and working out of the historical context. Also the publisher of *Rudolf Steiner-Nachlassverwaltung* [Administration of the Estate of Rudolf Steiner] and Walter Kugler must be thanked for their help so that in this way a thoroughly documented volume can appear.

The Natural Science Section sends this work out with its best wishes. Since the institute of that time, until today, hardly any fruitful work has appeared, with the exception of that of Lilly Kolisko, based on Goethean Natural Science and the instigations in method of Rudolf Steiner in the 1920s. Rudolf Steiner has deplored this more than once, for example in conversation with Dr. Fritz Kauffungen in St. Gallen on 12th April 1923: "…*I am having experiments done in Stuttgart—sadly the people there are not progressing fast enough…*" (GA 291a, 1990, S. 74.) Much must be seen as unfulfilled tasks. Ernst Lehrs described movingly how he could not work on the task given him, although he thought about it daily. Then he writes of a meeting with Rudolf Steiner: "*As we…brought up the question of a friend concerning the subject for his examination work, Rudolf Steiner sharply refused. Again and again he has agreed and then mostly it happens that nothing is really taken in hand. He has heard enough of dealing with such unreasonable requests. Then my conscience pricked me. I said that I was in a similar situation. To his question as to how this was, I explained what was preventing me from taking up the proposed task. The school leaves me no time for it* (Dr. Lehrs was a teacher in the Waldorf School—J. K.). *At this, with his eyes half shut, as if to himself, 'yes, yes, the school.' And looking at me with friendly warmth, 'but you are always thinking about it, and that is good.'*" ('*Gelebte Erwartung* [A Life of Inner Expectancy]', Stuttgart 1979, S. 229f.)

It seems good from time-to-time to measure one's own work and problems against that which Rudolf Steiner instigated as tasks for research. It seems also that without the teacher Rudolf Steiner at one's side the way to the questions must first be found independently that can lead to experimental work.

Johannes Kühl

Suggestions and the Setting Up of Tasks
for Natural Scientific Research
Given by Rudolf Steiner

The Schiller File

Paul Eugen Schiller, editor

Folio 1

Preliminary remarks

For the field of Natural Science Rudolf Steiner has given a large number of guidelines and practical advice. He has also, mostly on inquiry, set up concrete tasks for experimental research.

Much is to be found in the lectures of Rudolf Steiner. A greater part of the indications were given in conversations with personalities having a scientific interest. In the following pages, as many indications as possible are assembled and the undertakings of scientists made accessible.

This can therefore only happen with the supposition that this collection is treated confidentially, and only to be used as working material by the reader himself. Passing on such information to other people is only permitted after previous consultation with the management of the Natural Science Section. Care should be taken that in the case of death the compilation should be returned to the Natural Science Section.

It may be observed that the majority of the following texts deal not with verbatim records but notes, which were made by people of conversations with Rudolf Steiner, very often a long time later. Because of this all kinds of uncertainties and errors arise.

Finally, pages are added which belong here but have already been published and are contained in journals or books.

Should further indications and tasks of Rudolf Steiner become known, it is requested that these be offered so that continuing pages can be added to form a second collection.

Paul Eugen Schiller

Folio 2 a-d

What follows comes from the '*Akten des Stuttgarter Forschungsinstitutes* [records of the research institute in Stuttgart].' The first part, according to Dr. Rudolf E. Maier, is the reproduction of sketches by Rudolf Steiner. The second part contains notes that Dr. Maier made after the conversations. Unfortunately, the original sketches by Rudolf Steiner have not been found.

I. The notes of Dr. Rudolf Steiner

1) The four ethers —
Alum
Iodine solution in carbon disulphide
Æsculin solution
[See also the Notes from Rudolf Steiner on page 38 and the related anecdotal comments at the end of Folio 9 a-c on page 17, Tr.]

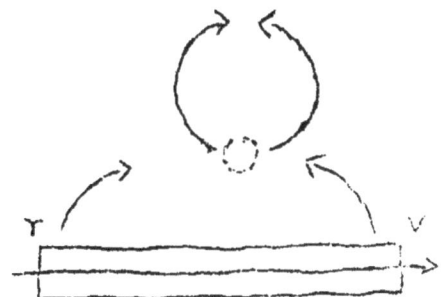

$r = rot$ [red] $v = violett$ [violet]

2) In every warmth reaction two streams can be detected: a terrestrial and an extra-terrestrial.
   Chemical reactions.
   Silver iodide: light speeds up the decomposition, warmth impedes the decomposition.
   Studies should be observed by day and night.

3) The small freely moving thin metal leaves under the influence of various strongly magnetic metal spheres—one metal with different strengths, different metals with equal magnetisation.

4) Plant ashes—fresh.
   Mineralised ashes.

5) Graphite and coal. Graphite is coal but altered so that cosmic forces have carried on the work of the earthly forces.

6) Investigate poisonous and non-poisonous plant substances and compare their forces. Especially their structural forces.

II. Notes of Dr. Maier

Tuesday, the 20th of April 1920.
After discussion with Dr. Steiner (from 12:00 until 12:45pm) about the research institute, he wrote notes on two sheets, which he gave me. The tasks are listed below under 1) to 6).

1):
Concerning the discovery of the four ethers by physical means.
   This concerned the closing of the spectrum into a circle by means of magnetic force—the red [*rot*] (*r*) and violet [*violett*] (*v*) ends together produce the colour of peach-blossom [*Pfirsichblüt*]. [See the diagram on the bottom right hand corner of the previous page, Tr.] I asked, where should the magnetic force be applied, at the light source, at the prism, or elsewhere; the greatest intensity of magnetic force would occur when the air space between the pole pieces is small. Thus for the most effective working the magnetic force close to the gap should be brought into activity.
   Dr. Steiner: *that would certainly be the case; perhaps the high intensity of magnetism could be obtained by the fast revolution of a dynamo or generator.*
   I ask whether he meant a three-phase generator, I was thinking particularly of the rotating magnetic field between the pole pieces.
   Dr. Steiner: *Yes, the best would be two generators.* (I failed to ask more closely how he thought of the arrangement with the generators.)
   Reagents for the observation of the nature of peach-blossom (life-ether).

2):

In every reaction with warmth, distinguish between the two kinds of warmth, fine and coarse; the former in the radiation and conduction of heat, which is related in the soul-realm to light, the latter, coarser, to the extra-terrestrial and terrestrial.

Study silver iodide decomposition by previous exposure to light and warmth—the rays cause this process of decomposition, which is speeded up by light, but hindered by warmth. These experiments to be set up during the night as well as the day, and the results compared.

I'm quite sure, Dr. Steiner added, at night when the darkened Earth comes between the Sun and the experimental process, then different results will appear.

3):

The small metal leaves are to be so suspended that they are as free as possible to adapt to the formative forces [*Gestaltkräfte*] of the magnetic forces.

Magnetised metal spheres. In what way can, e.g., a copper sphere be magnetised? When the two iron ends of an electro-magnet are fused there, then the magnetic forces will be affected. (Dr. Maier: *Modified?* Rudolf Steiner: *Yes.*) Outside the arrangement of the sphere in the plane, later the same thing in a further dimension (Space).

4):

Ashes from freshly incinerated plants can be compared physically to mineralised ashes (coal). The physical investigation will reveal essential differences, the chemical hardly any. I questioned Dr. Steiner on this: for example *"by spreading out the ashes,"* he meant on a screen, paper or something similar.

5):

Rudolf Steiner said further…*cosmic forces have completely won the upper hand over the earthly in the diamond.*

6):

Method of investigating poisonous and non-poisonous plant substances. Above all, mixtures are added (to weak solutions) out of which one allows crystals to be formed. The plant substances with respect to the mixtures will call forth distinct modifications in the crystals. The transition from mineral formative force of crystallisation to plant formative force can be seen.

Industrial use: plant pigments. The addition of poison is so small that it is not harmful. With further coatings with solutions of poisonous and non-poisonous plant substances of peach-blossom: changes will appear, namely beginning of life-activities.

Folio 3

The 20th of October 1920, Stuttgart. At a meeting of the 'College of Teachers' Werner Rosenthal asked Rudolf Steiner what tasks could be taken up within the framework of the College of Teachers. Below are reproduced the tasks set by Rudolf Steiner as they were subsequently written down.

Architecture: Research how the gothic style was influenced by the characteristics of the different guilds.

Chemistry: Examine the true difference between organic and inorganic compounds; especially cyanide compounds, which can be seen as transitional.

Construction of Machines: Verification of the laws of oscillation in machine construction, especially the transformation of small waves into large (detectable by flames).

Speech: It should be pointed out that in the speech of earlier times spirit and matter were not separated. As an example of this we still have: *"Ich brenne dem Tag die Augen aus* [To burn out the day's eyes]."*

Rudolf Steiner continued with the idea that everything rests on polarity in the inorganic world. Anthroposophy would carry the spirit-self into science (Chemistry for example). (See also the lecture of 12.28.1914, GA 275, 2003, pp. 65-91.)

Folio 4 a-c

Dr. Ehrenfried E. Pfeiffer reported that he had a series of conversations with Rudolf Steiner about experimental work in which he had taken part.

Rudolf Steiner was asked whether etheric formative forces [*Bildekräfte*] could be made available in the laboratory and also for technical purposes. This question arose from his lectures in which the Keely Motor and the future use of oscillations had been referred (e.g. 11.25.1917, GA 178, 2004, p. 178). Rudolf Steiner had answered: *"In the first place it is necessary to find a reagent for the etheric formative forces. One must be sure that the formative forces are active in any research arrangements. This could happen with phenomenon of warmth and light, and even with cultures of bacteria too, that is, living substances. (Dr. Pfeiffer suggested that Paramecium could also be used as a test medium.) Furthermore, for example, life-ether could be obtained so that animals [bacteria, etc., Tr.] brought into the evacuated vessel would be killed. The life-ether would then be extracted with ethyl alcohol."*

---

* The idiomatic expression *"Dem Tag die Augen ausbrennen"* is an Austrian/Viennese expression which means literally *"To burn out the day's eyes."* It is an expression for *"To leave the lights on in a room that you have left or during the hours of daylight,"* i.e. you're wasting electricity. Tr.

Rudolf Steiner referred to the book by Râma Prasâd: 'Nature's Finer Forces.' There are seven kinds of ether mentioned. Today, so said Rudolf Steiner, information about the first four kinds of ether only may be given because the premature knowledge and misuse of the three others could lead to the greatest catastrophes.

Rudolf Steiner recommended the study of resonance and wave motion (oscillation); likewise the influence of human rhythms on acoustic and magnetic phenomena. The transformation of delicate pulsations into larger waves. This means, above all, that substances must be found which react very sensitively. Here copper came into consideration.

Human vibrations could also be measured; for example by using a fine copper strip in an evacuated tube (Geissler tube) and the influence of the light phenomena observed (or measured with an electroscope). A telephone receiver could also be used. There lies another possibility here, to set up a connection between the human tongue and a flame (via a wire or thread) and observe the changes.

In connection with the above, Dr. Pfeiffer had set up an experiment and observed that the approach (not touching) of a discharge tube to various parts of the human body produced colour changes and shifts in the dark regions. When an evacuated glass globe was brought near the human body he noticed light phenomena too. These light phenomena are quite different for different parts of the body. Dr. Pfeiffer told Rudolf Steiner about all this; Rudolf Steiner said that the observed changes in the discharge tube could be traced in the first place to the influence of the astral body, that is to say not to etheric occurrences. However, he ruled out the course of the experiments up to that moment because the time was not yet ripe for the etheric forces to become operative. Dr. Pfeiffer asked: When would the time come? Dr. Steiner replied: when the threefold social order and Waldorf School education were realised and humanity had another moral constitution. Until then, these studies should be carried out in the greatest privacy and secrecy.

Finally Dr. Steiner mentioned that electromagnetic experiments would succeed better in America because greater concentrations of magnetic forces exist there.

In a further indication Rudolf Steiner suggested research into the reaction of the human being with a motionless burning flame (see Folio 10). One could also observe that when someone speaks the etheric body of the listener mimes the vibrations of the speech of the speaker. If one makes a eurythmical movement, the etheric body of the other mimes this movement in resonance. (In this connection see the lecture of 02.20.1917, GA 175, 1996, pp. 40, 42.) One must now investigate how far, for example, an 'I'-movement can be transmitted to a machine by means of resonance so that a lever arm, for example, of this machine mimes the 'I'-movement.

The Keely Motor was mentioned. Mr. Keely could not realise his assertions because his invention would have been exploited for egoistical purposes (war). Only certain people could set the Keely Motor in motion, and also many of them only when Mr. Keely touched them on the shoulder. With these experiments the moral side of humankind definitely comes into question. Only persons with an altruistic morality could and should serve such etheric oscillatory machines, otherwise great destructive mischief occurs.

In the Tibetan Mysteries a machine was constructed for demonstration purposes, not for technical use, that was so finely tuned to the movement of the Moon that it copied it. That is it moved according to the Moon rhythms.

One should also study changes in the blood, for example research the difference in camel and llama blood compared with dog and rabbit blood. One could easily get llama and camel blood from the zoological gardens. The speed of the pulse depends on bodily size. You measure from the ground to the coccyx. The greater the distance, the slower the pulse. The horse, with 40, is slow, the rabbit with 140 very fast. The human being with 80 stands in the middle, the height being measured from the ground to the coccyx, and so for all four-legged beasts.

All these experiments will only succeed if the laboratory is made into an altar. Only when this requirement is met may one do experiments whereby the inner nature of the human being becomes outwardly effective; otherwise only greater mischief will be wrought.

Folio 5 a-b

Dr. G. Wachsmuth in his book, 'The Life and Work of Rudolf Steiner' (2nd ed. 1955, pp. 421ff and 470ff), mentions many of the conversations reproduced in the previous folio.

Here it was specially noted what Rudolf Steiner said about the Keely Motor, that this only functioned when two exceptional conditions were existing: the particular disposition of Mr. Keely's etheric body, and the special Earth forces of the American continent.

With reference to apparatus which were built in Tibetan mystery centres, Rudolf Steiner said to Dr. Wachsmuth, that they could carry out movements similar to eurythmy (etheric larynx). This was unsuited to today. Indeed it could be harmful.

Rudolf Steiner warned expressly about the book by Râma Prasâd. It includes examples, which could be dangerous for modern humanity.

In answer to a question from Dr. Wachsmuth as to whether a new way of working with oscillations from the living could be achieved for example by transposing the human pulse-rhythm into greater oscillations, Rudolf Steiner replied: *do you now already want to hammer the astral vibrations of man into the cosmos out there?* (He emphasised especially the words *"now already."*)

Detailed information about the tasks Rudolf Steiner had set for Dr. G. Wachsmuth and Dr. E. Pfeiffer a year before the Agricultural Course* can be found in Dr. G. Wachsmuth's 'The Life and Work of Rudolf Steiner,' 2nd ed. 1955, pp. 469ff and 546.

It may be mentioned here that Dr. Wachsmuth asked the question whether one could eventually add to the specified preparations in the cow horns, for example metal additives. Rudolf Steiner said this was not necessary and pointed out that quicksilver [i.e. mercury, Tr.] could prove harmful even to the following generations.

---

* Eight lectures given on the large farming estate of Count Carl von Keyserlingk at Schloss Koberwitz [Castle Koberwitz], east of Breslau, Silesia, Germany (now Wrocław, Silesia, Poland), between the 7th and 16th June 1924 (GA 327). See also the translation based upon the notes of Lilly Kolisko at webpage: http://www.garudabd.org/Agriccourse/contents.html.

Below are the notes Dr. G. Wachsmuth made in 1924 from the instructions of Rudolf Steiner concerning single elements (these are in addition to the indications in the Agricultural Course):

The Earth does not entirely crystallise, but crystallisation is itself earthly. Silica has made the Earth the image of the cosmos whereas carbon has made it into plant bearing Earth.
Phosphorus has made the Earth into a greedy planet, which attracts the contents of the cosmos.
Nitrogen makes the Earth become a spiritual planet that can include the animals.
Oxygen turns the Earth into a life planet that draws in the life of the cosmos.
Sulphur makes the Earth a life-consuming bearer of thoughts.
Hydrogen brings the thoughts.
Chlorine brings the thoughts towards the metals.

(More important notes of Rudolf Steiner on Natural Science are to be found in the weekly journal 'Anthroposophie [Anthroposophy]', Stuttgart, 9., 10. and 11. Jr. [9th, 10th and 11th Yr.], 1927-1929.)

Folio 6 a-c

Dr. E. E. Pfeiffer's report on the conversation he had with Rudolf Steiner on the 29th of April 1921. It concerned the nature of electricity. Rudolf Steiner accompanied his answers with the sketches reproduced here. (The originals remain with Dr. Pfeiffer, of which there are photocopies in the deeds of the Natural Science Section.)

Rudolf Steiner: *"Electricity originated as an astral force. It comes from the undefined and goes into the infinite."*
(Here the long arrow was drawn, which goes from below to above.)
"This thrusts against something, which then becomes matter."
(The large curves.)

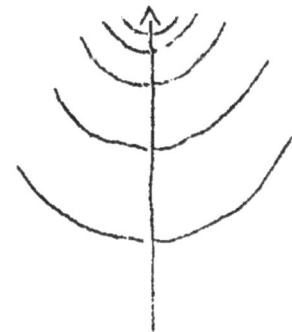

"So long as one swims with and in the electricity, it cannot be perceived, just as of what we are ourselves we have at first no consciousness. Consciousness comes about through polarity, of interrupting the current."

(See the arrow on the right which continues on a straight line and is intersected by two curves with a fine line above; first the long line was drawn = current of electricity, finally the figure of the arrow.)

"Polarity appears by interrupting the current."
(On the left two free lines and the signs + and − were added.)

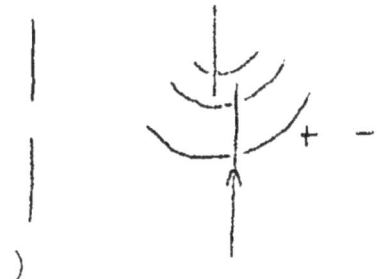

"In fact, electricity is a fourth axis in space."
(See sketch of the three axes of space with a fourth arrow pointing
below, left of the upward vertical.)

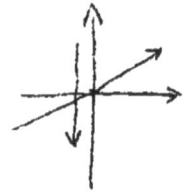

*"One can best observe the being of electricity in the cathode ray tube. Its radiating
form flows from the anode accompanied by light, that means the light and warmth
pole, into the vacuum."*

(See drawing of the anode with the radiating beam and the words *'hell'* [light]
and *'Wärme'* [warmth].)

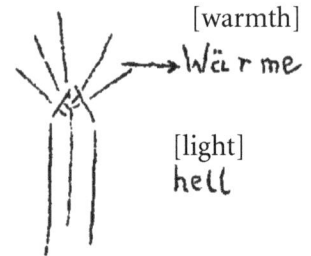

*"At the 'K' (Kathode) [cathode], the cold pole, matter is encountered and produces
levels of darkness and chemical activity in blue."*

(See diagram: *'K' (Kathode)* [cathode], and layers around the cathode with the
words *'dunkel'* [dark] and *'chem.'* [chemical].)

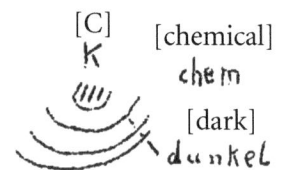

*"It always comes to the fact that one notices from the material side something
opposing the radiating path of the electric current which becomes pushed together."*

*"On this pushing together rests the shape of the Earth. As for example cosmic
astrality as cosmic electricity rays onto the Earth and by this means earthly
matter becomes pushed together and the mountains tower up by the force
from outside."*

The question was then asked whether the cosmic electricity, which is found in the air as static electricity,
could be used in technology.

Answer: *"One must first create a polarity and a potential, like putting a candle in a balloon, and letting
it climb to 100 metres. A flame attracts electricity. This could be brought down with a wire like Franklin, and
would have a potential to the Earth (negative pole). But one must find out whether forces would be withdrawn
which could be used elsewhere."*

Folio 7

In connection with indications given by Rudolf Steiner in the years 1919 to 1922, Henri Smits, who was a student at the time, was directed to select samples of various peat fibres and bring them to Rudolf Steiner in Stuttgart.

As Mr. Smits requested a realistic research task from Rudolf Steiner he was directed to the refining of peat fibres. This refinement should on the one hand make it possible to have peat fibres that could be spun into material and on the other hand a compressible material that can be cut for example and used for making picture frames.

At that time Mr. Smits and his colleagues carried out experiments in the Stuttgart research laboratory, which lead to testing peat fibres that could be spun. As a result, small samples of material were woven. Due to external circumstances, however, further development of the work for industrial application was not possible.

Folio 8 a-b

Rudolf Steiner often made the remark that certain natural processes of the daytime took a different course during the night. One of the tasks placed before the Stuttgart research laboratory in this respect can be found in Folio 2.

Dr. Hans Theberath of Hamburg, reported modifications to these suggestions as follows:

Rudolf Steiner presented the task in the following form: *"Hang up a hygroscopic substance in the form of a spiral."* The changes in the length and the shape of this spiral should be observed. Rudolf Steiner drew the expected curve in the following surprising form.

Dr. Theberath took a silver coil, i.e. wound a 0.1 mm silver wire into a spiral with about 100 turns, and hung this up at constant temperature. He sighted a telescope with a micrometer eyepiece on the bottom end so that the change in the length of up to 1/50th of a millimetre could be ascertained. On being questioned, Rudolf Steiner said that by *"hygroscopic substance,"* a metal wire was meant. The results of the whole series of observations showed a continuous elongation of the spiral. This elongation was interrupted at sunrise and sunset, respectively, by lengthening or shortening. This was the result Rudolf Steiner expected.

Rudolf Steiner said later that he had meant a conical spiral and particularly, though not exclusively, a spiral of gold wire.

Dr. Rudolf Steiner had also considered, so wrote Dr. Theberath, such a large spiral that the movement could be seen without optical means.

A second task was as follows: *"Hang a plate in steam."* The condensation process should vary according to the alteration of day and night. Dr. Theberath made the apparatus shown in the accompanying drawing, which demonstrated what Rudolf Steiner had said.

'A' is a vessel containing water above a narrow opening, which separates the steam space 'B.' Steam vessel 'B' is a hollow sphere. 'C' is a half-Moon shaped vessel with two tubes, 'E' and 'F.' Through these, water flows in and out. Inlet and outlet temperatures are measured, the difference will fluctuate according to the condensation temperature.

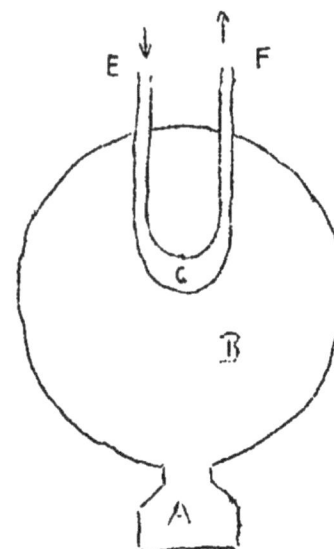

The completed experiments, which had to be discontinued, did not have any clear outcome.

Folio 9 a-c

Dr. Hermann von Dechend carried out research into electrical discharge phenomenon in a super-cooled vacuum at the research laboratory in Stuttgart. Unfortunately, the exact formulation of the indication given in 1922 or 1923 is no longer available. Dr. P. E. Schiller was working as an assistant. Two series of experiments were carried out.

1) The spectrum from Geissler tubes was investigated at room temperature and at –200°C. This demonstrated that not only single spectral lines disappeared, but also new lines appeared. Dr. P. E. Schiller had the opportunity in spring 1924 to show Rudolf Steiner a sketch of these variations. Rudolf Steiner advised that every position on the spectral band where these variations appeared should be carefully examined. He even mentioned that quite new colours could appear there. To clarify these he made the following sketch. The perpendicular line 'A' in the upper zone represents a spectral line at room temperature. With cooling, this disappears, and there appears a new line 'B' at another place on the spectral band. At the areas shown by the hatching below the upper line and above the lower line, Rudolf Steiner wanted these carefully investigated.

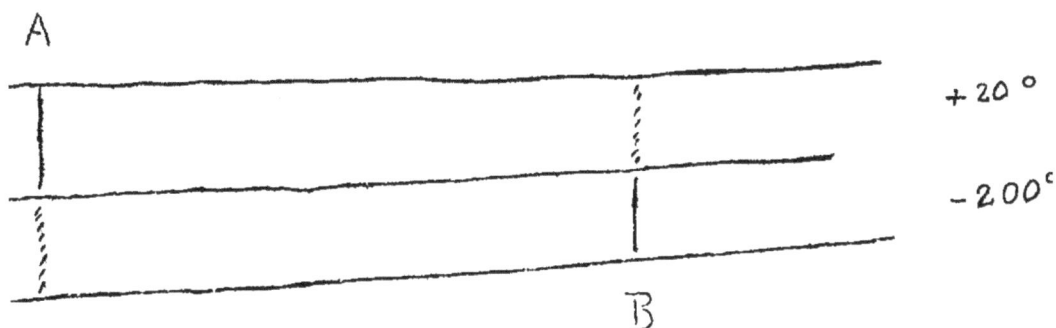

2) Discharge phenomena were produced in an evacuated glass sphere. By means of a fused copper tube the discharge area could be brought down to –200° C. This experiment was shown to Rudolf Steiner and pointed out that here also there are variations in the spectral lines especially in deep violet. After observing this, Rudolf Steiner remarked to Dr. P. E. Schiller that the middle of the sphere of light, which had formed at the end of the copper tube where it projected into the evacuated glass sphere, conditions could be observed which would correspond to the Sun's centre. At the edge of this sphere of light was something similar to the surface of the Sun to be seen.

Turning towards the elementary spectroscope used for these experiments, Rudolf Steiner then said: *"But with this instrument you will not be able to establish it."*

Sadly, up to the present time, it has not been possible to start with the construction of such a specially designed, costly instrument.

In a letter, which Dr. Walter Johannes Stein wrote to Mr. G. Hahn in 1948, there are a few sentences that refer to the task above.

Rudolf Steiner said: *"Set up a Torricelli vacuum for a certain temperature. Super-cool this. Then find out what difference there is: in just the vacuum and then in the super-cooled vacuum. You will see that in the super-cooled vacuum, the ether is present as a negative quantity, which can be measured."*

Those present asked: what kind of experiment should be done in the vacuum?

Dr. Rudolf Steiner did not answer; he believed he had said it. One must try everything: difference in pressure, difference in temperature, passage of light, thousands of other things. Chemical reactions. *"Outer space,"* said Dr. Rudolf Steiner, *"is a super-cooled vacuum. One must use a mercury vapour lamp in a quartz tube. Investigate the gases of the Sun in this manner in the super-cooled vacuum. Investigate the discharge phenomena with the spectroscope. Begin with slight super-cooling. Examine the temperature gradient accurately. Its effect on the phenomenon."*

A friendly doctor reported that Rudolf Steiner (1924) had prescribed the following for an eye injury:

Administer compresses on the eyes. In order to protect the eyes from the different ethers, compresses are used with 5% alum solution (warmth-ether), 5% potassium iodate (light-ether), 5% Æsculin (chemical-ether); soak a cloth in this and lay on the eyes.

Folio 10 a-b

Dr. E. E. Pfeiffer reports on the 24th of September 1924. First conversation took place between Dr. Steiner, Dr. Wachsmuth and Dr. Pfeiffer; Dr. von Dechend arrived soon after and the conversation continued.

Dr. Wachsmuth asked whether it would be possible to broadcast Dr. Steiner's lecture by radio, perhaps with a transmitter at the Goetheanum, in such a way that only the members of the Anthroposophical Society could receive the transmission. Would Dr. Steiner reject such an idea, or what were the requirements for carrying it out?

Rudolf Steiner: *"In the current use of radio the influence of the voice of the persons is lost. It must first be made possible that the personal nuances of the voice are kept and are not mechanised. This could be achieved by using a flame as a detector. This would be a necessary condition. One must work out a code so that only those could receive it whom one wished to allow."*

Dr. von Dechend reports this part of the conversation from memory as follows: Rudolf Steiner said he could only *"think of a solution that you take a flame and follow the effect of speech on the flame and express it in curves as it were and then allow different people to speak. Study the differences that appear. And then give the coherer the form that you discover—it is well-named coherer* [apparatus used in the early days of wireless telegraphy, Tr.]. *Then only those who have the coherer can receive the message."*

Dr. Pfeiffer reported further that he had asked Rudolf Steiner whether it would also be possible to use the fluidity of the Earth for wireless telephony and radio transmission because the conductivity is so much better. Rudolf Steiner: *"That is theoretically possible, but one must know more about the behaviour of terrestrial magnetism. I have already given out the task of studying rhythms of terrestrial magnetism, to some extent, by sinking measuring instruments into underground water. I must wait until I receive the results of this experiment. If one connects the terrestrial magnetism in the wrong way, one runs the danger that the Earth will burst apart."*

Dr. Pfeiffer pointed out that this utterance stood closely in connection with the remarks about formic acid in the 'Bee Course' lectures, given on 12.22.23 (Lecture 8), GA 351, 1998, p. 155. Rudolf Steiner describes the connection between formic acid in the ground and electromagnetic communication.

Work on the above task was carried out by Dr. P. E. Schiller in the Physics Laboratory at the Goetheanum.

Folio 11

October 1923. A member of the Anthroposophical Society, an electrical engineer by profession, had asked Rudolf Steiner what he could best do in the sense of the Anthroposophical impulse.

Once in his studio, Rudolf Steiner rose up and after walking to and fro, said: *"prepare a floating freely moving open flame on a fluid and then hold the hands so, like a gothic flying buttress over the flame."*

The person in question continued in his report: I had the impression that he considered the discussion at an end. Before taking my leave I asked a further question; if it mattered whether a healthy or sick person held their hands over the flame. He answered: *"Yes."* A few weeks later I said to him after his lecture, that I could recognise no regularity in the verified movements. After that he said: *"Add some music."*

Folio 12 a-c

Wilhelm Pelikan, of Schwäbisch-Gmünd, made notes which he wrote down after conversations with Rudolf Steiner.

March 15, 1922: *"I asked him* [Rudolf Steiner] *in connection with indications which appear in the lectures under the title 'Spiritual Science and Medicine'* where there are described the basic substances which go to form albumin in connection with the organic processes of liver, kidneys, heart, and lungs. Later, similar indications appear in the Agriculture Course.*

In connection with my question, Rudolf Steiner made the following suggestions: In connection with the effects of these substances one must distinguish between the upper and lower organisation. To the carbon of the physical body one can associate the limb metabolic organisation. The physical body is something, which is formed on the basis of the combustion process of the carbon. Then one can associate the hydrogen with the ego activity. In the head, nerves, sense system on the contrary, one should connect the physical body with the hydrogen, and the ego to the carbon."

April 28, 1922: *"I had requested a leading thought from Rudolf Steiner so that I could understand the nature of the so-called inert or noble gases: Helium, Neon, Krypton, Argon, and the various radioactive isotopes. The question arose directly in connection with problems I had with radioactivity.*

Rudolf Steiner answered without pausing to think: In the rare gases we have substances which become solid at very low temperature. These substances could be followed up through the most varied conditions: earthy, fluid, gaseous, heat-condition, but also a light-condition, etc. Now gases can be liquefied, liquids can be solidified, and so on. When light is solidified or hardened, the rare gases arise. Light in an amorphous state, not crystallised."

---

* Available on-line at webpage: http://wn.rsarchive.org/Lectures/SpiSciMed/SpiSci_index.html.

Mr. Pelikan added to this: If one considers how the heaviest rare gas is produced from alpha-rays, one can already find a way to understanding this statement and from there a bridge to helium in radioactive decay.

In the year 1927, Mr. Pelikan, in the Yearbook of the Natural Science Section: '*Gäa Sophia* [Gaia-Sophia],' has an article entitled '*Experimentelle Untersuchungen über die Gestaltung der Lebensprozesse aus dem Kosmos* [Experimental Research about the Formation of Life Processes out of the Cosmos].'

In this article he related that he could propose the question to Rudolf Steiner: The plant-form makes visible supersensible formative forces, could these be shown also as the etheric state of metals in characteristic changes of form or similar?

Rudolf Steiner was of the opinion that not only was a correct starting point for experimentation given, but he also added immediately a whole series of experiments that should be undertaken, and predicted at the same time what the results of the experiments would be one day.

"*You must strive*" so he said "*to have the metals in a gaseous condition, and then bring them in a small dosage to the air that is breathed by the plant. You will then get only effects on the form. If you take lead, for example, you will find areas of rank vigour in the plant, globular lattice shaped forms, which are full of rank growth, i.e. not normal. Copper shows rather the opposite effect. Globular shapes appear, enclosures that dried up: hardening and shrivelling-up processes.*"

Later Rudolf Steiner suggested that with metals that did not permit of an easy and fast vaporisation, another path could be followed. Soluble salts of such metals should be submitted to electrolysis, and fluid near the cathode drawn off, this is then poured on the appropriate plants.

The above-mentioned article by Mr. Pelikan reported further on the results of such experiments.

Folio 13 a-b

Dr. Oskar Schmiedel made notes of a conversation with Rudolf Steiner concerning the treatment of wood. He has Dr. E. E. Pfeiffer's permission to copy them. Dr. E. E. Pfeiffer reproduced them as follows:

To bring wood into a sound condition:
I.   Exposure to sunlight whilst carbonic acid is thinly spread underneath. Humus in a quite small quantity.
II. Then in status nascendi: 1% mushroom-juice, 1% oleander blossom, 1% larch sap, 1% beech leaf tea, 1% Ranunculus.

Add 1% humus – present in wood – moistened with rainwater on 350 grams of wood with 2 - 2.5% litres water.

(Carbon dioxide (CO_2) would be removed) = dependent on warmth and sunshine.

With development of the gas O_2?

Appearing as fluids from the wood: Manna-sugar, Xylose (wood-sugar), Lignin.

(Dr. Pfeiffer wondered whether this sentence originated with the first experimenter.)

Treatment I for one and a half months.

Treatment II: K = *Kiefer* [Scots Pine], B = *Buche* [Beech], T = *Tanne* [Fir].

Never use gum Arabic, but mallow mucilage as a medium for emulsion.

No alcohol.

Larch sap: emulsify with mallow mucilage down to a filamentary consistency, and then carefully put into a mortar.

If necessary use a stronger resin additive.

III. Antimony D3 or D4 [D3 = the 3rd and D4 the 4th decimal potency, etc., Tr.].

(Antimony (Sb) colloquium at *Chemische Fabrik von Heyden* in Radebeul-Dresden, Germany.)

Protect with larch sap and mallow mucilage. Stir.

IV. Hardening: Silicon Oxide (SiO_2), Calcium Carbonate ($CaCO_3$) or slaked lime treatment or sodium water gas (Sodium, hydrogen and carbon monoxide) or silicic acid gel.

Tearing of the cell walls: steam distillation or strong vacuum because of the semi-permeable cell walls.

Postscript to II: Stir plant mucilage vigorously in order to prevent mildew: Cochlearia in small quantities.

Dr. E. E. Pfeiffer added a further explanation in December 1959:

After the experiences of orthodox timber chemistry, the breaking down of the cell walls would be undertaken first, and the additions of IV would come later. The silicic acid treatment is today technically achieved: There are elegant procedures for it, also in vacuum technology.

Folio 14 a-b

Suggestions made by Dr. Rudolf Steiner in a discussion with Dr. Fritz Kauffungen on the 12th of April 1923 in St. Gallen:

Dr. Rudolf Steiner: "*If you would understand the process of peptonisation you must not begin with the inorganic acid reaction. You must start with the human being to first understand peptonisation and then discern the acid reaction as a special case. You must also be able to establish the day and night rhythm in order to use the remedy; so you begin with a synthesis in daytime, then interrupt this and carry on at night. In this way you include time as a factor, which has not happened so far."*

Dr. Fritz Kauffungen: *"What actually happens when a medicine, let us say Phenacetin, is taken? Is that an etheric process?"*

Dr. Rudolf Steiner: *"Medicines like Phenacetin are quite terrible remedies* (here Rudolf Steiner expressed extreme horror), *they are pure shock remedies. They are quite frightful and not to be desired. These remedies are moreover not taken up by the astral body. They remain quite detached. At the same time the body is ruined. They are certainly ether processes."*

Dr. Fritz Kauffungen: *"I am now studying the influence of temperature on substances produced in a living situation."*

Dr. Rudolf Steiner: *"I know substances derived from plants respond to the annual rhythm. When they are brought to body temperature, the annual rhythm ceases, and you observe only the day and night rhythm."*

Dr. Fritz Kauffungen: *"I have been very interested in pyrogenic decay at about 300°C."*

Dr. Rudolf Steiner: *"I have not investigated such high temperatures, but very probably at such high temperatures, a reversal in the sense of reviving will take place, so that really an animation is brought about. I am having experiments done in Stuttgart—sadly the people there are not progressing fast enough—to close the spectrum so that the ultraviolet comes to lie above the infrared. A quite singular colour must then arise which is vitally active. That must be tested on bacteria."*

Folio 15

Mr. G. Hahn asked Dr. W. J. Stein which suggestions given by Rudolf Steiner for Natural Scientific experiments were known to him.

Dr. Stein answered with two examples. The first is described at the end of Folio 9, the second example Dr. W. J. Stein gave as follows:

"Another suggestion: take a point of heat, a flame. Examine the outspreading warmth. Steadily heat a hollow metal sphere or globe. Measure the rate of heating. Next place, first 12, later 24, such heat sources around the sphere or globe. Once more investigate the diffusing warmth, this time towards the inside. Determine the specific heat capacity of the surface unit in a unit of time. Result: the realities of quantum theory will appear as the result of measurement." [See also the Comments for Folio 15 on page 95, Tr.]

Folio 16 a-b

Prof. Franz Halla of Brussels described the following:

In a conversation about diffusion of dissolved salts, Rudolf Steiner said in the year 1917: *"Only the properties diffuse, not matter itself."*

Referring to the wave character of light: *"Modern physics is fairly close to the truth, only that the waves do not exist physically but in the etheric."*

Prof. Halla added here:
In another place Rudolf Steiner spoke about it: that every rhythm comes about through the working of something spiritual into the material and through which there is a return into the supersensible. So that something of this kind can take place, something must exist so that this interchange can be accomplished. For example, the ponderous movement of the pendulum where the 'conversion' of kinetic into potential energy occurs.

Concerning a conversation that heat-conduction belonged to an object, Prof. Halla reported:
Heat-radiation is a continual wave-like process. Because of the working of the material into it, the wave front becomes evermore bent. Which means a transition from the wave to the particle.

Welle [wave]   Korpuskel [particle]

To this corresponds the fact that in order to describe sub-material processes (e.g. concentrated effects of X-ray interference in the crystal) the reciprocal (or inverse) lattice is brought in. A lengthening of the reciprocal lattice corresponds to a bending or curving in the physical lattice.

With conduction of heat following the wording of the 'Warmth Course' (GA 321), we are concerned only with cyclical elementary processes, whereby heat or warmth appears out of nothing, becomes visible for a certain part of the way, and disappears again. At the point of disappearance however, fresh warmth arises and so on. One half of the cycle lies beyond the material. [See drawing above with the words *'Welle'* [wave] and *'Korpuskel'* [particle], Tr.]

Towards a phenomenology of electricity: this can only be found indirectly, whilst the phenomena of light are imaged or expressed where electricity appears and magnetic phenomena are imaged or reflected in chemical action.

Folio 17

Dr. Oskar Schmiedel of Schwäbisch-Gmünd, provided the following notes after a conversation with Rudolf Steiner on the 16th of February 1920:

"Negative matter is non-physical matter that has sucking activity. On the Sun, positive matter—continuous processes of disintegration—transition into the spiritual—protuberances are not volcano-like eruptions, but are as it were the remains of processes of disintegration. (The scientists would be astonished if they went to the Sun for it is quite otherwise than they imagine.) For research: To heat 'elements' to higher and higher temperatures until a change arises of itself in the sodium (Na) line, for example in the 'reversed' entry, then one would have produced the Fraunhofer lines.
Atoms, or what are so-called, are crossing points of lines of force."

Folio 18 a-b

20th of December 1920, Dornach, GA 283, 1975, S. 90-91. Rudolf Steiner concluded a lecture by Prof. Dr. Franz Thomastik of Vienna, with a few remarks. These are printed in the '*Nachrichten-blatt* [News Sheet],' 1945, S. 117.

First the metals used for constructing musical instruments were dealt with. The moisture content where the wood is growing is of the greatest importance, *"not only the dampness of the Earth from which the root grows, but the air humidity. And in a certain sense we can see in the outer configuration of a tree whether the wood is suitable for higher or lower notes. The wood that comes from a tree that has more crenulated leaves is always better for higher notes than the wood that comes from a tree with more rounded leaves. For indeed the leaf of the tree is formed out of sound."*

Somewhat later: *"so we can say: it is necessary to study altogether how the tree originates. And furthermore because the structure of the wood comes especially from the watery elements which it embraces and is the actual bearer of sound—in this manner, wood should be studied…"*

In conclusion Rudolf Steiner described the various kinds of wood used in the building of the first Goetheanum, including the proportions of the building, which have an influence on the acoustics of a space.

Dr. Thomastik had proposed having the orchestra and organ in the middle of a space, but to arrange it underneath so that sounds would issue from the centre.

Rudolf Steiner commented: *"Also having an organ sunk into the Earth is an exceptionally ingenious idea, but it would cause a certain difficulty because the relatively neutral existence of the pipes in the open air would cease the moment when we really sank the organ into the Earth: it would in fact sound quite different in winter than in summer. It would have to be treated quite differently and tuned in winter as in summer. Above all, it would bring about an intense awareness of winter and summer."*

Finally Rudolf Steiner spoke about the influence of the geological formation on the soul-spiritual environment, which is a prerequisite for a quite special performance of music.

Additional very interesting details about acoustics and music are to be found in these remarks of Rudolf Steiner. (The transcript of the lecture contains no drawings. The sketch above comes from the notes of one of the participants.)

Folio 19

Dr. E. E. Pfeiffer has published in the weekly journal '*Das Goetheanum* [The Goetheanum],' 1940, S. 75, Rudolf Steiner's suggestions for stage lighting. For this Dr. Pfeiffer made Rudolf Steiner's sketch available. This shows the arrangement of the lamps in the small cupola of the first Goetheanum.

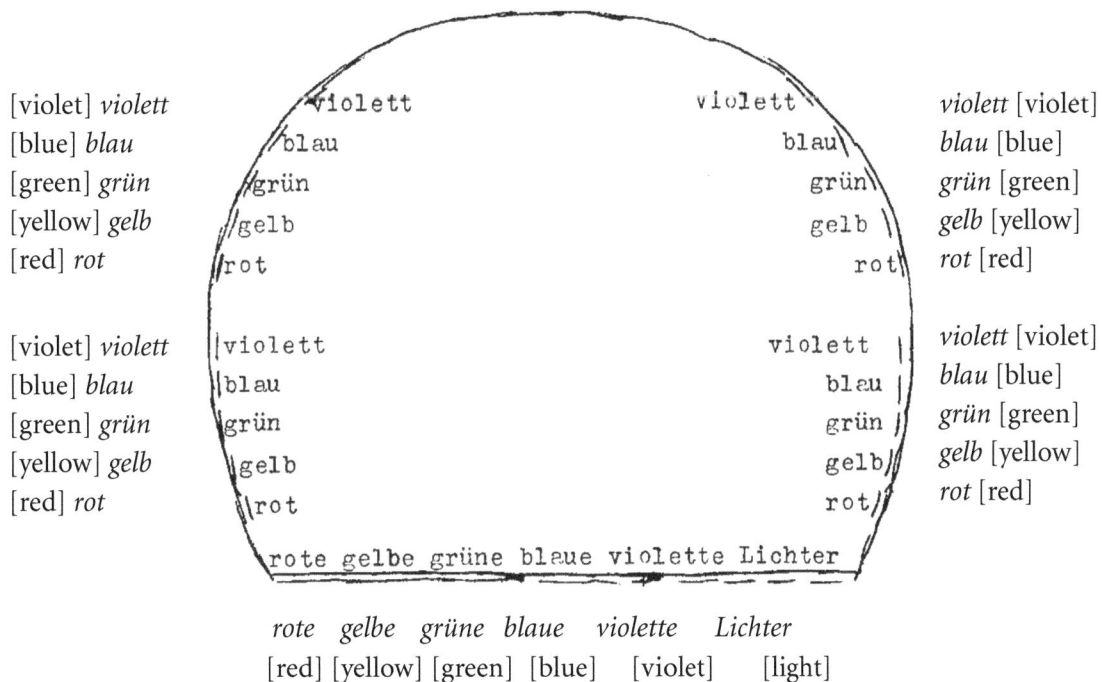

[violet] *violett*	violett	violett	*violett* [violet]
[blue] *blau*	blau	blau	*blau* [blue]
[green] *grün*	grün	grün	*grün* [green]
[yellow] *gelb*	gelb	gelb	*gelb* [yellow]
[red] *rot*	rot	rot	*rot* [red]

[violet] *violett*	violett	violett	*violett* [violet]
[blue] *blau*	blau	blau	*blau* [blue]
[green] *grün*	grün	grün	*grün* [green]
[yellow] *gelb*	gelb	gelb	*gelb* [yellow]
[red] *rot*	rot	rot	*rot* [red]

rote gelbe grüne blaue violette Lichter

rote   gelbe   grüne   blaue   violette   Lichter
[red]   [yellow] [green] [blue]   [violet]   [light]

25

With the next drawing Rudolf Steiner made the remark:
"Sunlight should be studied, not as a beam, but diffused, spreading out on all sides, as if falling through a window. Projectors with a converging lens are an untruth. The light should ray out on all sides, and not become concentrated."

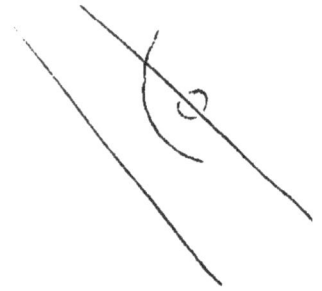

Dr. Pfeiffer commented on the diagram:
The circle = the Sun; and the curve the spreading out and correspondingly the source of light fixed to a convex body.

Folio 20

Dr. E. E. Pfeiffer reported:

In the spring of 1920, Rudolf Steiner suggested a formula for the study of etheric forces. He further said one should let a branch of a hyperbola slide over a solid and discover how it relates to the other branch. One could construct an axis system out of lead, and make an astroid out of copper.

$$x^{2/3} + y^{2/3} + z^{2/3} = a^{2/3}$$

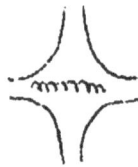

aus Cu

eine Astroide

From a copper [Cu] Astroid

(Unfortunately, it cannot be confirmed whether Rudolf Steiner himself wrote down the formula and the accompanying diagrams. In addition, it is no longer known to whom Rudolf Steiner made these suggestions. It is very probable that this proposition somehow stands in connection with the Strader Machine.) [See also the sketch of the Strader apparatus that is reproduced on the front cover and frontispiece of this book, Tr.]

Folio 21 a-c

The following is connected with Rudolf Steiner's article: '*Die Atomistik und ihre Widerlegung* [Atomism and its Refutation],' (GA 38) printed in: '*Anthroposophie und Psychoanalyse* [Anthroposophy and Psychoanalysis]' (Zeitschrift [Journal] '*Anthroposophie* [Anthroposophy]'), Buch [Book] 3 und [and] 4, April-September 1935. Reprinted in '*Beiträge* [Supplements]' Nr. 63, Dornach 1978; English translation published by The Mercury Press, Spring Valley, New York, 1975. See also webpage: http://wn.rsarchive.org/Articles/AtmRef_index.html. It must be emphasised that the reprinting of any of this material for unauthorised use is forbidden.

Answers to Six Questions about the nature of some fundamental Natural Science concepts by Rudolf Steiner for the year 1919. [See also the Comments for Folio 21, page 99, Tr.]
With permission of Frau Marie Steiner for the application made by Dr. Ing. Herberg, Stuttgart. The text of the actual questions is no longer available, and must be assumed from the answers.

I) Atoms are to be regarded as ideal contents of space. The contents are the results of force-directions meeting each other, e.g., directions of force. [See also Folio 17, page 24, Tr.]

'*a, b* and *c*' are active in space, and by their meeting a resultant force is carried which is effective as an atom of tetrahedral character.

Elements are the expression of certain meetings of forces; that they manifest themselves as such is due to the fact that one force, in meeting another, produces a result, while other effects of forces on each other are without result.
Crystals are the result of more complicated meetings of forces, atoms the result of simple meetings.
Amorphic masses result from the neutralisation of force-directions.

II) Force is the revelation of spirit viewed in a one-sided way. One cannot say that force has an effect on matter, since matter consists merely in the effects of the force-rays when they meet. Never does one form of energy pass over into another one; as little as the activity of one person goes into that of another. What passes over is merely the arithmetical expression of measure.
When 'mechanical energy passes over into heat energy' the real occurrence is as follows: a certain quantity of mechanical energy in the non-material condition reveals itself as heat, bringing about a definite quantity in this manifestation. (This is so in a healthy fashion with J. R. von Mayer. It was only Helmholtz who confused the issue.)

III) Neither sound, nor warmth, nor light, nor electricity are waves, just as little as a horse is a sum of gallop paces. Sound, for instance, is a real suffering [*wesenhaften Quale*] and the effect of this real suffering in its passage through the air is vibration [*die Schwingung*]. For a human being as a sensing being, the oscillation is the occasion for imitating the suffering; therein consists the perception of sound. It is similar with others: light, etc.

IV) Light is that by which it is perceived. (See my 'Einleitung zu Goethes Farbenlehre [Introduction to Goethe's Theory of Colour],' GA 1d, Vierter Band [Volume 4] (Erste Abteilung [Part One]), 4. Auflage [4th Edition] Dornach 1982, S. I-XVI.) The vibration is the revelation of light in the ether.

The refraction of light is the result of the effect of a certain force-direction upon the light-direction. Newton's colour rings (circles), phenomena of interference, are results of light-radiation (effect of light in the ether), and of the effects of other forces found in the path of light (weakening effects, gradually weakening effects of other forces). The same goes for phenomena of polarisation. One should not seek the polarisation figures in the structure of the essence of the light but in the structure of the medium, which places itself in the path of light.

The speed of transmission is the result of a kind of friction of the light against the medium.

V) Light is not to be considered as a function of electricity, but the latter is to be considered as a kind of corporeal carrier of light.

Electrically charged matter: certain accumulations of force retain those accumulations of force, which manifest as electricity.

VI) Mathematics is the abstracted sum of the forces effective in space. If one says, "*Mathematical propositions are valid a priori*," this comes from the fact that human beings exist within the same lines of force as the other *beings*, and that he can disassociate himself from everything that does not belong to the scheme of space, etc.

Folio 22 a-d

Index with reference to lectures of Rudolf Steiner

The following references are given in date order. In no way do they provide a complete picture of the remarks of Rudolf Steiner connected with experimental research. They should be considered in any research undertaken.

Many of the lectures below contain impressive indications on the necessity for developing the right mood in the laboratory, which is making the workbench into an altar.

P. E. Schiller

Lecture date	Contents	GA No.
02.12.1906	Moral Culture – Keely Motor – Moral Technology.	97
10.22.1906 morning	Organic products can be changed into highly developed inorganic (milk-like) products.	96

09.22.1907	Experimenting on a higher stage of morality becomes the transition where inorganic to organic can be realised (a living situation not produced by fertilisation).	--*
12.04.1907	The moral requirements for the preparation of plants in the laboratory.	98
12.27.1907	The preparation of living creatures in the laboratory. The transfer of vibration belonging to the ether-body.	101
01.12.1908	Moral requirements for bringing about the living.	--*
01.29.1908	In sacramental acts, life could be generated (power of thoughts).	102
06.28.1908	Artificial generation of plants will become possible, but first the moral requirements must be created.	104
09.24.1909	In experiment guiding and directing powers are working (Masters), also when the researcher has absolutely no idea of them.	114
04.13.1910	After the development of higher moral forces, the scientist will be able to let life stream into the forms, which he has combined together.	118
09.28.1911	The aura of the alchemists altered during the experiment and by means of it.	130
11.04.1911	In future research, the right feelings must accompany the experiment.	130
12.27.1911	As 11.04.1911	134
11.24.1915	Plant seeds can only be produced artificially in the laboratory with the incorporation of the star constellations.	174b
11.12.1916	Future machine construction (and with their manufacture, the creation of elemental *beings*) must be bound up with what happens within the human being. Likewise the treatment of chemical substances, for example medicaments.	172
03.13.1917	The arising of living forms in the laboratory will only be possible in connection with the corresponding star constellations.	175
11.25.1917	The spiritual-etheric shall be placed in the service of outer practical life—The emotion in a human mood will be transmitted in wave movements to machines—between the dying forces of the nervous system and the external power of the machine, a union will be produced—in future the difference between morning and evening current and midday and midnight currents must be observed—the danger exists that the dead can become united with vibrating mechanical appliances.	178
12.25.1917	The application of human forces in the laboratory in earlier times. Then there arose Luciferic elemental *beings*. Today Ahrimanic elemental *beings* arise as a result of the purely technical-mechanical, physical, chemical thought forms. Especially when these are connected with nationalism.	180
04.29.1918	The laboratory experiment must be pervaded by reverence for the harmony of the Universe.	181

* Not published.

10.09.1918	By means of the harmonisation of certain oscillations, great forces from machines will be unleashed. Great danger arises through the egotism of humankind.	182
12.31.1919	The difference between sound and wave. The sympathy with the phenomena must be researched (pendulum clock, thought transference, etc.)	320
03.07.1920	Definite experiments are to be carried out by day and by night in order to indicate the difference between earthly and cosmic forces.	321
03.13.1920	An exceptional arrangement should be found whereby the twelve-fold spectrum is produced.	321
04.25.1920	The present results of research at issue (especially in America) should be regrouped and developed further from the spiritual-scientific point of view.	201
01.16.1921	An active phenomenalism should be fostered with a new inner understanding of the phenomena. It is also necessary to develop new methods of research.	323
01.18.1921	Research should be undertaken to differentiate those forces which arise from within as against those which arise from outside (heat, optical, magnetic and planetary processes, etc.).	323
06.24.1921	To study the line of leaf stipules: their positions form a picture in miniature of planetary motion.	205
06.26.1921	Synthesising and analysing must become a spiritual skill pervaded by the highest morality.	205
09.24.1921	By means of appropriate intermixing of colours of the spectrum, these could take on life.	207
07.29.1921	Notes on the Anthroposophical research institute and its work.	206
11.25.1921	As 07.29.1921	209
12.23.1921	As 07.29.1921	209
01.16.1922	As 07.29.1921	210
01.23.1922	As 07-29.1921	210
01.24.1922	As 07.29.1921	210
05.07.1922	The godless technology and science must be so replaced that spiritual and moral forces are called forth and brought into activity.	212
09.30.1922	We must again come to regard all research as intercourse with the spiritual world.	216
12.17.1922	Work in laboratories and clinics have become incomprehensible to the gods. In this work too, we must seek new bridges to the spiritual world.	219
01.06.1923	The mechanics of human motion are to be studied anew.	326
01.26.1923	In the lectures about the philosophy of St. Thomas Aquinas (ca. 1225-1274) most important suggestions are made. These must be adopted, otherwise research institutes will remain unproductive.	220

03.12.1923	Chemical processes, for example in medicines, are only understood when one goes into the events of the elemental world.	222
06.17.1923	With experiments spiritual *beings* are at work, often a whole host. Sometimes there are unexpected results (inspired). (For example: the physicist J. R. von Mayer, 1814-1878.)	258
08.30.1923	Science should already find the spiritual in the physical-sensible realm. See L. Kolisko: '*Physiologischer und physikalischer Nachweis der Wirksamkeit kleinster Entitäten** [Physiological and Physical Proof of the Effectiveness of the Smallest Entities].'** Significance for knowledge of medicines.	227
10.08.1923	Experiments with air travel must arise from studies of butterfly wings.	351
10.13.1923	Research on the air breathed out through the nostrils. Figures comparable with snow would appear. These are formed through the mucus.	351
10.20.1923	The active principles of eagle, lion and cow may not work one-sidedly. An ill-balanced cow principle would lead to oscillatory machines, which would work back on the whole planetary system.—"*The frightful law of the harmonisation of the oscillations…*"—Peripheral activity, star influences will be destroyed. The lion impulse one-sidedly employed would lead to influences on the weather. The eagle impulse, one-sidedly used, would lead back to a primitive clairvoyance.	230
10.24.1923	In the cow, and in the dog is inner light. It should be possible in a freshly laid egg, in a cow or dog embryo, to identify a light-effect (yellowish) with the appropriate instrument (photographic).	351
12.22.1923	The influence of the reverential mood on experiment – intercourse between cosmic intelligences and nature spirits becomes possible – Rosicrucian work in the laboratory. (For example: medicine, oxalic acid, formic acid.)	351
12.23.1923	In Rosicrucian research, there exists not only a connection to the nature spirits, but also to higher cosmic intelligences. (Gold, silver, and the mystery of carbon.)	232
12.31.1923	Concerning the necessity for financial requirements for the Anthroposophical research institute.	260

[See also the survey by Walter Kugler in '*Mechanischer Okkultismus, Keely-Motor, Technik der Zukunft im Vortragswerk Rudolf Steiners* [Mechanical Occultism, Keely Motor, Technology of the

---

* '*Entitäten* [Entities]' was Steiner's expression for what is more generally referred to as high dilutions or potencies.
** "*Der Kommende Tag*" [The Coming Day], *Wissenschaftliches Forschungsinstitut* [Scientific Research Institute], Mitteilungen Heft 3 [Reports Number 3], (*Herausgegeben von der Biologischen Abteilung* [Published by the Biological Department]), Der Kommende Tag A.-G. Verlag, Stuttgart, Erste Auflage [First edition] 1923; Arbeitsgemeinschaft anthroposophischer Ärzte [Working Association of Anthroposophical Medical Doctors], Stuttgart, 2. Auflage [2nd edition] 1959; Mit beitrag von [With contribution from] Gisbert und [and] Friedwart Husemann, Verlag am Goetheanum, Dornach, erweiterte Neuauflage [expanded new edition] 1997.

(continued on following page)

Future in the lectures of Rudolf Steiner],' in '*Beiträge zur Rudolf Steiner Gesamtausgabe* [Supplements to the Collected Edition of Rudolf Steiner],' Heft [Issue] No. 107, Michaeli [Michaelmas] 1991, S. 22-23.]

See also L. Kolisko's later paper: '*Physiologischer Nachweis der Wirksamkeit kleinster Entitäten: In Fortsetzung der 1923 und 1926 hierüber erschienenen Arbeiten* [A Physiological Proof of the Activity of Smallest Entities: In continuation of the work about this that appeared in 1923 and 1926],' Mitteilungen des Biologischen Instituts am Goetheanum [Reports of the Biological Institute at the Goetheanum], Herausgegeben von der Medizinischen Sektion am Goetheanum [Published by the Medical Section at the Goetheanum], Orient-Occident-Verlag, Stuttgart, Nr. 1, Juni 1932; English translation by Harold Jurgens published under: 'Homeopathy – Research and Theory,' in 'Mercury,' Journal of the Anthroposophical Therapy and Hygiene Association (A.T.H.A.), Spring Valley, N.Y., Number 11, 1991, pp. 1-27.

Notes from 2nd of July 1984

Paul Eugen Schiller

Concerning Heat

It should be noted that Rudolf Steiner, when characterising the *being* of heat, again and again used new descriptions.

The zone of warmth lies between the spiritual and material realms.

Extra-terrestrial current of warmth and terrestrial current of warmth.

Living warmth (blood-heat) and dead warmth (mineral warmth).

The inner fire of the soul, external perceptible fire, and in between, neutral warmth.

Especially important is the description in 11.07.1911, GA 132, 1996, p. 183.

To grasp warmth it is necessary to go out-of-space, see for example the Warmth Course, Lecture IV of 03.04.1920, 2005, GA 321, 2005, p. 47.

See also: '*Vom Wesen der Wärme* [On the Nature of Heat]', 1961, by Dr. P. E. Schiller.

Concerning Cold:

Is there a polarity, warm-cold, like the polarity light-darkness? The understanding of super-cooling is of importance for finding the answer. See Folio 9 a-b.

To be included: *"Displeasure is only a diminished pleasure; just as cold is a diminished heat."* ('Theosophy', Chapter 3. The Three Worlds: 1. The Soul World, GA 9, 1994, p. 106; http://steinerbooks.org/research/archive/theosophy/theosophy.pdf.) In the same way: *"If there arises in nature an effect such as heat, so this heat must be drawn from another part of the environment; cold occurs there as a counter-effect."* (10.19.1905, GA 93a, 'Foundations of Esotericism', 1982, Lecture XXI, p. 156.)

Observations:

External warmth is perceived through the bodily senses (such as the airy, fluid, and solid), inner warmth must be grasped by the soul-experience. (04.12.1909, GA 110, 1996, p. 43.)

We have no 'zero-point' in us. *"If we did then a quite different state of consciousness would be the result. Just because this 'zero-point' is hidden from us, we live our lives as we do."* (Lecture I 03.01.1920, GA 321, 2005, p. 4.) *"When we subjectively judge the condition of warmth in our environment, we do not experience the true condition of warmth, but we experience differences."* (Lecture I 03.01.1920, GA 321, 2005, p. 10.)

Inner and Outer Warmth:

'External' warmth may not penetrate the human organism unchanged. It is allowed to work only as a stimulant, the human being must produce his 'inner' warmth himself. *"In that moment when you are merely an object, not producing your own warmth or cold yourself, but when somewhere within you the warmth continues to work as for example with any external object, then you will become ill from the outer warmth itself..."* (12.30.1923, GA 233, 1997, p. 123.)

The mineral, plant, and animal substances that are for example taken up as nourishment by the human organism must be so far metamorphosed, transformed *"that throughout a certain period it is pure warmth and indeed united with the warmth that the human being develops as his own warmth towards his surroundings."* (11.10.1923, GA 230, 2001, p. 183.)

Not only the substances but the forces too must be worked upon by the human organisation. *"I must at every moment be in the position to lay hold of the warmth and immediately make it my own over my entire skin. If I am not in the position to do this, then the cold enters."* (11.10.1923, GA 230, 2001, p. 187.)

Heating:

The architect Aisenpreis reported how he had proposed to Rudolf Steiner that the Goetheanum building should be heated by electricity. In principle, Rudolf Steiner had no objection, but pointed out that in this case *"the heat must be allowed to radiate through water."*

In the Agricultural Course said Rudolf Steiner: If trees are planted without understanding, *"then they do not give us such sound heat as when we use wood that has been planted with understanding."* (06.07.1924, GA 327, 1993, p. 26.)

Cooking:

In connection with the use of certain materials and forces as sources of heat for the cooking of human food, there are unfortunately many erroneous and senseless ideas circulated. Most important, Rudolf Steiner warned against the use of electrical heat and in its place recommended the use of coal, wood or gas. Dr. P. E. Schiller held a lengthy correspondence over this and attempted in many conversations with practising doctors, pharmacists and scientists, to clarify these questions. (This correspondence and the reports from such discussions are in the hands of P. E. Schiller.)

The following has been confirmed: Circa 1917 an electric oven was installed in the home of Rudolf and Marie Steiner, *Haus Hansi* [House Hansi], near the existing gas cooker and coal stove. These and the regular use of the electric oven were obviously known to Rudolf Steiner.

During Rudolf Steiner's illness in the '*Atelier* [studio],' in a room next door an electric hot plate was installed on which small meals could be prepared for Rudolf Steiner. This too was self evident to Rudolf Steiner.

Dr. Margarete Kirchner-Bockholt, a co-worker of Dr. Ita Wegman, remarked that it was quite impossible that Dr. Wegman would have allowed the 'electric-cooker' when the slightest hint from Rudolf Steiner against the use of an electric-cooker would have been known.

Dr. E. Pfeiffer reported in 1928 on experiments whereby the use of wood, coal, gas and electricity were shown to affect the growth of wheat; various values being established.

Dr. Rudolf Hauschka carried out similar experiments and reported substantial differences. (See 'Nutrition: A Holistic Approach,' Sophia Books, Forest Row, East Sussex, 2002, p 150.)

Dr. P. E. Schiller and co-workers have from 1952 to 1954 carried out similar research on gas heating on the one hand and on electrical resistance heating on the other. Prolonged observations on the growth of wheat produced the same values for both kinds of heat. Those taken for the plant extracts in copper chloride crystallisations also showed no difference. Similarly with measurements of viscosity, surface tension, and conductivity.

Tasks:

Folio 2 a-c: *"In every heat reaction there are two currents, a terrestrial and an extra-terrestrial."* This should also be observed by night and day. This task was given shortly before (03.07.1920, GA 321, 2005, pp. 88-90) investigations were instigated into day-warmth [*Wärmetag*] and night-warmth [*Wärmenacht*]. See also Folio 8 a-b in this connection.

Folio 9 a-b: Cooling to low temperatures was mentioned. What should appear? Will light phenomena (spectra) or electrical discharges behave differently when the effect of heat is largely cut off?

Folio 9 c: Use of definite temperature shifts.

Folio 14 a: Body temperature, high temperature, day and night rhythm.

Folio 15: Outspreading warmth. In this connection examine the speed of the outspreading warmth: a) towards the centre of the Earth, b) in the opposite direction. No difference could be confirmed.

Folio 16 a-b: Reference to the conduction of heat.

Wachsmuth Wundt should guide the radiation from a source of heat through a pyrites-prism. Different qualities of warmth were ascertained with plants.

Dr. Rebmann investigated the influence on current-forms.

Dr. A. Heertsch carried out experiments on dew point in connection with day-warmth [*Wärmetag*] and night-warmth [*Wärmenacht*].

Comments and Documents on the Separate Tasks Given by Rudolf Steiner

Stephan Clerc

Comments for Folio 2

Wholly in agreement with his fundamental works concerning the rendering of the concept of ether-body as *formative forces time-body*, Rudolf Steiner placed this dual nature of the etheric at the beginning of the research programme in this folio. The first task outlined there consists, on the one hand, of identifying *formative forces* in natural phenomena (only directly perceptible supersensibly) with physical-chemical methods and suitable processes or reagents, and on the other hand to examine more closely the influence of *rhythms* (e.g. day-night) on these experiments. With this the two pillars of anthroposophically-oriented Natural Science were set up: *formative forces and rhythm research.*

1) Four kinds of ether

The directions of Rudolf Steiner for the work in the research laboratory of the 20th of April 1920, repeated by Dr. Rudolf E. Maier, concerns the question of the discovery of the four kinds of ether through the closing of the spectrum by means of magnetic force. As answer to the question, how one can arrive at the four ethers in one experiment, Rudolf Steiner, one month before in the Second Natural Scientific Course (GA 321, 2005, Lectures VIII, p.104, IX, p. 115 and XII, pp. 149-150 on the 8, 9 and 03.12.1920) and once again in the Astronomy Course (GA 323, Lecture IX on the 01.09.1921), proposed that the light-spectrum itself *"be bent in a certain manner"* with a strong electromagnet.

The fundamental idea behind these expressly stated assignments is the following: In the straight colour-band of the visible light spectrum as one usually has in the laboratory, only three of the four kinds of ether are directly present and manifest in the experiment. Already Goethe, and later Eugen Dreher,* investigated the fundamentally different warmth, light and chemical effects respectively in the red, yellow and violet part of the rainbow. According to Rudolf Steiner, the fourth kind of ether, life-ether, is only active where the violet and red run off at each end of the spectrum and meet together, which, with the linear colour band, is only the case at infinity. By means of a special bending of the straight spectrum by magnetic force, the meeting place of violet and red will now be

(continued on page 40)

---

* Rudolf Steiner returned to this series of experiments by Dr. Eugen Dreher. First in a commentary on Goethe's colour theory in the 1890 Kürschner edition of '*Goethes Naturwissenschaftliche Schriften* [Goethe's Natural Scientific Writings]' 5. Bd. [Vol. 5], 2. Abt. [Part 2], S. 147 (Berlin 1897, Nachdruck [Reprinted] Dornach 1975; 1982) and then, in addition to the places mentioned above, on the 08.08.1921 (GA 320) during a discussion (See the footnote on page 104 of this issue and pp. 172-185 + Notes, pp. 195-196 in the downloadable pdf file of 'The Light Course', (first natural scientific course): http://steinerbooks.org/research/archive/light_course/light_course.pdf).

In his book, 'Gelebte Erwartung [A Life of Inner Expectancy] (S. 194-195),' Dr. Ernst Lehrs describes an extension of Dr. Dreher's experimental series as follows (summarised): A task of L. Kolisko consisted of letting plants grow in darkness in order to investigate the changes in growth predicted by Rudolf Steiner. However, no changes were confirmed by her. Whilst visiting the laboratory, Rudolf Steiner remarked that the darkening produced in the cellar was only an absence of light and not active darkness. He recommended taking a strong lamp that is surrounded with a glass sphere having a double wall filled with iodine solution. After this the expected changes took place.

1

4. August.

Alaunlösung
[alum solution]

Wärmefanger
[heat trap]

Tod im Schwefelkohlenstoff
[death in carbon disulphide]

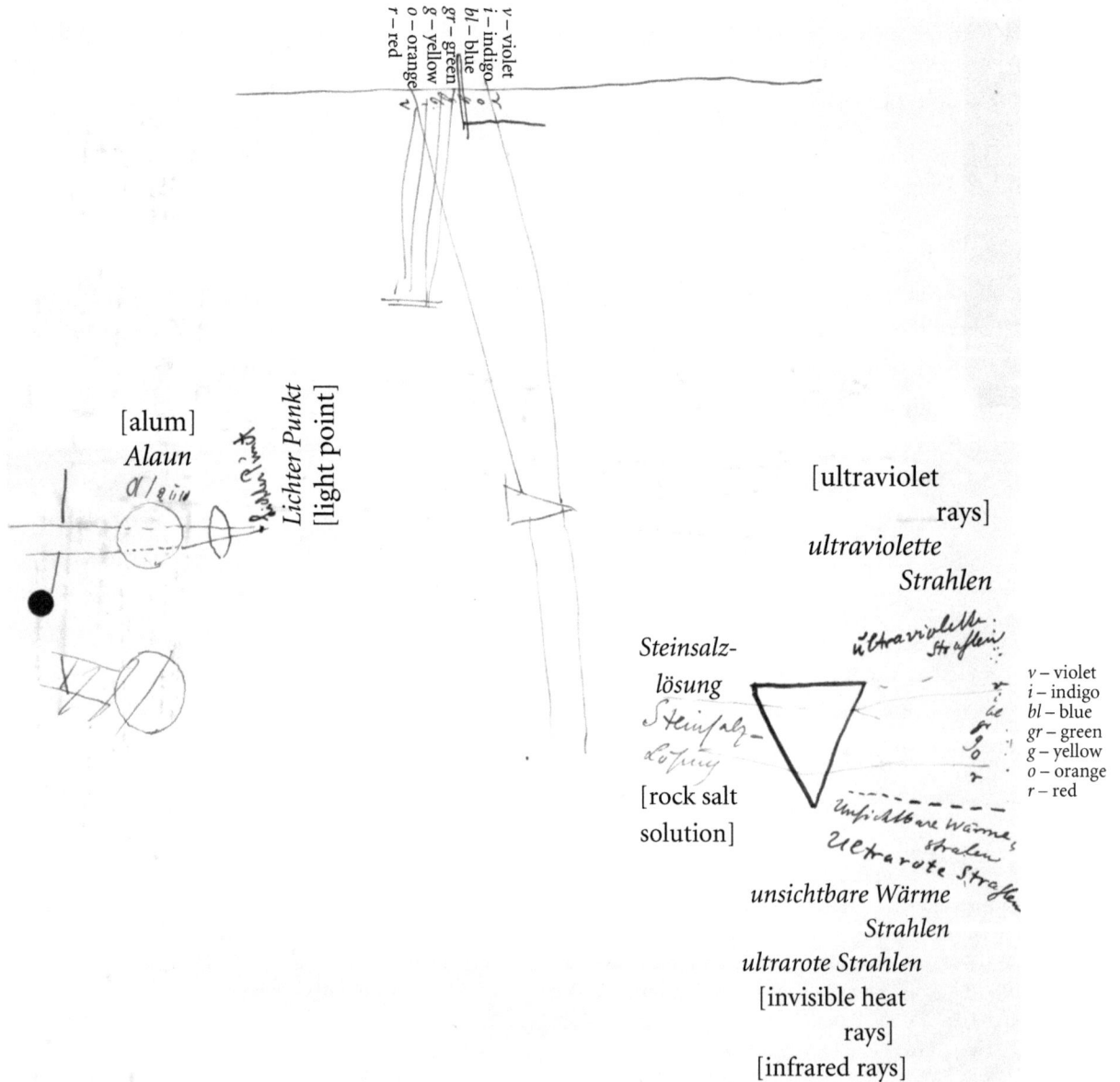

v – violet
i – indigo
bl – blue
gr – green
g – yellow
o – orange
r – red

[alum]
Alaun

Lichter Punkt
[light point]

*Steinsalz-
lösung*
[rock salt
solution]

[ultraviolet
rays]
*ultraviolette
Strahlen*

v – violet
i – indigo
bl – blue
gr – green
g – yellow
o – orange
r – red

*unsichtbare Wärme
Strahlen
ultrarote Strahlen*
[invisible heat
rays]
[infrared rays]

365
348
‾‾‾‾
17

290
58
‾‾‾‾
348

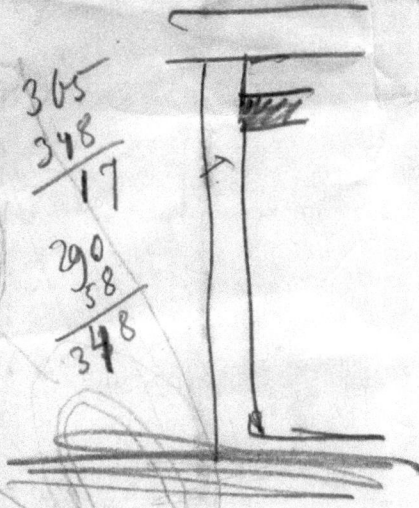

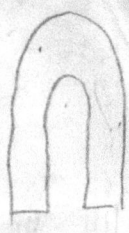

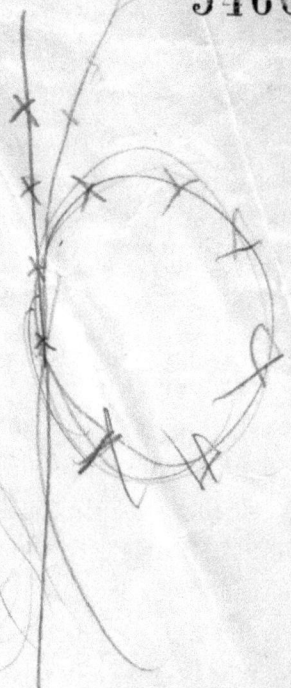

280
260
228
056
58
‾‾‾‾
336

4
2

300
00

periphery into the laboratory. After the problem at the end of Folio 2, investigations could be made into *"the beginnings of life-effects."* Organisms such as Paramecium were suggested as reagents for observing the nature of the peach-blossom colour which arises from the superimposition of red and violet (see also Folio 4 on page 10). In Folio 8 Rudolf Steiner's statement is noted that bacteria are also suitable *"reagents for the peach-blossom colour which works in a strongly vitalising manner."* At a meeting of *'Der Kommende Tag A.G.** [The Coming Day plc],' illustrating the meaning of the experiment, he said: *"If you bring a fly into a glass in the space of the peach-blossom colour of the spectrum, it would become exceptionally lively."* (See *'Beiträge zur Rudolf Steiner Gesamtausgabe* [Supplements to the Collected Edition of Rudolf Steiner],' Nos. 95/96, Ostern [Easter] 1987, S. 33.)

Pilot tests by Dr. Rudolf E. Maier and his assistant Hans Buchheim in Stuttgart, during the summer 1923 and a few months later in Einsingen bei Ulm [a village south-west of Ulm in Germany, Tr.], partially showed the expected effects. Rudolf Steiner was extremely pleased about these first results, and, in this connection, said once to Mr. Buchheim that these experiments were far more important than Einstein's theory of relativity. He then spoke in conclusion about these first results as an important beginning of a series of experiments to be further carried out and to those co-workers taking part, that the name Einsingen with its experiments would one day be world famous.

To clarify the task presented here short references to the appropriate sections of the Second and Third Natural Scientific Courses follow.

On the 12th of March 1920 (GA 321, 2005, Lecture XII, p. 150), Rudolf Steiner put the process of the bending of the colour band in concrete terms: he emphasised that it was not only a bending together of a single dimensional straight line into a two dimensional circle, but it must be much more in the one case a right-angled deviation on the one side with violet, and in the other case towards the opposite side with red. In practice, this would better be achieved with a rotating electromagnet. In conclusion he said that for the understanding and description of this *"doubly complicated bending together"* an attempt should be made using hyperimaginary numbers.**

Another time Rudolf Steiner referred to the complicated structure of this intertwining colour circle in the Third Natural Scientific Course (GA 323, Lecture IX) on the 01.09.1921 and spoke of having to *"somehow bend the spectrum into itself."* Directly after this, he pointed to the necessity of also having to consider very irksome uninterrupted procedures. As an example of this, he describes the metamorphosis of the form of the lemniscate. In the Cassini curve with two branches where one leaves space in order to keep the totality of the whole curve in mind.

Further details about the realisation of these experiments can be found in the *'Beiträge zur Rudolf Steiner Gesamtausgabe* [Supplements to the Collected Edition of Rudolf Steiner],' Heft [Issue] Nr. 95/96, Ostern [Easter] 1987. Concerning the twelve-colour circle, see also the lectures on 'Colour,' of the 12.05.1920 (Lecture Six) and 05.07.1921 (Lecture Two), GA 291, 1996, as well as the *'Unterredung mit Zeylmans van Emmichoven* [Discussion with Zeylmans van Emmichoven]' in the *'Beiträge* [Supplements]' already mentioned. Dr. Walter Landensperger, 50 years later, carried out the Einsingen experiment again in a Weleda laboratory. He expanded the original research project

---

* A.G. = *Aktiengesellschaft* [joint-stock company] the equivalent being public limited company (plc) in the UK.

** Hyperimaginary numbers i, j, and k form the vector (imaginary) part of generalised *quaternions* of the form $q = a + bi + cj + dk$, discovered by Sir William Rowan Hamilton in 1843. a, b, c and d are arbitrary real constants and $i^2 = j^2 = k^2 = ijk = -1$. Non-commutative multiplicative algebra requires that $ij = -ji = k$, $jk = -kj = i$ and $ki = -ik = j$.

so that the *Faraday effect* became active, with the hypothesis that fundamentally light cannot be influenced by magnetism. ('*Das Experiment von Einsingen* [The Experiment of Einsingen],' *Elemente der Naturwissenschaft* [Elements of Natural Science], 1990, Heft [Issue] 1, Nr. 52, S. 51-55 and 1991, Heft [Issue] 2, Nr. 55, S. 55-61.)

Throughout the 19th century, there was speculation by generations of natural scientists that light and magnetism were as closely related as electricity and magnetism. Already Michael Faraday had repeatedly attempted to alter the light of candle flame only with a magnet. The conclusions at the threshold of the new century of a great number of such magneto-optical experiments were that light is not magnetisable, except in a few special cases, where either the light travels through a magnetised crystal (*Faraday effect*) or where the source of light is situated in a magnetic field (*Zeeman effect*). The theorists who at that time had just learnt from the newly arrived mathematical apparatus of the Maxwell equations that light as well as electromagnetic phenomena (for example radio waves) could be calculated, failed in the attempt to also deal with magnetised conditions of light and electricity.

Quite recently, under the title 'Light Bent by Magnets' in the renowned science journal 'Nature' (Vol. 381, No. 6577, 2 May 1996, pp. 27-28), it was announced that scientists of the *Max Planck Institut für Festkörperforschung am Hochfeld-Magnetlabor* [Max Planck Institute for Solid State Research at the Hochfeld Magnet Laboratory] in Grenoble had, for the first time, succeeded in deflecting light with a magnet. In their experiment, a ray of light passes through a diffuse gas mixture (for example air), and with a sufficiently strong magnetic field orientated at right angles to the ray, more light escapes into the third dimension (that is at right angles to the ray of light and the magnetic field).

Æsculin:

(6,7-Dihydroxycoumarin-6-glucoside), $C_{15}H_{16}O_9$. Colourless, bitter tasting, needle shaped crystals. The aqueous solution fluoresces at pH > 5.8 blue, which is why Æsculin was used as an optical brightener already in 1929. Æsculin, isolated from the shell of the Horse-chestnut (*Æsculus hippocastanum*), is also the raw material for natural protection from light and Sun. Æsculin is completely transparent to visible light. Immediately below the perceptible violet part of the spectrum (from wavelength of 400 nm), however, it begins to strongly absorb UV light, between 335 and 222 nanometres (for the exact measurement, we are grateful to the author Dr. Judyth Sassoon).

In the lecture of 04.06.1920 (in '*Geisteswissenschaft und Medizin* [Spiritual Science and Medicine],' GA 312, 1999, Lecture 17, pp. 236-237 or see webpage: http://wn.rsarchive.org/Lectures/SpiSciMed/SpiSci index.html), Rudolf Steiner says that highly diluted Æsculin taken internally works in a regulating way on tooth preservation. This substance releases the chemism, i.e. removes the chemical-ether, so that only mineralisation remains, which is desirable for tooth formation, where there should be nothing etheric. Finally he made the suggestion: "*these are things which must be tried out, which when they are brought before the world as statistical results would make a significant impression.*"

2) Day and Night Trials with the two Warmth Currents:

As already mentioned in the introduction, close to the formative forces research is the rhythm research, i.e. studying the influence of daily and annual rhythms in organisms as well as various natural processes, especially warmth, the second fundamental area for work in ether research. These natural rhythms would play an important role in future technology, said Rudolf Steiner in his lecture of 10.12.1918 (GA 184, 1985, Lecture Five, p. 100): *"Through the penetration of natural rhythms one comes also to a particular use of the rhythmical in technology. That is then the aim of technology in the future: through harmonised oscillations that are produced small, and are then translated into large, and by means of simple harmonising could carry out enormous work."*

With these studies, one comes next, according to the remarks of Dr. Rudolf E. Maier, to the special characteristics of warmth-ether, with its 'two currents.' In the Warmth Course (Lecture X of 03.10.1920, p. 122), Rudolf Steiner mentions that in many heat effects there are two different heat currents to be found simultaneously. *Radiant heat* appears in connection with the extra-terrestrial (cosmic) and the living (blood-heat), the warmth that is related to light or to soul-fire. *Conducted heat* on the contrary represents the more externally perceptible (coarser) fire, the dead (mineral) warmth or also the terrestrial warmth.

Once again in the Astronomy Course on 01.08.1921 (Lecture VIII), Rudolf Steiner considers the two kinds of warmth: the Earth is the place for ponderable matter that causes pressure. We have air and the effects of gravity. He provides these conditions with a positive sign. In place of ponderable matter, the ether is found on the Sun with a negative sign and light effects and repulsion. With most heat phenomena, both conditions are present at the same time: warmth is related to ponderable matter just as much as it is to the ether. It is otherwise with air (positive) and light (negative) and we must *"with warmth…positive and negative change over then it becomes transparent what we are used to seeing as conducted heat and radiant heat, etc."* (GA 323) For this reason Rudolf Steiner introduced in the Warmth Course, an imaginary coefficient ($\sqrt{-1}$) for the equation of heat conduction (see Lecture XII of 03.12.1920), which in quite another place as a wave equation became later an indispensable instrument of quantum mechanics.* [See also Comments for Folio 15 on page 96, Tr.]

More about the varied qualities of warmth, apart from the numerous indications in the Warmth Course, are to be found in 01.07.1924 (GA 316), 03.16.1908 (GA 102), 10.24.1923 (GA 351), 05.16.1920 (GA 201) and 10.15.1921 (GA 207).

Silver Iodide

The next matter that arose was to study the difference in decomposition of silver iodide by day as well as by night. Four weeks earlier Rudolf Steiner in the 'Warmth Course' had proposed research into whether crystallisation processes occur differently by day as by night. He coined the terms '*Wärmetag* [day-warmth]' and '*Wärmenacht* [night-warmth]' (See Lecture VII of 03.07.1920 in GA 321, p. 89):

"You see, with such matters we will have to establish our research institute. In addition to our usual thermometers and hygrometers and so on, we will have to invent instruments which will indicate that certain processes which take place within the earthly, especially within the fluid and gaseous material nature, occur differently by night than by day.

---

* See Lecture XII, p. 149 in the 'Warmth Course,' GA 321, Mercury Press, Spring Valley, New York, 2nd edition 1988; reprinted 2005.

You see then, we are led to an appropriate physical method of observation so that once and for all it can be grasped and for suitable measuring instruments to demonstrate the fine differences between day and night that arise for all phenomena, especially those occurring in fluid and gaseous states. In the future, we must be able to do a certain experiment in the day and repeat it in the corresponding hour of the night; we must have the delicate instruments that can show that the phenomena are different by day and night. For by day there are not the forces that tend to crystallise the Earth passing through our phenomena, which are just there at night. By night, forces appear which come from the cosmos. These cosmic forces attempt to crystallise the Earth and this must be seen in the phenomena. Here a way of experimenting is opened up for us to establish again the connection of the Earth with the Universe.

You see, the research institute that must in the future be set up in the sense of our anthroposophically-orientated world conception will have significant tasks. You must really reckon with matters that are today reckoned with least of all in certain phenomena. Of course with light phenomena we already do that, at least with certain phenomena, when we create an artificial night, darken the room, and so on, but we do not attempt it with other phenomena that occur below a certain 'null-sphere.' Instead of this we come to the idea, that what we would find as visual results, if it really existed visually, to then transfer to the insides of bodies and to speak of all kinds of forces which play themselves out between atoms and molecules. The whole thing only rests on the fact that we can investigate everything by day. We will discover for example the difference in crystal forms, when, in this way, we carry out the same experiment first by day and then by night." (From Lecture VII of 03.07.1920 in GA 321, 2005, pp. 90-91.)

Rudolf Steiner also spoke of the cosmic influences on water in the Agricultural Course, and said there the crystallisation forces (form-forces) are different above and below the Earth, and further it can be observed that the influences in the course of the day are different; the tendency to freeze being the greatest on February 1. To better research the two different warmth qualities, see the second experimental arrangement in Folio 8.

Working directly from this suggestion, Dr. Ehrenfried Pfeiffer in 1927 in Dornach made crystallisation experiments with a solution of sodium sulphate, which was allowed to crystallise at different times of day and night. He observed definite differences in the arrangement of single crystals at different times of the day and night, later published in '*Gäa Sophia* [Gaia Sophia],' Band [Vol.] II, 1927. In addition to this, Lilly Kolisko presented the results of her own research in her book titled '*Sternenwirken in Erdenstoffen, Experimentelle Studien aus dem Biologischen Institut am Goetheanum* [Working of the Stars in Earthly Substances, Experimental Studies from the Biological Institute at the Goetheanum],' Orient-Occident Verlag, Stuttgart 1927, Seite [page] 9. Over many years she had allowed the crystals to grow during the most varied times of day and night, *"always with the same result. In the night the process was quicker and the forms appeared more strongly than during the day,"* she wrote looking back. In the course of one year, she always found a weight maximum for the substance crystallised out in February, and a minimum in August.

These pioneers of rhythm research have been followed in the course of the century by other anthroposophical scientists; they tried with most varied apparatus to make visible the influences of days and seasons, also in connection with the Moon and then the rhythms of the planets and their positions in the zodiac. Similarly in the Mathematical-Astronomical Section for many years, exact differences have been established by the drop-picture method developed by Theodor Schwenk, showing dependence on certain planetary constellations (e.g. conjunction of Jupiter and Saturn). Lilly Kolisko noticed for the first time in 1936 that also an eclipse of the Sun affected her reagents. More recently, Lawrence Edwards in Scotland could show experimentally that there is also an influence on living substance: he researched for years with the change in the forms of buds and established that during every Mars/Moon conjunction the shape of the bud was different than before. In addition, the so-called 'chronobiology' concerns itself with the influence of rhythms on living things. A pioneer of this still young scientific discipline, Eugen Kolisko, was told by Rudolf Steiner: *"If you would study life, study rhythms!"*

Recently, in current orthodox science, new connections have been discovered between natural rhythms and living things. Thus, researchers have pointed out statistically significant correlations of Moon phases with numerous meteorological measurements such as temperature, pressure and also concentration of ice-crystals in the atmosphere ('Influence of Lunar Phase on Daily Global Temperatures,' Science, Vol. 267, No. 5203, 10 March 1995, pp. 1481-1483, and 'A Mysterious Monthly Temperature Cycle,' New Scientist, Vol. 145, No. 1962, 28 January 1995, p. 18). Ernst Zürcher of the *ETH-Zürich* [Swiss Federal Institute of Technology Zürich] connected regular variations within the diameter of trees, which were in the region of 1/10th of a millimetre, with the position of the Moon ('Tree Stem Diameters Fluctuate with Tide,' Nature, Vol. 392, No. 6678, 16 April 1998, pp. 665-666). The effects of the already long known 11-year cycle of the Sun's activity can be seen in many natural phenomena. (

See also e.g. *'Mathematisch-Physikalische Korrespondenz* [Mathematical-Physical Correspondence]' Nr. 47a, Frühling [Spring] 1964, S. 5 and D. R. Barber, 'Apparent Solar Control of the Effective Capacity of a 110-V. 170 AH Lead-Acid Storage Battery in an 11-Year Cycle,' Nature, Vol. 195, No. 4842, 18 August 1962, pp. 684-687.)

In connection with the inquiry into the nature of heat, Dr. Ehrenfried Pfeiffer and Lilly Kolisko also set up experiments about the quality of warmth in various heating materials. See the Notes of Dr. P. E. Schiller on pages 33-35.

A few years ago scientists discovered that water reacted very differently depending on whether it was heated by wood, coal or on an electric stove: the growth of wheat sprouts in variously pre-treated water tests served as a unit of measure in a research project at the University of Fulda [in Germany, Tr.]. (*Die Weltwoche* [The World Week], Zürich, Nr. 12/98 vom [of] 03.19.1998.)

3) The Magnetism of Metals

In 1778, Brugmans observed the repulsion of bismuth in the proximity of a magnet. In 1827, Le Baillif described the repulsion of antimony. Similarly, Seebeck, Becquerel and others observed this phenomenon. In 1845, Michael Faraday generalised this observation when he showed that all matter could be more or less magnetised. He found too, that there are two kinds of substance. The one can be attracted, the other repelled, by a magnetic pole. Faraday called the origin of these inherent and constant forces in the substance, diamagnetism for repulsion, and paramagnetism for attraction. These forces are of the order of six times weaker than the ferro-magnetic forces, which appear in iron, cobalt and nickel.

Further details of this problem are to be found in a letter of the 26th of November 1955 from Dr. Paul Eugen Schiller to Peter von Siemens (p. 81):

"*In connection with magnetism, Rudolf Steiner recommended a study of the formative forces appearing there. A magnet, whose poles are covered alternately with coatings of copper, tin, lead etc., shall be investigated. The task has to do with the fact that magnetism is the counter-image of the chemical-ether. Very probably this is also connected with the indications about the use of magnets in the healing of certain illnesses. Closely linked to this are also the experiments with electricity. To what extent can we demonstrate that we are dealing with a sub-physical force? Some years ago I began relevant experiments including those concerning the influence of electrical fields on plant growth. The first results were very interesting, and it would be important to continue these experiments further.*"

4) Ashes of Plants

Very probably, the research into the physical differences between plant and mineral ashes is a kind of pre-study to the crystallisation experiment with and without plant substances. How the crystal shapes were influenced by the etheric formative forces, would then be investigated later. A trivial physical difference between mineral and plant ashes: carbon appearing in the plants is partly radioactive. However, when it has not been found for a long time in a living organism, the radioactivity decreases.

More about ash formation may be found in: 10.06.1923 (GA 229); ashes (weed-control): 06.14.1924 (GA 327); carbon formation: 03.31.1920 (GA 312); connection of human beings with surrounding world: plant kingdom; formation of carbon: 01.21.1921 (GA 203).

See also the reference in Folio 7 to Mr. Henri Smits where investigation of incinerated peat fibres can demonstrate whether the previous treatment of the fibres became etherically effective or not.

5) Carbon, Graphite and Diamond

Carbon heated in a vacuum becomes fluid, which when rapidly cooled solidifies to graphite. When carbon is dissolved in molten iron and the temperature further raised to white heat, small diamonds are found when this molten iron is rapidly cooled. The opposite is also acknowledged. When a powerful electric current is passed through diamond, causing a small flash, then it turns to carbon.

Rudolf Steiner often spoke about the metamorphoses of carbon. On 12.23.1923 (GA 232, 1997, Lecture 14, pp. 229, 231) he said that the counter-pole to gold (Sun) is carbon. The alchemists therefore call carbon 'the precious stone of the wise': "*and if one were to convey a piece of common carbon to the Moon, at that moment it would become silver.*" This metamorphosis of carbon to silver is mirrored in the blood stream.

On 12.30.1923 (GA 233, 1997, Lecture VII, p. 113): With crystal formation, not only forces of gravity but form creating forces are working; these are related to earthly forces, so that these substances are subject to earthly conditions. "*Who does not keep such things firmly in mind will come and point to a piece of coal, black coal. What is this in reality? It is black coal only near the Earth, it is no more so in that moment when it is only a relatively short distance from the Earth. Everything about coal that makes it coal, are the forces of the Earth.*"

01.03.1924 (GA 316): The forms of antimony resemble the etheric forms of common plants. Antimony is responsive to etheric forces. Another example: coal (Earth), graphite (Moon), diamond (Sun).

01.14.1921 (GA 323, Lecture XIV): By means of the plant the activity of the Sun is carried into the Earth, causing mineralisation, for example coal.

6) The form-forces of plant substances

In 1925, Dr. Ehrenfried Pfeiffer together with Erica Sabarth quite by chance came across copper chloride that crystallised well between glass plates. With this equipment, the formative forces could easily be studied. In initial experiments, they used plant extracts of water lilies and chamomile. Later they also investigated the crystal forming forces in human and animal blood. Today Dr. Pfeiffer's copper chloride crystallisation is established as a standard method worldwide so that the vital quality of foodstuffs can be determined and in a reproducible form. More about this technique is to be found in the extensive literature, which has since become available under the theme of 'Image-creating Methods.'

Industrial Use of Plant Colours

At that time, the newly appearing synthetic colours in the textile industry displaced the widespread tradition of plant colours. Dr. Guenther Wachsmuth describes in his book, 'The Life and Work of Rudolf Steiner' (Whittier Books, New York, 2nd ed. 1955, p. 408), one of the earliest tasks of a scientific nature in the following way:

"Amongst the initiatives for the development of art and medicine are included the manufacture of new plant colours. *On his advice, in order to produce paints from plants a small laboratory was already set up in 1912 through the initiative of Dr. Oskar Schmiedel and Baroness I. von Eckardtstein in Munich, where the first experiments were made. This was re-sited at Dornach in 1914, where Oskar and Thekla Schmiedel also made all the colours for the painting of the two cupolas of the* [first] *Goetheanum building. Rudolf Steiner frequently visited the laboratory by the canteen and gave further advice on the development of the* plant colours. *On this basis, further attempts were made later by W. Scott Pyle and Mieta Pyle, Dr. Otto Eckstein and colleagues with the 'Anthea'* colours."* See also the chapter '*Herstellung von Malfarben aus Pflanzenstoffen* [Manufacture of Pigments from Plant Material]' in Rudolf Steiner's '*Farbenerkenntnis* [Knowledge of Colour],'** (GA 291a, 1. Auflage [1st Edition], Gesamtausgabe Dornach [Collected Edition Dornach] 1990, S. 403-421), edited and commentated by Hella Wiesberger and Heinrich O. Proskauer.

Comments for Folio 3

Cyanide compounds as a transition from organic to inorganic chemistry

---

* Anthea (from the Greek word *Antheia* meaning 'flower, blossom').
** In German only. Supplement to '*Das Wesen der Farben* [The Being of Colour],' GA 291 published in English as 'Colour,' 1992; second edition 1996.

The physical body of a living *being* is made up of chemical substances. If the physical basis for the life functions has gone, a process of decay sets in. There arise in the framework of protein metabolism very poisonous cyanide compounds. In the dying leaves of plants, for example, there appear alkaloids (nicotine, etc.). Also in the kernels of fruit, that is to say, in those parts which are least penetrated by life activities, we find compounds of prussic acid. In this sense the appearance of cyanide compounds in the protein metabolism of living *beings* can be seen as a border where the etheric draws back for the benefit of physical considerations. In modern school chemistry all carbon compounds are counted with organic chemistry, and inorganic chemistry is concerned with the remaining substances and compounds. This classification, which today has solely an historic significance, originated in the 18th century where the chemist did not to begin with succeed in producing substances artificially from living *beings*.

Transformation of small oscillations into large

See in the corresponding commentary in Folio 4 under the heading 'Keely Motor.'

Philology [Sprachwissenschaft]

In the German tongue many expressions can be found that have a meaning connected with spirit and matter. So for example one can find in every etymological German dictionary something about a *negation of seeing*. See also Rudolf Steiner's lecture of 12.28.1914 in GA 275, 2003, pp. 84-85. (The author Pascale Didier provided this reference.) [See in addition Folio 3 on page 10, Tr.]

Comments for Folio 4

In this folio the reported conversations between Rudolf Steiner and Dr. Ehrenfried Pfeiffer took place between October 1920 and spring 1921.

…the age is not suitable for making etheric forces workable.

In addition there are three documented versions of answers to the same questions:

1. Report from Dr. E. Pfeiffer on the 27th of February 1955, published in Alla Selawry's, 'Ehrenfried Pfeiffer – A Pioneer in Spiritual Research and Practice – A Contribution to his Biography,' Mercury Press, Spring Valley, New York, 1992, pp. 11ff.
2. Dr. E. Pfeiffer in his last lecture in Dornach on the 10th of October 1958 published in 'Sub-nature and Super-nature in the Physiology of Plant and Man: The True Basis of Nutrition,' Mercury Press, Spring Valley, New York, 1981, p. 21.
3. Dr. E. Pfeiffer's autobiography '*Ein Leben für den Geist: Ehrenfried Pfeiffer (1899-1961)* [A Life for the Spirit: Ehrenfried Pfeiffer (1899-1961)],' edited and with a preface by Thomas Meyer, Perseus Verlag, Basel, 1999, S. 121; 2. Aufl. [2nd Ed.] 2000; 3. Aufl. [3rd Ed.] 2003.

Reference from 1: Dr. Ehrenfried Pfeiffer reported on 27th of February 1955:

"The question raised by Rudolf Steiner, before the work began, was for an inquiry into the etheric realm: How are the etheric formative forces to be demonstrated and in such a form that they can be utilised? How can the etheric realm be introduced as a new natural force into technology? For it lies in the nature of the etheric that it does not destroy but creates and thereby a constructive technology could be brought about. How does one gain the knowledge to do this, and later manage the etheric realm?"

These were the original questions raised by Rudolf Steiner in 1920 and 1921. The answers with reference to the ether-forces went as follows: organisms should be used for detecting the effects, and the influence of rhythm on life-processes studied. Formative forces should be made visible.

Reference from 2:

Dr. Ehrenfried Pfeiffer described in his last lecture 'Sub-nature and Super-nature in the Physiology of Plant and Man: The True Basis of Nutrition', given in Dornach, on the 10th of October 1958, the following memories (p. 21):

"It was my idea that through the discovery of such energies [meaning the etheric formative forces, Note W. K.] *a new technology and social order could be created. Rudolf Steiner's answer was to propose a few quite simple experiments which I carried out for him, and upon their completion he had, through these experiments, received the answer from the spiritual world which was: the time was not yet ripe that these etheric energies can be made known and introduced."*

Reference from 3:

"I must carry out certain experiments which I may not describe in detail. The results of these experiments were shared with Rudolf Steiner whereupon he remarked with the greatest seriousness: 'The result of this trial points to another force, not the etheric, but to an astral force' (i.e. to forces that are in living substance, having sensation such as nerve and brain). That the experiment led to this result was for him the answer of the spiritual world and it meant that the time was not yet ripe to make use of the power of the ether."

Keely Motor

John Worrell Keely (1827-1898), independent researcher in U.S.A. (Philadelphia) working in the realm of acoustics. He invented in 1872 the Hydro-Pneumatic Pulsating Vacuo Engine, an improved steam engine, which, in connection with a vacuum, steam can be rapidly cooled. The condensed steam in a super-cooled vacuum is then used as a motive power. Certainly, in the course of the first trials, the machine exploded. Rudolf Steiner referred to Mr. Keely in several lectures when discussing future technology. Anything further on this theme may be found in the Comments for Folio 20 in this issue (see page 98) and especially in Issue No. 107 of the '*Beiträge zur Rudolf Steiner Gesamtausgabe* [Supplements to the Collected Edition of Rudolf Steiner],' entitled: '*Der Strader-Apparat, Modell – Skizzen – Berichte* [The Strader Apparatus, Model – sketches – reports],' Dornach, Michaeli [Michaelmas] 1991. Contained therein is a chronological overview of Rudolf Steiner's statement concerning 'Mechanical Occultism, the Keely Motor and Technology of the Future,' as well as numerous references on the same subject.

Notes to the report by Dr. E. Pfeiffer:

See lecture of 11.25.1917, GA 178, Secret Brotherhoods, 2004, p. 178: *Mensch und Mechanisierung* [The Human Being and Mechanisation]; p. 191f: *Maschinentiere, kosmische Kräfte und Maschinen* [Machine-animals, Cosmic Forces and Machines].

Paramecium

Paramecium (caudatum), from the family of Protozoa, is only just recognisable as a living *being* to the naked eye. In order to move about it uses hundreds of small sensitive hair-like 'cilia' whose coordinated movements in the animal body are converted into a rotatory transposition. Biologists have researched thoroughly the behaviour of the paramecia towards various external influences such as electric current, acids, heat and the gravity field of the Earth. It has been shown that paramecia react sensitively to all these influences; therefore they are especially suited as reagents.

Life-ether extracted with ethyl alcohol

The uncertainty of the information must be specially pointed out at this stage. All three documents (lecture, notes and autobiography) by Dr. Ehrenfried Pfeiffer already cited rely on the agreement of the first two points whereas with the last point it is always animals, or in this case bacteria, as *reagents* which are spoken of. It may be assumed that here also this is what was envisaged. See also in the notes to Folio 2 the idea that the activity of life-forces would be identifiable through their vitalising affect on bacteria and flies. The final comment on these conjectures we owe to Dr. Guenther Wachsmuth ('The Life and Work of Rudolf Steiner,' Whittier Books, New York, 2nd ed. 1955, p. 421):

"*To give a slight insight into the endless problems of these initial gropings, I would like to relate how I with Dr. Ehrenfried Pfeiffer and a thirst for knowledge, equipped with a primitive laboratory, went to Rudolf Steiner and put the questions how could we recognise the life-forces or formative forces, which he named life-ether, in nature and then get to know them through research. I no longer know how far our highly aimed questions (all beginners' questions reach for the stars at first) were taken by Rudolf Steiner in complete seriousness, or with a hearty dash of friendly humour. In any case he replied that the answer was simple, for example we only have to put a fly into a vacuum. Armed with a more or less correctly understood research set-up and in the excitement of the moment, we scrambled down to our cellar. We soon caught the required fly and brought it into a vacuum. However, after this was done, the same question arose in our minds: what next? Perhaps we had indeed the life-force in the vacuum, but what we lacked was the possibility of verifying and testing it, measuring or using it. This small experiment, to be seen perhaps in a more humorous light, nevertheless had a decisive influence on us, for now we realised: what we needed above all is a reagent, a test, something that indicated where and how these forces were present, whether increasing or decreasing, etc.*"

Rudolf Steiner and the book by Râma Prasâd, 'Nature's Finer Forces,' where mention is made of seven kinds of ether (Part One, V. Prâna (II), p. 41):

In the English original (The Theosophical Publishing Society, London, 1915*) on page 7, only five kinds of ether, the five principles (*Tattvas***) of Indo-Hindu tradition are described which later in the book are brought into connection with the classical occidental elements:

1. Âkâsha	sonoriferous ether	sound (dark)	'ether'
2. Vâyu (Pavana)	tangiferous ether	touch (blue)	gas
3. Tejas (Agni or Raurava or Pitta)	luminiferous ether	colour (red)	fire
4. Apas (Varî)	gustiferous ether	taste (white)	liquid
5. Prithivî	odoriferous ether	smell (yellow)	solid

When in a whole series of lectures (GA 177, etc.) Rudolf Steiner quotes from C. G. Harrison's 'The Transcendental Universe' (James Elliott & Co., London, 1894; Second edition, George Redway, London, 1896; reprinted, Temple Lodge, London, 1993), widely read in Theosophical circles at the time, it may be assumed that in discussing this work he was also referring to the footnote (on *Seite* [page] 25 of the German edition***) in connection with the so-called 'Sevenfold Mysteries of the Forces of Nature' in Râma Prasâd's book.

Dr. Guenther Wachsmuth devoted a whole paragraph to this sevenfoldness in his work 'The Etheric Formative Forces in Cosmos, Earth and Man' (Anthroposophical Publishing Co., London, 1932, p. 39). He states there (the whole paragraph is stressed by him):

"In fact there are altogether seven etheric archetypal or formative forces active in the cosmos, but of these only four are revealed in the processes of space and time at present."

Literature

Hermann Beckh, '*Der übersinnliche Organismus im indischen Yoga (Lotosblumen, Kundalini) im Lichte der Erkenntnis der ätherischen Bildekräfte* [The Supersensible Organism in Indian Yoga (Lotus Flowers, Kundalini) in the Light of the Knowledge of the Etheric Formative Forces],' in '*Gäa Sophia* [Gaia Sophia],' *Jahrbuch der naturwissenschaftlichen Sektion der Freien Hochschule für Geisteswissenschaft am Goetheanum Dornach* [Yearbook of the Natural Science Section of the Free High School for Spiritual Science at the Goetheanum Dornach], Band [Vol.] III, 1929, S. 196ff.

Günther Schubert, '*Indische Bezeichnungen für die Ätherarten* [Indian Descriptions of the Different Kinds of Ether],' in '*Gäa Sophia* [Gaia Sophia],' loc. cit., Dornach, Band [Vol.] I, 1926, S. 342ff.

The reaction of a quietly burning flame:

In a note of the 24th of April 1960, Dr. Guenther Wachsmuth mentioned that Rudolf Steiner on another occasion has spoken of a *"very mobile flame."* See also Folio 11 where a *"freely moving"* flame is mentioned.

---

* Original 1890 edition available on-line at webpage: http://www.rexresearch.com/prana/essays.htm or download in pdf format from: http://www.hermetics.org/pdf/NaturesFinerForcesTheScienceofBreathRamaPrasad.pdf.
** *Tattva* is a Sanskrit word meaning 'principle,' 'thatness,' 'reality' or 'truth.'
*** '*Das Transcendentale Weltenall* [The Transcendental Universe],' Ackermann, Munich, 1897; (a photo-mechanical reproduction of the edition of 1897 is published by Engel & Streffer, Stuttgart, 1990).

Comments for Folio 5

Folio 5 refers to further important notes by Rudolf Steiner on Natural Science, that were published in the periodical '*Anthroposophie* [Anthroposophy]' (Edited by Dr. Kurt Piper) in Stuttgart over the years 1927-1929. Below they are reproduced, partly in facsimile.

Comments for Folio 6

Referring to the anode-cathode polarity and its correspondence to the antithesis of Sun and Earth mentioned in this folio, see notes to Folio 8.

Candle in a Carboy…

At that time the electric field was measured with so-called flame inductors, whilst the following two facts were made use of simultaneously: 1. In the case of an insulated, electrically conducting rod in an electric field, the freely moving positive and negative charges separate, i.e. the rod is polarised. 2. A burning candle intensifies the electrical conductivity of the surrounding air. When one brings a candle to one end of a polarised conductor through the electrical field all the accumulated charges emerge so that only one kind of a charge remains in the conductor. The strength of this charge can be read with an electrometer and is an immediate measurement of the existing field strength.

Negative Charge of the Earth

The electric field of the Earth was discovered about 200 years ago. In 1803 Prof. Erman of Berlin showed with a gold leaf electrometer that the Earth was negatively charged (*Gilbert's Annalen* [Gilbert's Annals], Vol. 15, 1803, S. 386). Later, research into the electricity of the atmosphere began. Viktor Franz Hess in 1911 was the first to show that the atmosphere has a positive charge, increasing with height, after many balloon trips up to 5,400 metres. Numerous measurements in further research showed that the charge is smaller in summer and greater in winter. From these measurements it could be seen that a certain proportion of these free charges flowed down to Earth. This vertical stream with a total current of circa 1,400 amps shows regular daily variations over the whole globe. Prof. Hess postulated once: *"the existence of radiation coming from above with an extraordinary penetrative power of probably extra-terrestrial origin."* At that time the causes of these charges were unknown. For his later work on cosmic radiation and the discovery of its cause, Prof. Hess was nominated and subsequently awarded the Nobel Prize in Physics 1936, and is considered as the pioneer of all the atomic research that followed. The source: Ferdinand G. Smekal: *Österreichs Nobelpreisträger*, Wien 1968 [Austria's Nobel Prize winner, Vienna 1968].

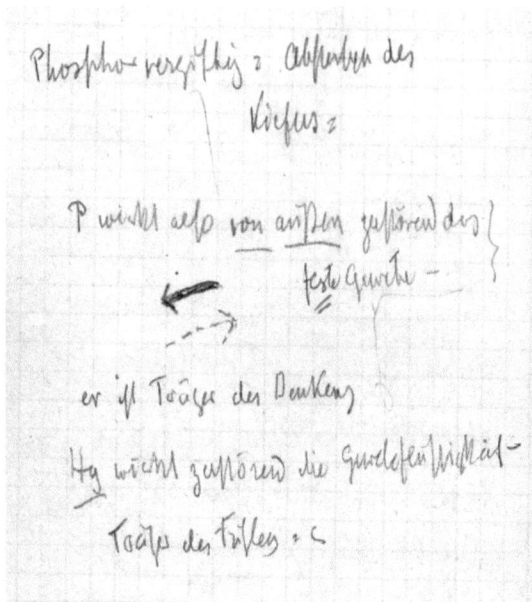

Phosphorus poisoning or contamination: The dying of pine trees.

Phosphorus works thus from outside destroying firm tissue.

It is the bearer of thinking.

Quicksilver [mercury, Tr.] causes the destruction of tissue-fluidity: it is the bearer of feeling.

From a Notebook

(*'Geistessaat aus Rudolf Steiners Notizbüchern: Aus einem Notizbuche vom Jahre 1923* [Spiritual Seeds from Rudolf Steiner's Notebooks: From a notebook for the year 1922]' in '*Anthroposophie* [Anthroposophy],' *Stuttgart, 11. Jahrgang* [11th Year], *Nr. 14, 31. März* [31st March] *1929, S. 105-106)*

Will is hunger, conceptualising is appeasement.
Will forms carbon dioxide (CO2).
Conceptualisation consumes phosphorus which is in light.

Notebook Archive No. NB 309, 1922/23

In spring the active forces are cosmic, making the human head similar to the body, which in autumn make the body similar to the head. Therefore, more carbon dioxide (CO2) is exhaled in winter than in summer.

*Notebook Archive No. NB 310, 1923**

The world-plant-animal expires in porphyry, then the plant *being* dies away in slate, the animal *being* in lime, and in salt the human *being* is extinguished; the other pole is sulphur where the mineral is burnt-up.

Mineral burns-up in sulphur.
Plants put down layers of warmth in slate.
The plant-animal finds sensation ingrained in porphyry.
The animal preserves its structural form in lime.
The human *being* composes his thoughts in salt.
Man enters the earthly realm by means of sulphur.
By means of slate he correctly brings about conformity to the earthly.
Aroused feeling (porphyry-like) organises itself and makes its human model in lime in order to create the basis for thoughts in the depositing of salt.

* First published under the title 'Geistessaat aus Rudolf Steiners Notizbüchern: Aus einem Notizbuche vom Jahre 1923 [Spiritual Seeds from Rudolf Steiner's Notebooks: From a notebook for the year 1923]' in 'Anthroposophie: Wochenschrift für freies Geistesleben [Anthroposophy: Weekly Journal for the Free Spiritual Life],' Stuttgart, 9. Jahrgang [9th Year], Nr. 41, 9. Oktober [9th October] 1927, S. 173-174; English translation published in 'The Living Earth: The Organic Origin of Rocks and Minerals,' by Walther Cloos, Lanthorn Press, 1977, p. 26.

The mineralising process goes from front-to-back in the animal (Sun), the vitalising process from behind to the front (Moon).

The mineralising process is an earthly one that the powers of the Universe have taken up and organised.

Plant poisons: They draw the astral towards themselves:

in them lies the power to give particular spiritual form to the chaotic-spiritual.

They work directly on the lower human being so that they produce universal forms that appear negative as the upper human being becomes conscious of them.

The digestion is already poisoned but not yet in any exact form. Coming from the upper human being the forms become exact.

Comments for Folio 7

Rudolf Steiner's Suggestions for the Refinement of Peat

1. Origin and purpose of the task

An essential characteristic of the proposition is the fact that it arose from Rudolf Steiner's own decision and not on account of questions brought forward by various persons, as was often the case. Henri Smits, the editor for this project in '*Der Kommende Tag A.G.* [The Coming Day plc],' wrote subsequently on the 15th of November 1964, that through the initiative of Dr. Paul Eugen Schiller, he gave a lecture on (26.11.1960 Stuttgart) on 'Rudolf Steiner's Suggestions for the Refinement of Peat':

"From my sister, Frau Lory Maier-Smits, I have quite recently heard the following about the beginnings of the peat question: 'during the First World War Dr. Rudolf Steiner visited an exhibition of artificial materials in Berlin; he was accompanied by Albert Dibbern, a committee member of the Hamburg branch. There, amongst other exhibits, were fibres of stinging nettles to be seen, which Dr. Steiner described as good; he added however that peat fibre would be still better. Not only warmer, but almost untearable and could also give undoubted protection against radiation.' Through the connection of the families of Dibbern and Maier, Dr. Maier heard of this conversation and told me how he was led to set out experiments with peat before Dr. Rudolf Steiner."

Mr. Henri Smits described further conversations with Rudolf Steiner about this project right at the beginning of his lecture:

"Forty years ago Rudolf Steiner was at the Guldes-Mühle, a farm in the district of Neresheim, in order to participate in experiments, which he had inaugurated, for finding a remedy against foot-and-mouth disease.* At the time the farm belonged to my relatives, and on this occasion Dr. Rudolf Steiner mentioned that there were good prospects for producing material that could be spun from peat fibre. My relations made it possible for me to obtain tests from Upper Swabia in order to submit them to Dr. Rudolf Steiner. From what I know today I must say that I brought unsuitable peat. I brought fenland peat. Rudolf Steiner, however, declared the peat as suitable.** I considered my task finished and returned to Berlin in order to complete my studies. When I came back the research institute was about to be established. This interested me very much and I was pleased to be summoned there. I had studied mining and heard lectures about mineralogy, geology, etc. I was given a list of the tasks of the research institute, and looked for one that met with my interests. I thought of crystallisation. Then I requested an interview with Dr. Rudolf Steiner. He greeted me with the words: 'It is terrible here, nothing is happening. Neither is the work on peat progressing.'

---

* See Kolisko, Eugen M.D. (Vienna), 'Foot-and-Mouth Disease: Its Nature and Treatment,' Published by The British Weleda Co., Ltd., London, No date, circa 1925. This pamphlet was revised and enlarged by L. Kolisko and reprinted as Chapter XVII (Part III) in 'Agriculture of Tomorrow' by E. Kolisko and L. Kolisko, Kolisko Archive, Stroud, 1st edition 1946, pp. 348-377; Kolisko Archive Publications, Bournemouth, 2nd edition 1978; 1982, pp. 263-282.

** In the transcript of his lecture, Mr. Henri Smits added the following: *"I should like to mention that once more I had the opportunity to submit peat experiments that I had carried out in north Germany to Dr. Rudolf Steiner in Dornach; this time with the correct moorland peat with abundant fibre bundles. On this occasion Dr. Rudolf Steiner said that one would find that the peat-bundles would become longer the further north one went. In fact, the fibre-bundles from north Germany were altogether longer than those from the Black Forest or Upper Swabia. Later I was involved with a peat experiment in Finland which involved considerably longer peat-bundles than I found in Germany."*

57

I began to say my little speech but he carried on talking about peat, so that in the end I asked whether he meant me to undertake this role. He confirmed this, speaking with animation, gave me the first instructions."

With the war over, the production of substitute material was no longer a priority. It was much more a concrete research task set up by Rudolf Steiner that for the first time one could deal with the etheric realm.* This becomes still clearer in the statement of Rudolf Steiner made to Mr. Henri Smits:

"Once I asked him: 'Should we not build a new etheric body on the peat fibres?' I went from the implicit assumption that the peat is dead, containing nothing of the living, i.e. etheric. He replied however: 'No, it is not like that, in peat the etheric has a descending tendency that must be changed into an ascending one.'"

In a written report Mr. Henri Smits added later:

*"The brittle fibres should be strengthened by the addition of cosmic forces to the earthly process of destruction."***

Dr. Rudolf Hauschka, who later took on this task from Dr. Ita Wegman, considered in his 'Heilmittellehre [Treatise on Medicines]' that the formative forces that build up the plant produce flower and fruit, and in autumn are again released and drawn back into the Earth. Arising from this natural cycle is humus for the next generation of plants. In exceptional circumstances, with the exclusion of air, the plant fibres become peat where the plant building forces, especially their mediator, the elemental *beings*, become bound to these plants for thousands of years. Dr. Hauschka reported later from conversations that Dr. Ita Wegman had with Rudolf Steiner, that through the refinement of peat fibre one would succeed, *"in freeing the fettered elemental beings and that these, out of thankfulness to human beings, would protect them from what stood before them in the not too distant future, namely: that the atmosphere would be pervaded with electricity, magnetic fields, aeroplanes, and still much worse, and in such a way as to bring suffering to human life on Earth. Clothes made from peat fibre, however, could protect human beings from these influences."*

2. The elaboration and setting up of the tasks for the scientific research institute 'Der Kommende Tag A.G. [The Coming Day plc]'

From the first, at the instigation of Rudolf Steiner at Guldes-Mühle, Mr. Henri Smits, with the help of relatives, had peat experiments carried out in Upper Swabia. In March 1921 he submitted this to Rudolf Steiner, on the occasion of his first discussion, and spoke about it in his lecture (See also the identical data in Folio 7 and Document 1 'First discussion,' on page 64 of this issue):

"Now I should like to repeat to you the nature of the task which Rudolf Steiner presented for the refinement of peat. Rudolf Steiner said to me: '1. The fibres contained in peat from the remains of Eriophorum

---

* Alexander Strakosch reported in his book 'Lebenswege mit Rudolf Steiner [My Path of Life and Rudolf Steiner]' (Zweiter Teil 1919-1925 [Part 2 1919-1925], Dornach 1952, S. 79), that Rudolf Steiner once said to him, *"that it was important to him that one succeeded in finding a considerably mineralised substance which could again be given a plant-like character (particularly the suppleness), so that it could be penetrated with etheric formative forces."*

** This also makes it understandable why Rudolf Steiner in the Agriculture Course (GA 327, in lecture 4 and in the Question and Answer session on 12th June 1924) advised, *"use peat for loosening the soil, because peat blocks the ascending and descending stream in the plant, because it holds the etheric fast."* Peat is much better suited to the conservation of processes in matter. He said further: *"Peat, spread in thin layers in the compost heap, holds together what would otherwise evaporate."*

vaginatum (cotton-grass) so strengthen that they could be used for making textiles. 2. One can make a compress-ible material out of peat, that can be cut, from which something like picture frames could be made.'"

On the 1st of April 1921, Mr. Henri Smits became a co-worker in the research institute and immediately began with the first experiments in confined temporary conditions, but supported by another co-worker, Mr. Hans Buchheim. First of all the fibres were steeped in a caustic solution, and then treated with acid. After these baths the bunches of fibres were then thoroughly beaten and brushed, then bleached with chlorine gas. This led to no result.

During a second discussion with the new co-worker, Rudolf Steiner made the following recommenda-tions for refinement and especially strengthening the peat fibres in order to achieve an almost un-tearable raw material for textiles: The treatment with plant saps from thread forming plants such as creeper and climbers (vetch, flax and linseed, hemp) and the addition of siliceous substances should cause a gluing action. But not merely the substances but more the dynamic-etheric influences must be removed from the peat to be replaced by cosmic powers. On account of the first concrete suggestions further experiments followed which once again produced a negative result. The peat fibre refining with pressing from fodder peas, vetches, and hops led to no result because, in spite of a certain gluing effect, they could always be washed out.

There were probably more conversations with Rudolf Steiner in the summer and Mr. Henri Smits also showed him new trials in Dornach. It was arranged by means of experiment to replace silica by asbestos, chrysolite or hornblende.

At the beginning of September the Peat Fibre Department was given new premises in the basement of the school hut. Still in the same month (See Document 2 'Suggestions from Dr. Rudolf Steiner on the 21st of September 1921,' on page 64) Rudolf Steiner further advised taking a salt from grey antimony and Robinias, laburnum grown on lower new red sandstone or the white bark of the birch, with which the fibres could take up the plant essences in a lasting way. To improve the straightening out of fibres electric fields were mentioned.

In a members' discussion of the 17th of December 1921, Mr. Henri Smits demonstrated new trials and told of his latest fibre treatment experiments with asbestos, the above mentioned plant substances and anti-mony, but which did not lead to a particularly un-tearable fibre. Rudolf Steiner was of the opinion that the plant saps used must be from an earlier stage of growth, harvested when possible before flowering. He added further: *"One is concerned here with obtaining the force in the antimony."* Mr. Henri Smits asked in connection with the replacement of silica whether chrysolyte powder would not be still better because asbestos was so difficult to handle. Rudolf Steiner supported this, *"because there the fibre tendency is even better lived out… if you do experiments with chrysolyte, you are more likely to get something from them."* A further indication: temperature above 37°C should be avoided.

From December 1921 to February 1922 a detailed series of experiments were made with all kinds of treat-ment of peat fibre. At times a concentrated solution was taken and diluted to the 29th potency. In one of the first series of experiments the solution, with the same potency, consisted of: Convolvulus sap and Sb_2S_3 in Na_2S. In this solution the fibres are allowed to lie for 23 to 29 hours. The result of the experiment was that there was a great variation in the strength of the fibres, whilst clearly different thicknesses of fibres were measured separately. A second and a third series of experiments (with all the potencies from D1 to D29) with chrysolyte and Convolvulus produced greater elasticity without increasing the strength.

On the 28th of April 1922, Rudolf Steiner recommended that Mr. Henri Smits (See Document 3 'Discussion with Dr. Rudolf Steiner on the 28th of April 1922,' on page 65), should entwine three fibres into a plait and then measure the tensile-strength because with different thicknesses of fibre the variations in the measurements were too great. Furthermore, that antimony should be evenly distributed in the fibres, which could best be established by incineration of the fibres. If the fibres burned uniformly instead of sputtering, then that should be the case.

Mr. Henri Smits describes it in his lecture:

"A method which he indicated was that the fibres were burnt completely and the ash-skeleton observed. After the burning, untreated fibres formed a disintegrating ash-skeleton, whilst with the treated fibres there was a cohesive ash-skeleton."

Compare Folio 2: the problem of investigating the physical differences between plant and mineral ashes!

In the spring of 1922 all the necessary plants could be obtained for the first time and a new series of experiments could be put in hand. Rudolf Steiner was informed of the situation and he promised to consider additional ideas, so that the antimony could bestow a more radiant power. At first sloes or hairy seeds, for example thistles or dandelions were used. Whilst the experiments with thistles gave negative results, with the dandelion seeds and roots an increase in the average strength of about 130% was achieved.

In September 1922 Rudolf Steiner produced more ideas and he gave the following formula: Plant sap + larch resin + Horse-chestnut. With this recipe there were problems of the mixing of resin in water (with Horse-chestnut) and about this he said that gum Arabic should be used as the dissolving medium. In December 1922 he advised that the emulsifying agent gum Arabic should be replaced with mallow mucilage and, *"in order to make the action of these substances permanent,"* make use of an oxygen-ozone bath. With this treatment no substantial increase in strength took place.

At the beginning of 1923 Rudolf Steiner looked at the fibres treated with his formula through a microscope and remarked that the image showed a positive effect. As a demonstration he compared the treated fibre with a waxed thread and the untreated with an unwaxed one. Next Rudolf Steiner gave the proportions for his formula as follows: related to the weight of fibre, 1% resin, 1% Horse-chestnut (*Æsculus*) and 0.1% antimony. This must be stirred continuously until it emulsifies and afterwards bleached in an oxygen-ozone bath. It was forgotten to ask about the wild Convolvulus juice, and 10% was chosen. The completed formula showing a big increase in strength averaging 70% (400-500% had been hoped for), and was patented five years later in England by Dr. Ita Wegman. Rudolf Steiner recommended: five fibres twisted into a bundle and ten such bundles made into a cord or thread. The measurements of those of about 40 cm long threads showed an average increase in strength of up to 100% (127% to a maximum of 256% with thick threads and 84% with threads of thin fibres). Finally he advised rhythmically alternating the oxygen and ozone (about 18 times per minute) whilst allowing them to work on the fibres and to use chrysolite for further experiments.

From a letter of the 23rd of October 1923 (Document 4 *'An die Centrale, Hier,'* page 65) it is stated that Rudolf Steiner made a visit on October 17. Mr. Henri Smits proposed to him a project for extracting cellulose from peat fibres. Further plans were discussed for extending the refining baths for 3-4 tons of fibre material.

Just before the liquidation of 'Der Kommende Tag A.G. [The Coming Day plc],' the research workers had succeeded in refining the peat fibres to such a degree that small samples could be spun and woven. Olga Smits, the wife of Henri, reported later that a *"knitted scarf from the yarn of the treated fibres delighted Dr. Rudolf Steiner and gained his approval."* (Zeitschrift [Journal] 'Die Kommenden [The Coming Generations],' Nr. 4 1989, S. 23.)

Modestly, Mr. Henri Smits himself speaks about the results in his lecture:

"Dr. Rudolf Steiner declared himself to be very pleased about the results, even more than those in other laboratories. I am certainly of the opinion that these expressions were to be thought of as encouragement to strengthen our aims and take the wind out of the sails of the slight opposition which held sway among many managers. In any case I am sure that this result was only the beginning but I could not continue with the experiment because of the dissolving of the institute and the possibility did not arise again in my life-time."

Also looking back over the result of this series of experiments Alexander Strakosch writes ('*Lebenswege* [My Path of Life],' 2. Teil a.a.O. [Part 2 loc. cit.], S. 79):

"To a certain degree the task was completed but not for industrial use; meanwhile the importation of cotton on a sufficient scale had begun again, with further consequences."

Similarly, Hans Kühn relates:

"During the time of Der Kommende Tag [The Coming Day] only smaller fabrics were produced. Later Mr. Hans Buchheim and others carried the research further.—A further suggestion of Rudolf Steiner concerned the use of horn, which was first developed in Einsingen. The horn was brought into a honey-like condition with the intention of producing a spin-able thread. Had these experiments been carried further, a sound textile thread could have arisen."

('*Dreigliederungszeit* [The Time of the Threefold Commonwealth],' Dornach 1978, S. 114.)

Suggestions of Rudolf Steiner to Henri Smits for the refinement of peat

+ One can in peat, as the remains of Eriophorum vaginatum, so strengthen the fibres contained in it that they could be used for making textiles.
+ Out of peat a compressible material suitable for cutting can be made from which something like picture frames could be made.

From the 'Zeitschrift für Moorkultur und Torfverwertung [Journal for Bog Culture and Peat Utilisation],' XV. Jahrgang, Wien [XVth Year, Vienna] 1917

"…Also the use of sufficiently pulverised peat instead of sawdust as filling material in magnesia cement and zinc oxychloride compounds was not carried out. Similarly, 'artificial wood from peat,' made in a hydraulic press, consisting of a slowly dried mixture of peat-powder, sulphate of alumina and lime. It could be beautifully polished, drilled, sawn and worked, had an astounding capacity to withstand fire but swelled up in water and was much too expensive to be a suitable substitute for oak or other quality woods."

From A. Hansdingl's '*Handbuch der Torfgewinnung und Torfverwertung mit besonderer Berücksichtigung der erforderlichen Maschinen und Geräte nebst deren Anlage- und Betriebskosten* [Handbook of peat extraction and utilisation with special consideration for the available machines, equipment and their installation, including running costs],' Berlin 1917:

"…doors, telephones, kiosks, etc. manufactured from moulded peat bricks and panels…as binding agents the normal building materials, lime, cement, mud, etc, were used…thus peat-bog huts were so made in Sweden (Christiana) that the walls of peat bricks were built with mortar and covered with planks both inside and outside…building materials made from pulverised peat and mixed with cement, gypsum, magnesium or zinc oxychloride compounds proved to be commercially non-viable. 'Artificial wood made from peat' had a similar fate…."

Postscript

In 1932 in Germany there started an industrial undertaking for insulation boards, etc., made out of wood-fibre board. These boards were produced by strongly compressing a pulp consisting of woody fibres, obtained predominantly from fir and deciduous trees. With the utilisation of a wood-derived binding agent, one ended up, to a large extent, without additions of foreign substances (binding agents). (See also Folio 13 by Ehrenfried Pfeiffer the suggestions of Rudolf Steiner for wood treatment.)

3. Resumption of research after the liquidation of Der Kommende Tag [The Coming Day]

In his book, '*Heilmittellehre* [Treatise on Medicines]' (Vittorio Klostermann GmbH, Frankfurt am Main, 1965; 1990; 2004) we learn from Dr. Rudolf Hauschka that the work was continued at the Knopf factory in Einsingen, *"where Mr. Smits, later, was active. After the liquidation of Einsingen, Dr. Wegman entrusted me with the continuation of the work. I was not happy about taking over what had been achieved up to then. Later, I tried to incorporate Mr. Smits in the work again. From Dr. Wegman I know that we were not dealing with an artificial thread but with a material that was intended for 'healthy clothing.'"*

In London on the 1st of December 1928, Dr. Ita Wegman had Rudolf Steiner's formula patented. (See Document 5 'Process of Manufacturing a Textile Fibre from Peat,' Patent No. 36,250/28.)

Proceeding from Dr. Rudolf Hauschka's remarks about the healing effects of peat, Johannes Kloss, in the 1960s in Sweden, took up the topic anew. For the further processing of larger amounts he developed special machines to refine and comb the fibres that had been treated with Rudolf Steiner's formula. He also had equipment for spinning and weaving set up that suited the peculiarities of peat fibre. From 6 cubic metres of raw material he could only manufacture about 60 kg of thread. In Hettenschwil, Switzerland, Ruth Erne herself spun refined peat fibre, mixed with wool or silk, into a yarn that was later woven into material and articles of clothing, principally used for therapeutic purposes. Recently, in Finland, where the widespread production of peat occurs as a waste product, there is a renaissance in the use of natural raw material for textiles. The Finnish firm *Kultaturve Oy** [Kultaturve Ltd.] in Sammatti uses fibres mixed with wool or cotton for making clothes, coats, blankets, etc. For their main products see webpage: http://www.ecotopia.be/yearbook/fashion.html.

4. *History of the production of peat fibre*

After Pliny had spoken of peat as early as the 1st century, it was at the turn of the millennium with the rapid spread of Cistercian monasticism which settled and enclosed marshy landscapes of middle Europe that indigenous peat was treated so as to produce filling and insulating material for buildings as well as fuel. At the end of the 19th century the fibrous part of peat was researched for the first time with a view to its incorporation as a textile thread or in paper-making. There were several formulae for peat refinement. On the 12th of April 1890, Georges Henry Béraud was the first in London to patent a process for the manufacture of peat-thread for the textile industry: Boiling in a caustic solution under high pressure followed by rinsing in water produced a friable, hard and brittle peat wool. The Viennese firm Karl A. Zschörner and Company used this Béraudine method in the manufacture of hats, carpets, curtains and covers, decorative materials and tiles. In Vienna in 1898, at a Jubilee Exhibition, the firm showed their whole range of products and the various stages of peat extraction. In a cloth factory in Düsseldorf a further treatment with caustic and acid was given making the fibres decidedly flexible. This Düsseldorf peat hair could easily be mixed with wool and cotton for further manufacture. Even so, the turnover was not very large whilst there was an abundance of wool until the Great War began when, in the absence of imports, thoughts turned again to peat fibre, above all, for the manufacture of horse blankets and overcoats.

5. *Some physical qualities of peat*

Ninety years ago Rudolf Steiner had already spoken of the *"great warmth-giving quality"* of peat on account of the numerous hollow spaces of the fibres, visible in the microscope. Also, because of its high specific heat capacity, it had been used for a long time in the treatment of rheumatic-sclerotic diseases. This capacity to store heat is mainly to be attributed to the high proportion of humin substances in the fibres. These dark-brown substances are closely related to the brown skin-pigment melanin; these could transform the energy-rich short-wave radiation from the ultraviolet part of the spectrum into the long-wave heat radiation. These substances are semi-conductors and are thus active in the electron-photon interchange. Peat fibres can therefore not only transform ultraviolet light but also electric particles into heat. In a recent report of the 'Südkuriers [South Courier],' Konstanz, Germany, it was noted that houses insulated with peat had the disadvantage of a wireless telephone (NATEL®)** being practically cut off from the world.

---

* No longer in business. See alternative peat fibre products manufacturers' *Älma Torvtextil* in Rydöbruk, Sweden, at website: http://www.naturtextilien.se/ and WANDIL in Oettern (approximately 3.5 miles from Weimar), Germany, at webpage: http://www.wandil.de/shop/about.php.

** NATEL® (*Nationales Autotelefon* [National car telephone]) is the name of the Swiss mobile phone company.

Document 1

First discussion
[from Dr. Rudolf Steiner suggestions about the use of peat, Manuscript Archive]

Peat can be used for the production of fibres and the manufacture of a material that can be compressed and cut (picture frames, etc.). The fibres could be used for woven fabrics, not in the way they have been up to now, but having different characteristics. The fabric would retain heat more than was usual. It would therefore be possible to use a lighter material for clothing than hitherto.

   Dr. Rudolf Steiner has the impression that the fibres were more suitable, the further north one went. The Swiss peat, he said, had too short a fibre. The Swabian, on the contrary, he termed useable.

   Concerning the treatment of the peat, he said it must be passed through a magnetic (electric?) field and the structure investigated before and after.

Document 2

Suggestions from Dr. Rudolf Steiner on the 21st of September 1921
[from Dr. Rudolf Steiner suggestions about the use of peat, Manuscript Archive]

Referring to the problem of which part of the plant should be used in order to obtain an adhesive substance, he said, this would be established by experiment.

To the question how the plant substances would be taken up by the fibres, he said one must experiment by treating with a salt of grey antimony (stibnite) (Sb_2S_3). Tartrated antimony ($C_8H_{10}K_2O_{15}Sb_2$) was proposed. Dr. Steiner was not keen, he seemed to have doubts. Mr. Stockmeyer spoke of the addition of certain plant substances from the Robinia to which Dr. Steiner replied, yes, the bark, but better still laburnum, which gets its propensity for yellow from the lower new red sandstone, could provide substances which could cause the fibres to take up leguminous compounds. The white bark of the birch could also come into consideration. Finally the question arose of bringing adhesive substances into an electric field in order to also make it capable of penetration.

Document 3

Discussion with Dr. Rudolf Steiner on the 28th of April 1922

[from Dr. Rudolf Steiner suggestions about the use of peat, Manuscript Archive]

Under consideration is the matter of the fibres becoming <u>stronger</u>. To the objection that it was perhaps more concerned with pliability of the fibres, Dr. Rudolf Steiner said that the elasticity would increase with the strength..

So that the variation in the strength of the raw fibres was less evident, the fibres should be plaited in threes and then torn apart.

The combined action of the antimony and plant substance is specific. It is essential that the antimony is <u>uniformly</u> dispersed in the fibres. This should be achieved by heating the fibres after the soaking; the degree of heating must be determined. The reagent for this, as to whether the antimony has been uniformly dispersed, lies in the combustion. Usually the fibres spark when burnt, but if they have been properly soaked, gradually burn out.

Document 4

23rd of October 1923

An die Centrale, Hier.

We thank you for yours of 19th of October and the peat fibre experiment. This experiment is certainly more sensitive than the fibres from Dorenwaid, but up to now there is no likelihood of getting larger quantities of this peat.

When Dr. Rudolf Steiner made a visit on the 17th, Mr. Smits, according to instructions, presented the project concerning the extraction of cellulose from peat fibre and added two questions:

1. Is it in the interest of the present course of the peat fibre work, that *Der Kommende Tag* [The Coming Day] makes a closer connection with such a peat enterprise?

2. Arising out of the Anthroposophical outlook are there not better methods for producing cellulose than with the means of modern technology?

To the first question Dr. Rudolf Steiner replied that it would be better to proceed with a 'peat enterprise' when the fibre refinement techniques were ready for further development.

Dr. Rudolf Steiner promised to reflect on the second question and comment later.

With friendly greetings
Scientific Institute of Research.

[Addendum to the letter of the 23rd of October 1923]

The work in the Peat Fibre Laboratory has now reached a stage that provision must be made for such large amounts of the substances required in the treatment of the raw fibre, so that bigger experiments can be carried out.

The raw material in greatest demand is mallow mucilage, that is obtained from the hollyhock (*Althaea rosea*). This mucilage is used in the proportion 1:10 with the processed fibres.

It is absolutely necessary to sow immediately after the harvest of the plants in the late summer of 1924, for use in the year 1924/25, because the hollyhock blooms in its second year.

As a rule hollyhocks are sown during May and June in boxes and planted out in October after a series of transplants. About 30,000 plants can be cultivated in an area of 3,300 square metres. If one would harvest from approx. 3 *Morgen* [morning]* the next year, then some 100,000 plants would need to be sown immediately, that when placed close together would take up initially 2.5-3 *Ar* [are].**

Thus a garden of 4 *Ar* [are] had to be made available immediately with hot beds covering 2.5-3 *Ar* [are]. In October the field of 3 *Morgen* [morning] must stand ready for transplanting with sand available, and indeed the hollyhock requires a sandy, dry, sunny position, so the question arose whether the valley of the Neckar river was a suitable place for cultivation.

Now it cannot be denied that this special culture, which can be made in sufficient quantities, immediately encountered certain difficulties in the technical sphere.

If the season is fairly far advanced; this reason is not too serious, for June can be cold and raw and therefore, in any case, unsuitable for sowing. Furthermore, a certain time must pass until sowing time so that staff, sand, seed-trays, the seed etc., can be made ready.

Also, until then, there had not been the opportunity to determine how much mucilage can be obtained from a hollyhock and we still do not know whether the mucilage can be used only once or more often for the fibre treatment. Likewise it could be seen that tests should be recommended for determining which varieties were specially rich in mucilage.

It should also be made clear concerning such a sudden undertaking, that the danger of failure cannot be excluded, calling into question the success of the operation.

On the 12th during Dr. Rudolf Steiner's visit, this question of the hollyhock cultivation was tackled, without of course the opportunity of going into the difficulties. Dr. Rudolf Steiner was totally convinced that the cultivation should take place.

On account of this it seems to us, in spite of the existing difficulties, desirable to start immediately with the cultivations.

It remains to be said that a rough estimate of the yield from about one hectare of hollyhocks was calculated to produce at least 300-400 kilograms of mucilage, enough to refine three to four tons of peat fibre.

---

* *Morgen* [morning] is a traditional unit of land area equal to about 0.6309 acres. It is derived from the German word *Morgen* [morning] and represented the area of land that a yoke of oxen could plough in one morning.
** *Ar* [are] is a metric unit of surface area equal to 100 square metres (m2) commonly used in German speaking countries.

Document 5

PATENT SPECIFICATION
325,904

Application Date: Dec. 8, 1928. No. 36,250/28.
Complete Left: Oct. 5, 1929.
Complete Accepted: March 6, 1930.

PROVISIONAL SPECIFICATION.

Process of Manufacturing a Textile Fibre from Peat.

[...]

COMPLETE SPECIFICATION.

Process of Manufacturing a Textile Fibre from Peat.

I, Ita Wegman, a citizen of Arlesheim, Canton Basel, Switzerland, Dutch subject, do hereby declare the nature of this invention and in what manner the same is to be performed, to be particularly described and ascertained in and by the following statement:—

The invention described here-in, is dealing with the production of a fibrous material, which, spun and woven, will be suitable for every kind of texture. The raw material consists of the so-called peat-fibre, remainders of the leaf-stems of eriophorum vaginatum. They are to be extracted from the adhering peat and other not spinnable remainders of plants by mechanical means, either by hand or by suitable machinery. That might be done for instance as described in the specification numbered 9408/02 or chemically cleansed with alkalis and acids as described in the specification numbered 20501/95. The so extracted and cleansed fibre is not yet fit for spinning and for manufacturing valuable yarns and tissues. It is the object of this invention to improve the spinning properties, tensile-strength, appearance and suppleness. In order to improve the fibrous material, it has to be treated by chemical-biological methods.

It has been found, that a treatment with extracts from plants has a very good effect on the tensile-strength, the appearance and the spinning properties of the peat-fibre. For this purpose preferably plants belonging to the families of Labiataes,* Aristo-lochiaceaes and the like may be used. Also resins in a suitable preparation, for instance in an emulsion, can be applied with advantage. The process consists of immersing the fibrous material in a diluted solution of extracts from plants and/or an emulsion of resins. The treatment has to be done in wooden vats and takes about 20 to 30 days.

It has been found furthermore, that the efficiency of the extracts from plants and/or of the emulsions of resins is supported by small quantities of earth-alkali- and/or metal salts. These salts have to be added to the solution of extracts from plants and/or to the emulsion of resins.

Finally it has been found, that the effect, gained by the treatment as described will be increased or, so to speak, fixed, if the fibres are subsequently treated with oxygen in any form or oxygen-producing substances.

---

* Note most botanists now use the Latin name 'Lamiaceae' when referring to this Mint family.

After having been dried, the fibre is ready for spinning.

The result of the treatment as described above, will be a high tensile-strength, a pleasant, glossy appearance and a woolly structure of the fibre. The tensile-strength is 16-24 kg. per sqmm, whereas the tensile-strength of the untreated fibre is only 6-10 kg. per sqmm.

The following is an example:

The extracted and cleansed fibrous material is immersed in a solution consisting of

Galeopsis Ladanum	–	–	0.1%	
Emulsion of resin		–	–	0.1%
Chloride of lime		–	–	0.5%

The treatment takes place in wooden tanks and is lasting about 20 days. Instead of Galeopsis Ladanum also Clematis vitalba or similar plants or mixtures of these plants may be used. Instead of Chloride of lime also salts of Magnesia or metals or mixtures of these salts may be used.

After having been treated in the way described and rinsed for a short while, the fibrous material is put on shelves and treated with oxygen for about two hours. The same effect may be obtained by immersing the fibrous material in solutions of oxygen-producing substances, for instance Peroxides.

Having now particularly described and ascertained the nature of my said invention, and in what manner the same is to be performed, I declare that what I claim is:—

1. The process of treating fibrous material from peat for spinning, consisting in immersing it for a substantial period in a diluted solution of extracts from plants and/or emulsions or resins.

2. The process claimed in claim 1, adding a small proportion of earth-alkali- and/or metal salts.

3. The process claimed in claims 1 and 2, the fibrous material being subsequently treated with oxygen in any form.

Dated the 2nd day of October, 1929.

I. WEGMAN.

Comments for Folio 8

About the first task in the folio, Dr. Hans Kühn has written in his book '*Dreigliederungszeit* [The Time of the Threefold Commonwealth]' (Dornach 1978, S. 116):

"In another laboratory Dr. Theberath carried out similar tests for the day and night effects, such as star influences on metals. For instance, I remember a series of experiments with spirals of fine silver wire that led to certain measurable movements corresponding to the course of the planets. These experiments were extremely difficult to perform because they were concerned with influences that were hardly detectable. Rudolf Steiner expected that the variation in the Moon influences* on the

---

* Concerning the existing daily variations of the Earth's magnetic field, there are super-imposed rhythms exercised by the Moon. We will have more to say about these rhythms of Earth magnetism in the notes to Folio 10.

magnetic and electric Earth-currents would be followed up, just as the intensity of magnetic iron gives different values through the influence of the Moon. (According to Mr. Hans Buchheim, these experiments were carried on for years.)"

Letter from Hans Theberath to Rudolf Steiner concerning his experiments with copper and silver wire spirals:

14th of July 1924, Stuttgart

Dear Dr. Steiner,

For a long time we have observed copper wire spirals which were wound onto a double cone, following the *e*-function [exponential function, Tr.]. Sometimes two spirals wound in opposite directions were also observed. At present an observation is also being made at the apex of the spiral. In none of these cases were repeated deflections observed bigger than those which were caused by the small vibrations, i.e. at the most up to 1/10 of a millimetre. This is so little with a spiral 80 centimetres in height, that I am afraid of having made a cardinal error. I must therefore ask, Herr Doktor, for advice on the continuation of the experiment. May we expect Herrn Doktor in the Institute or can I ask for advice in Landhausstraße?

Respectfully,
Hans Theberath

[Without Place and Date]

Dear Dr. Steiner,

My measurements on a silver wire spiral and a hair showed distinct effects in the transition from day-to-night. I must ask you for a brief discussion about how to continue the research.

Respectfully,
H. Theberath

In the diary of Joachim Schultz, it is noted that Dr. P. E. Schiller in 1935 *"was working on the spiral experiments."*

In a letter** from Dr. Paul Eugen Schiller to Peter von Siemens dated the 26th of November 1955, we hear more about them:

"A third undertaking was the research into spiral forms. Rudolf Steiner was of the opinion that, for example, a correctly formed silver spiral would carry out a movement at Sun and/or Moon-rise. For this purpose an instrument comparable to a barometer would be constructed which would record the changes of energy in the etheric sphere, just as the barometer does for the air pressure. This task appears to be the preliminary stage of the Strader Motor, resting on the fact that various metals combined in appropriate forms produce an etheric 'power station.'"

---

* Reproduced in full on pages 81-82.

Joachim Bramsch added to the above on the 7th of September 1997:

"Dr. P. E. Schiller…made experiments with 'screw-windings' which progress axially, the radius of the windings remaining constant. As a student I was acquainted with this, as Dr. P. E. Schiller with his assistant, the mechanic Wolf, had his laboratory in one of the two towers in the Heizhaus [boiler house]. There he used mostly the planetary metals. There must be much to be found in Dr. P. E. Schiller's estate.*"

See also the remarks in the report from Paul Eugen Schiller of the 5th of July 1984 under the heading '*Rhythms of Earth-magnetism,*' on page 91.

Comments for Folio 9

Gas discharge experiments and the opposite nature of Sun and Earth

In the memoirs of Dr. Walter Johannes Stein is found the following statement of Rudolf Steiner: *"You will see that in the super-cooled vacuum, the ether is present as a negative quantity, which can be measured…. In cosmic space is a super-cooled vacuum."* This stands in direct relation to Rudolf Steiner's Whitsun lecture 06.04.1924 (GA 236), The Festivals and their Meaning, 1981, p. 313, where he says: *"The Universe begins with the etheric organisation…the physical is found only on Earth."*

Presumably with the experiments described in Folio 9 these peculiarities of universal space will be produced in the laboratory in order to be able to research the predicted characteristics (still only etherically present).

Folio 9 shows how the relationships on the Sun as described by Rudolf Steiner could be researched by gas discharge experiments. In many places in the lectures especially in the Warmth and Astronomy Courses, detailed descriptions are found of the conditions on the Sun.** Often in the same lecture—

---

* Unfortunately no further details about these experiments were found. Dr. Georg Maier told the author that he took part in these experiments for about a year. Concerning the result of the experimental set-up in the *Heizhaus* [boiler house], he said that the spirals were so sensitive that they registered the coming and going of trains in the Dornach railway station, which was more than the expected Moon and planet influences.

** Further references to the opposition of Sun and Earth, and on the constitution of the Sun: 01.18.1921 (GA 353, Lecture XVIII) "Negative (suction) Sun substance"; 06.09.1923 (GA 350) "Space between Sun and Earth with gas forming burning metals, anode, cathode: light phenomena, difference between bodies that radiate and those that emit waves"; 05.15.1920 (GA 201) "Negative matter of the Sun"; 03.30.1924 (GA 239) "Negative space of the Sun and nature of the Sun"; 5, 6 & 03.13.1910 (GA 118) "Macrocosmic opposition of Sun and Earth as head and limb polarity in the human *being.*"

Concerning spectral analysis, burning metals and the so-called '*Documents de Barr* [The Document of Barr],' see Hans Reipert's, '*Über die Stellar-Spektralanalyse: Eine kritische Untersuchung* [Concerning Stellar Spectral Analysis: A Critical Review],' *Mitteilungen aus der Anthroposophischen Arbeit in Deutschland* [Reports from the Anthroposophical Work in Germany], Stuttgart, 16. Jahrgang [16th Year] / Heft 3 [Issue 3], Nummer 61 [Number 61], Michaeli [Michaelmas] 1962, S. [pp.] 161-167 and Walther Cloos, 'The Living Earth: The Organic Origin of Rocks and Minerals,' Lanthorn Press, 1977.

Note: The Document of Barr actually consists of three documents. One of them, the 'Autobiographical Sketch,' written by Rudolf Steiner at Barr, Alsace, France, dated 9 September 1907, was translated into English and published in 'The Golden Blade,' London, 1966, pp. 1-7. The two other Barr documents, one which is quite short deals with the origins of Rosicrucianism and the third document contains a history of the Theosophical Movement, have not yet been translated into English. Hans Reipert's report refers to the Barr document on Rosicrucianism.

or a short time later—the opposing nature of the Sun and the Earth with the polarity of anode and cathode in a gas discharge tube was brought into relationship by virtue of peripheral and point-centred forces active along an infinite line. So it is described in the Astronomy Course on 01.18.1921, GA 323 (Lecture XVIII):

"With electrical phenomena this finds expression in that we get the cathode on the one hand, the anode on the other. On the one hand we can only explain the light by regarding it as a piece of a sphere, the radius of which is given by the direction in which the electricity is working whilst the other pole is given as a small part of the radius itself. It is not justifiable to speak of a simple polarity of poles, but we should speak in quite another way, namely whenever anode and cathode make their appearance, this will belong to an entire system; purely and simply by virtue of the whole arrangement it belongs to an entire system."

Two days earlier (Lecture XVI) the constitution of the Sun was described:

"The phenomena at the anode and cathode have not the same direction, but something else underlies them, and to discover what the difference is we must follow this path…that a real line in its totality may not be thought of as having two ends but with one end, and by virtue of the real conditions, the other end goes into a continuation which must lie somewhere."

In the same course it is also pointed out that this antithesis can be discovered everywhere. As examples, Rudolf Steiner cites experiments whereby electrical phenomena appear at the anode and cathode of gas discharge tubes and experiments with heat conduction *"from inside towards the outside"* or from the periphery inwards (Lecture XVIII, 01.18.1921). In the last lecture it is made clear that: *"In the spectrum itself we have an image of the opposition of Sun and Earth…"* The solar spectrum is placed between Sun and Earth in actual space. (For the solar spectrum see also Folio 2 on page 7.)

The following quotation, probably referring directly to the tasks in Folio 9, shows just how important the discovery of new provisions for research in these areas was for Rudolf Steiner:

"When we founded our institutes in Stuttgart, I said: one of the first tasks is to establish that where there is a star, there is absolutely nothing, there shines 'nothingness,' while all around where nothing is, a kind of light is seen." (09.10.1923, GA 350, 2000, Discussion 15, p. 278.)

Likewise Dr. Hans Kühn related in his book, '*Dreigliederungszeit* [The Time of the Threefold Commonwealth]' (Dornach, 1978):

"The Hamburg physicist Dr. Hermann von Dechend was given an interesting task, namely to concern himself with the solar structure and especially the interior of the Sun."

To follow are the notes for these experiments from the estate of Dr. Paul Eugen Schiller, with statements by Mr. Joachim Bramsch about the resulting discharge experiments in the 1950s, as well as supplementary documents.

From Paul Eugen Schiller (24th of May 1984)

"As reported in Folios 9 a-b, experiments with electrical discharges in a super-cooled vacuum were carried out at the Stuttgart laboratory in 1924. The phenomena could not be investigated spectroscopically. In the spring of 1924 it was possible to demonstrate something to Rudolf Steiner and to present him with photographs of alterations in the spectrum. It had been shown that with low temperatures (-200°C), certain spectral lines disappear and others, previously not perceptible, appear afresh. Rudolf Steiner looked at the experiment, where the spectrum of an oxygen mixture could be

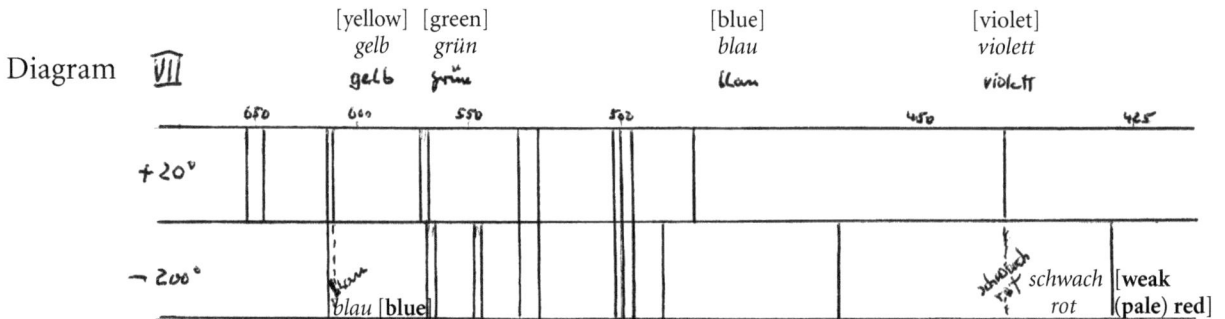

Diagram VII

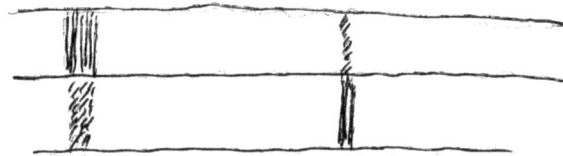

Diagram VIII

*observed, simultaneously at normal (20°C) and also at the lower temperature (-200°C). The two spectra were then discussed, using a rough sketch, and above all, the disappearing and newly appearing lines. Seated at a desk Rudolf Steiner took a pencil, drew with it on a red-yellow line (at about 610) and said where this line disappears in the super-cooled spectrum, if looked at exactly, a blue line would appear. Indicating likewise the blue-violet line at 437, he said there a red line must appear. He must have noticed the consternation of Dr. von Dechend, Dr. Maier and Dr. Theberath and therefore took the pencil and wrote on the sketch under the red-yellow line the word 'blue' and 'red' under the blue-violet line. (In Diagram VII, I have written these words in **bold** for emphasis.) In order to make this clear he took his short, thick pencil from his pocket and drew vigorously three lines (see Diagram VIII), drew in the upper area a line that disappears, in the lower area, one that appear anew, and said once more that one should observe exactly where lines disappear and then appear afresh!*

    As a young and inexperienced assistant, I did not have the courage, nor the knowledge, to then ask how it could be possible to perceive in the blue area a red and in the red area a blue line. Sadly the older gentlemen Dr. von Dechend, Dr. Maier and Dr. Theberath did not have the presence of mind to question this. Before Rudolf Steiner departed he pointed to our spectroscope and said: 'But with this instrument you won't find them!' He had already uttered a similar warning in 1921 (See Lecture XVIII, 18 January 1921 in GA 323).

What was Rudolf Steiner pointing to in his words and diagram? The observation of a coloured line or coloured band in the spectrum must, like any other colour, lead to the interaction of 'light' and 'darkness.' Did he assume or did he observe that through the cooling one of these two effects would be extinguished or called up in the perceptibility, as the case may be? Since the spectral lines and bands arise from the superimposed movement of fringe phenomena, the close study of these fringe phenomena might perhaps be of further help.

In any case, it seems to me Rudolf Steiner was interested in the changes of the energy structure caused by the cooling the gases under investigation. In another experiment, a globe of light (about 50 millimetres in diameter) was formed at the end of an evacuated glass vessel with a copper tube projecting into it. Observing this Rudolf Steiner said: in the middle of this you can observe conditions that correspond to the centre of the Sun. At the edges it may be seen to be similar to the Sun's perimeter. Was attention brought to etheric conditions in this investigation? In Folio 14 b the remark is quoted: 'I am having experiments done in Stuttgart—sadly the people there are not progressing fast enough—to close the spectrum so that the ultraviolet comes to lie above the infrared. A quite singular colour must then arise which is vitally active. That must be tested on bacteria.'

This experiment was broken off as I had to undertake another task instigated by Rudolf Steiner. In the early summer of 1955, Dipl. Ing. J. Bramsch repeated these experiments using Geissler tubes and reported in detail. I still have this report."

*

June 15, 1955, Dornach

Report of

discharge experiments in a super-cooled vacuum

A. First experiment

In the spring of 1924 experiments with electrical discharges in a high vacuum at low temperatures were carried out at the Stuttgart Research Laboratory. The spectra of these discharges were observed subjectively as well as being observed photographically.

Two kinds of apparatus were in use: First a large tube (diameter about 200 millimetres) with necks for anode and cathode. The cathode was a hot-cathode, the anode developed from copper tubing which could be filled with liquid air.

In the experiments with these tubes there appeared at the anode, *inter alia*, spherical discharges. On a visit, Rudolf Steiner, after observing the changed spectrum during cooling, made the remark that a difference between the light-sphere edge and the light-sphere centre could be established which corresponded to the conditions in the centre and on the surface of the Sun. He pointed out that in any case such confirmation is not possible using a spectroscope.

At that time Rudolf Steiner had often spoken of the surface of the Sun and its interior in connection with positive and negative matter, the supposition being that here was an experiment which, he thought, illustrated both conditions.

The second layout consisted essentially of a Geissler tube immersed in liquid air whose spectrum was compared with a similar one open to the atmosphere. It was possible to take photographs of both these spectra.

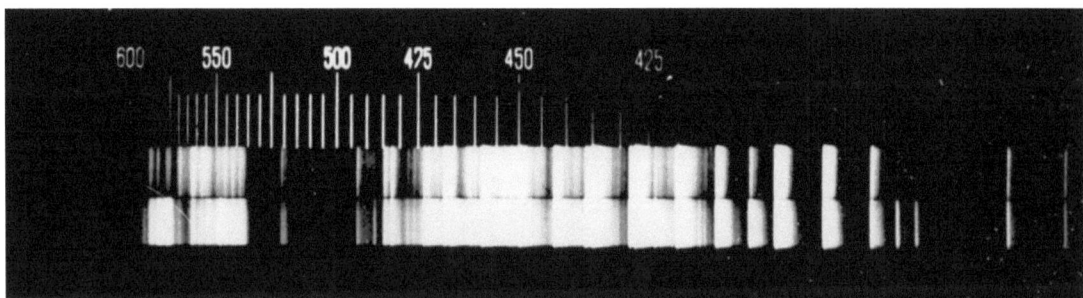

Figure 1

These photos show that with the cooled tube not only lines disappear but new lines appear. (The results from the very simple film camera were less clear than personal observation.) Having personally observed the change in the spectrum, Rudolf Steiner made the following sketch:

Figure 2

He indicated those places where a line had disappeared and recommended a special investigation. Where a new line appeared it *"must be followed exactly"* he advised, because it must indicate something important.

In consideration of Figure 1 and Steiner's sketch and his remarks about the Sun's surface and interior show that in this series of tests he saw the possibility of acquiring more knowledge of the formative forces.

The tests could not be continued at that time because of the lack of financial support. It must be appreciated that for its realisation, apart from a new spectroscope, probably one of modern construction, a larger high vacuum pump, an installation for heating and also for cleaning the tubes employed, and the equipment for cooling to low temperatures are all required.

Physics Laboratory
at the Goetheanum, Dornach
Paul Eugen Schiller

*

Private and Confidential Material
June 15, 1955, Dornach

Report of
discharge experiments in a super-cooled vacuum

B. Repetition of the experiments

1. Setting up of the work

In his Natural Scientific Courses Rudolf Steiner contrasted the universal etheric formative forces with the then known physical/chemical centred-forces. Particularly in the cycle about 'The Relationship of the Various Branches of Natural Science to Astronomy,'* he explains where and how the etheric

---

* See 'The Relation of the Diverse Branches of Natural Science to Astronomy,' Third Natural Scientific Course, (18 lectures, Stuttgart 1-18 January 1921, GA 323), Typescript of a translation by George Adams can be found in The Library, Rudolf Steiner House, London. This translation is available on-line at webpage: http://www.awakenings.com/jcms/anthroposophy-and-goethean/45-rudolf-steiner-third-cycle.html; Also available from the library is an American edition entitled 'The Relationship of the Diverse Branches of Natural Science to Astronomy,' Eighteen lectures given in Stuttgart from January 1 to 18, 1921, Translated by Rick Mansell from shorthand reports unrevised by the author, Transcribed & edited by Fred M. Mathews & Donald C. Hosier, The Rudolf Steiner Research Foundation, Redondo Beach, California, 1989.

can be concretely grasped. Starting with warmth, two conditions were described: a positive or ponderable, i.e. more material that is connected with pressure and ordinary space, and another, negative or imponderable, which is related to the etheric and connected with counter-space. Furthermore, this was brought into connection with the constitution of the Sun, whereby the activities do not pass from the centre to the outside, but run from outside towards the centre-point and disappear there.

So one must imagine the Sun as a hollow space enveloped by matter. In contrast to the positively oriented earthly matter, one has to think of a negative intensity within the Sun. Thus the Sun is not only an empty space, but a 'place' where space ceases, less than empty space.

Experimental investigation of astro-physical conditions is carried out by means of the spectroscope. Similar light phenomena as can be observed in the stars can be produced under earthly conditions by means of electrical discharges in gas filled tubes. Vessels having a high exhaustion can be seen as an experimental reproduction of the rareification of matter on the Sun. The heat conditions beyond the Earth-organism point towards lower temperatures. All these relationships as mentioned in the preceding report by Dr. P. E. Schiller, lie close to what Rudolf Steiner saw in bringing about such attempts to find experimental methods of demonstrating the positive and negative conditions in connection with the Sun's surface and interior.

Thus the whole task can be comprised under three headings:
a) Experimental investigations into spectroscopy of gas discharges *in vacuo* at low temperatures.
b) Treatment of existing astro-physical material about the 'core of the Sun' and the 'surface of the Sun.'
c) Comprehensive overview in depth on the basis of Rudolf Steiner's spiritual science.

2. The carrying out of the experiments.

In order to continue the early research of 1924 in the Stuttgart research laboratory, the undersigned, after discussion with Dr. P. E. Schiller on the 3rd of August 1954, in Dornach, wishes to convey his gratitude to the following: Dr. P. von Siemens in Erlangen, for the financial arrangements and the Nuremberg Rudolf Steiner School for the time given to familiarising itself with the experimental research.

For this purpose the undersigned prepared himself, formerly an engineer in the main laboratory of Siemens & Halske A.G. [plc] Berlin and now teacher of mathematics and physics at the Nuremberg Rudolf Steiner School, by study and experimenting. Through the friendly agency of Prof. Trendelenburg of Siemens-Schuckert-Werke A.G. [plc], Erlangen, he could take part during the winter semester of 1954/55 in practical physics at the University of Erlangen. In this way an effort was made to acquire the fundamentals of spectroscopy and optics within the framework of the weekly exercises. The Nuremberg teaching staff obligingly allowed him to do the actual work from Easter 1955 for eight to ten weeks. During this time besides the required teaching they (i.e. the staff) had previously given additional afternoon periods.

The experiments themselves began on the Tuesday after Easter, the 12th of April 1955. In the first weeks, following the cleaning and overhaul of the spectroscope, setting up a high voltage installation with Geissler tubes, and preliminary practice in using the spectroscope and taking photographs, the spectra of various tubes under changed conditions were photographed in order to acquire the technique of scientific photography and gain practical experience in gas discharges and spectroscopy. Vacuum pumps and Dewar flasks were also acquired, literature about liquid air studied and after further practice a technically useful arrangement was set up for the complete experiment with two discharge tubes.

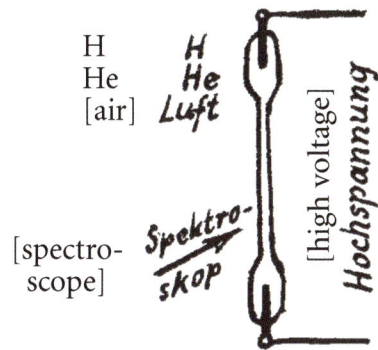

Figure 3a

In those four weeks the spectra, partly in liquid air, could be carefully studied and compared. The indications of the desired changes in the lines were found using the prepared helium-tubes. [See Figure 3a with the chemical symbols H (Hydrogen), He (Helium), words '*Luft*' [air], '*Hochspannung*' [high voltage] and '*Spektroskop*' [spectroscope].–Tr.]

With immersion in liquid air, the green lines disappeared, the red became weaker and the violet somewhat wider and stronger (See Figure 3b).

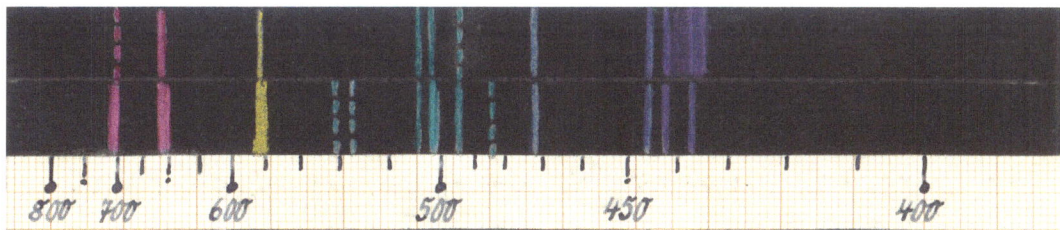

Figure 3b

In addition, it was found that the installed Geissler tubes proved to be of no use for continuous experiment. Not withstanding the reduced current, they showed irregular discharge phenomena and other effects after two hours due to hidden defects in the apparatus.

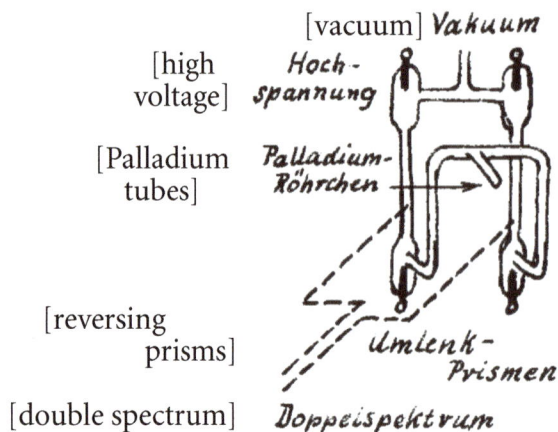

[high voltage] — Hoch-spannung
[vacuum] Vakuum
[Palladium tubes] — Palladium-Röhrchen
[reversing prisms] — Umlenk-Prismen
[double spectrum] — Doppelspektrum

Figure 4a

Hence the experiments with vacuum equipment were rearranged and carried out with a double-tube from old parts with additional pump and a small palladium tube. [See Figure 4a with the words 'Vakuum' [vacuum], 'Hochspannung' [high voltage], 'Palladium-Röhrchen' [Palladium tubes], 'Umlenkprismen' [reversing prisms], and 'Doppelspektrum' [double spectrum]. –Tr.] After overcoming the initial difficulties with the vacuum and the inaccuracy of the wavelength scale *inter alia* as a result of the relatively simple apparatus, the observations began again and indeed this time showed stronger indications of the sought-after line-alterations (Figure 4b).

Through immersion in liquid air the merging bands in the red part separated into weaker, single bands, whilst in the violet, lines appeared wide to the right and washed out to the left.

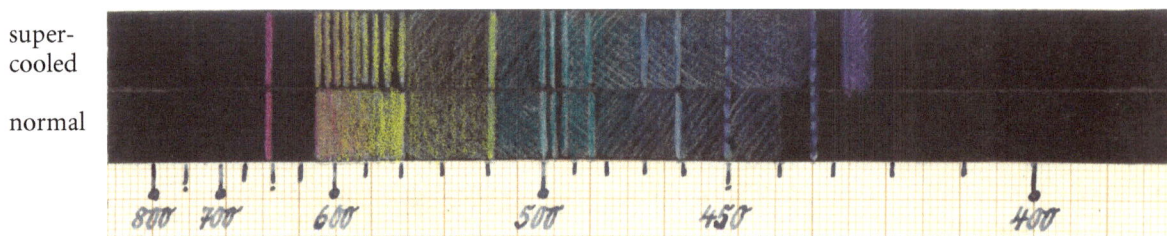

super-cooled

normal

800   700   600   500   450   400

Figure 4b

Neither admission of hydrogen nor increase of air pressure brought any new results, probably on account of the imperviousness of the small palladium tube as well as the permanent presence of hydrogen lines close by.

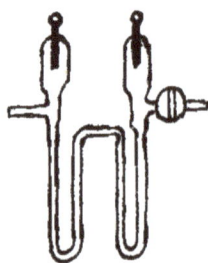

To overcome these shortcomings, a new tube was designed and the apparatus rearranged for high voltage direct current with reversible polarity (Figure 5a). After tests and corrections to the equipment with the old tubes and new installations, the experiments with liquid air were repeated in the seventh week. With both alternating and direct current and the pole-reversal of the latter changes in the lines appeared, and with immersion in liquid air a fading of the red and a strengthening of the violet, which must still be confirmed, were observed, as well as shadows of new lines in the interspaces. The existing apparatus was not adequate to bring these out more clearly (Figure 5b).

Figure 5a

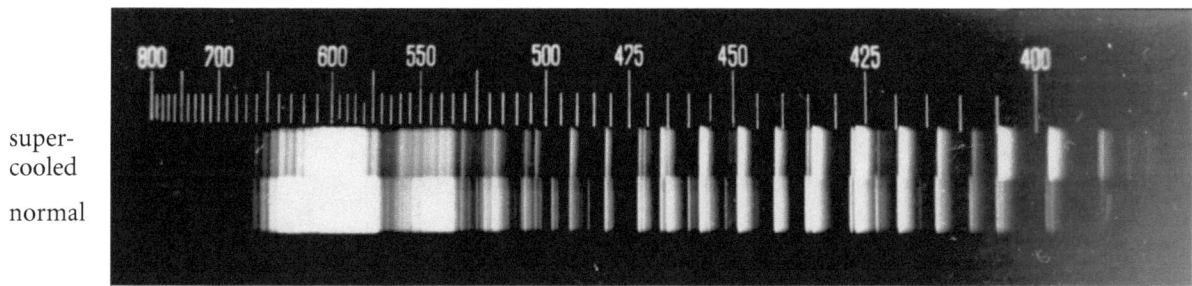

Figure 5b

These results and their comparison with earlier photographs (Figure 1) justify, together with Rudolf Steiner's instructions, the resumption of the experiments with more advanced apparatus.

This required carefully set-up discharge tubes following recent new designs, arrangements for annealing and purifying same and means for producing a high vacuum with two stages of pumps. In addition, the transfusing and purification of different gases, a high-tension installation for generating DC voltage with reversible polarity as well as apparatus for the super-cooling of the discharge tubes by means of liquid gases were required. Above all, an efficient spectrometer was necessary for ocular and photographic observation and also, after the remark Rudolf Steiner communicated in the preceding report, an instrument that would provide new features required for further experiments arising from the viewpoints of physics and spiritual science.

For those carrying out this task, therefore, professional knowledge and skills are necessary in the fields of gas discharges and vacuum technique including glass blowing, electro-technology at high-tension, low temperature work, spectrometry and scientific photography.

Finally the undersigned would like to warmly thank those who made it possible for him to become acquainted with the aforesaid task through his own experimentation: the Natural Science Section at the Goetheanum for their approval of the work, Dr. P. E. Schiller for advice and help in the experiments themselves, Dr. P. von Siemens for generous financial support and the Nuremberg Rudolf Steiner School for their long-term permission.

Physics Laboratory
at the Goetheanum, Dornach, Switzerland

Joachim Bramsch

*

Row 1 annotations (right): 10.5.55. vm. Luft, 3mm Hg 3 mA — 5.10.55 morning Air, 3 mm Hg 3 mA

Kontrollmessung in Zimmerluft — Control measurment at room temperature

Row 2 annotations (left): Flüss. Luft — Liquid Air; Zimmerluft — Room temp.
(right): 10.5.55. vm. Luft, 3mm Hg 3 mA 1. Verfuch — 5.10.55 morning Air, 3 mm Hg 3 mA 1st experiment

Row 3 annotations (left): Flüss. Luft — Liquid Air; Zimmer-luft — Room temp.
(right): 10.5.55. vm. Luft, 3mm Hg 5 mA 2. Verfuch — 5.10.55 morning Air, 3 mm Hg 5 mA 2nd experiment

Row 4 annotations (left): Flüss. Luft — Liquid Air; Bunfenfl. schwach — Bunsen flame weak; Zimmer-luft — Room temp.
(right): 10.5.55. vm Luft, 3mm Hg 5 mA 3. Verfuch — 5.10.55 morning Air, 3 mm Hg 5 mA 3rd experiment

Row 5 annotations (left): Flüss. Luft — Liquid Air; Bunfenfl. stark — Bunsen flame weak; Zimmerl. — Room temp.
(right): 10.5.55. mtg. Luft, 3mm Hg 5 mA 4. Verfuch — 5.10.55 midday Air, 3 mm Hg 5 mA 4th experiment

Row 6 annotations (left): Flüss. Luft — Liquid Air; Zimmer-luft — Room temp.
(right): 10.5.55. mtg. 5 mA 5. Verfuch Luftdruck gesteigert — 5.10.55 midday. 5 mA 5th experiment Air pressure increased

November 26, 1955, Dornach

Dear Dr. von Siemens,

Many thanks for your letter of the 16th of November. It is a pity that you cannot be here on the 3rd of December, so I am all the more pleased that you can be here in the beginning of January. I have booked a room for you in the guest house Friedwart for the 2nd and 3rd of January.

I have informed Dr. Wachsmuth of your visit. I hope very much that it will be possible for him to take part in our discussions. One can be grateful that you give Mr. Bramsch the opportunity to take part in the week for mathematicians.

Doubtless you have heard from Mr. Bramsch himself about the work and his discussions with other laboratory assistants. The questions connected with all this lie heavily on my soul. It has indeed shown that manifold preparations are necessary in the area of experimental arrangements (apparatus, equipment, etc.) as well as for Mr. Bramsch himself who had to become familiar with the fields of spectroscopy, vacuum technique and low temperatures which were new to him. I would not deceive myself about the extent and duration required for such work. I do not believe that any results would be achieved without an annual budget of 15,000 to 20,000 [Swiss] francs and within a shorter time than three to five years. The idea is not just to show a few new lines in the spectrum, but to reach a new well-founded insight into the forces of nature.

I can only be pleased and thankful when such a work is made possible and can be carried out. With regards to the experimental work, I can well believe that this or that detail could be dealt with in an industrial or university laboratory. However, I consider it to be quite impossible to carry out the entire undertaking in such a laboratory. This must lead to misunderstandings and finally to a negative view of the entire work of Rudolf Steiner. The thoughts that are fundamental to his proposals are so new and so often at variance with contemporary ideas that there is no alternative but to find the solutions in our own institutions, and place the well-founded results before our contemporaries. Then these will take effect and show people the way to a new conception of the world.

Just with this task there are exceptional difficulties and very complicated experimental requirements to be fulfilled. As has been shown, Mr. Bramsch had need to familiarise himself with this fundamentally new subject. The question therefore arises whether another task of Rudolf Steiner could be chosen whose solution would lie relatively nearer. I will briefly indicate three that could be considered in our discussion.

In connection with magnetism, Rudolf Steiner recommended a study of the formative forces appearing there. A magnet, whose poles are covered alternately with coatings of copper, tin, lead etc., shall be investigated. The task has to do with the fact that magnetism is the counter-image of the chemical-ether. Very probably this is also connected with the indications about the use of magnets in the healing of certain illnesses. Closely linked to this are also the experiments with electricity. To what extent can we demonstrate that we are dealing with a sub-physical force? Some years ago I began relevant experiments including those concerning the influence of electrical fields on plant growth. The first results were very interesting, and it would be important to continue these experiments further.

Another area lies in the treatment of warmth phenomena. Rudolf Steiner speaks of two kinds of warmth, an extra-terrestrial and a terrestrial. He pointed to day and night experiments that would show the difference. With this question was also connected the continuation of experiments concerned with the qualities of warmth (wood, coal, electricity, etc.).

A third undertaking was the research into spiral forms. Rudolf Steiner was of the opinion that, for example, a correctly formed silver spiral would carry out a movement at Sun and/or Moon-rise. For this purpose an instrument comparable to a barometer would be constructed which would record the changes of energy in the etheric sphere, just as the barometer does for the air pressure. This task appears to be the preliminary stage of the Strader Motor, resting on the fact that various metals combined in appropriate forms produce an etheric 'power station.'

I only point out these possibilities so that consideration can be given to their undertaking, should the means for a really thorough realisation of the 'spectrum-task' be lacking. If need be, we could speak about all this in detail in January. I am very pleased about this.

With best wishes for your work and warm greetings,

Yours,

Paul Eugen Schiller

September 19, 1966, Dornach

Dear Mr. Bramsch,

Many thanks for your letter of the 21st of August, and forgive me that I am so late in replying. Sadly my health is not as I would wish and therefore I am not always master of my time and strength. Luckily it is nothing serious and will soon pass.

Concerning the expression 'colour-ether,' I know only of the place it is mentioned. However, I am firmly convinced that Rudolf Steiner was referring to the light-ether. I believe you are correct when you say that the light-ether is to do with the 'geometrical-constructional' and the chemical or sound-ether* with the arithmetical and rhythm-producing activity. One can also say: the light-ether is the activity of the Spirits of Form and is therefore connected with creating forms and bringing about shapes. The chemical-ether is the activity of the Spirits of Movement and has to do with the relationship things have to one another. The shapes Dr. Wachsmuth has given: square, crescent Moon, triangle and circle, I must accept as symbols which refer to the different activities. However, I cannot accept the view that the four kinds of ether produce such forms under all circumstances. Only the light-ether can bring about form, the warmth-ether dissolves form, chemical-ether deals with the relationships of things to one another and the life-ether gives the sense of meaning, the 'life.'

The connection between the light-ether and what is for us perceptible colour is not so simple, as many of our friends have believed. Once and for all one must be quite clear that Rudolf Steiner said explicitly that the term 'light' is often used to imply a combination of the entire etheric forces as opposed to the term 'darkness' that implies a combination of the sub-physical forces. What we have in the visible perceptible world of colour is the situation between the etheric world and the sub-physical.

_____

* The chemical-ether has several different names. It is also called the sound-ether, tone-ether or number-ether. Tr.

It is noteworthy that Rudolf Steiner in a lecture to doctors (Dornach, 04.12.1921, GA 313*) says that the name light-ether was chosen on account of the priority given to the sense of sight. We would have chosen another name if the majority were blind. The light-ether has quite different effects than those that can be perceived with the sense of sight.

So much for today. Hopefully you can soon come to Dornach again so that we can discuss these questions. With best wishes and warm greetings.

Yours,

Paul Eugen Schiller

Gas Discharges

Under normal conditions and in weak electric fields, gases are insulating. However, when electricity of the same field strength is allowed to pass through rarefied air or even a vacuum, then the gas becomes an electrical conductor and so-called gas discharges appear. An evacuated vessel, usually of glass, is employed for the experimental observation of these phenomena. In order to conduct electricity into the vessel, two metal electrodes are brought inside and are lead outside with wires through the glass. When a voltage is applied to these electrodes (minus pole: cathode; plus pole: anode) light phenomena appear as glow discharges.

With a pressure of about one to two millimetres of mercury (1/1,000 normal air pressure), a blue-violet glow appears round the cathode. A shining red-violet extends from the anode, partly grouped in single equidistant discs. Between the two light phenomena, a 'Faraday dark space' is found. Such experiments were made for the first time in 1854 by Gassiot in France. In 1858, Plücker of Bonn researched gas discharges from variously shaped glass tubes, which he had received from the glass-blower Geissler. Such Geissler tubes became the core of spectrum investigation of a gas.

Since the beginning of the 20th century, work has been carried out on the spectroscopy of gas discharges dependent on pressure and temperature at the astrophysical observatory in Potsdam ('Einstein Tower'). [See H. Schlüter, '*Anregung von Spektren zur Untersuchung von Hyperfeinstrukturen* [Activation of Spectra for the Investigation of Hyperfine Structures],' Zeitschrift für Physik [Journal for Physics], Bd. [Vol.] 59, (1929), S. 149-153.]

Postscript
In 1944 C. E. R. Bruce noticed an analogy with electrical discharge effects from a large number of phenomena in the Sun's atmosphere. (See also: C. E. R. Bruce "A New Approach in Astrophysics and Cosmogony," Unwin Bros., London 1944.)

A friendly doctor…

Presumably Dr. Otto Palmer, who in 1924 treated a child (Nik Fiechter, 1914-1998, later became a doctor) that had contracted a severe eye injury.

---

* Anthroposophical Spiritual Science and Medical Therapy, Second Medical Course, 1991, Lecture II, p. 19.

The sensitive flame as a reagent for the human voice

This group of tasks from Folio 10 were not all directly instigated by Rudolf Steiner. With the advent of radio transmission, on the basis of questions from co-workers about the usefulness of this new technology, he had instigated experiments with sensitive flames on the grounds that this pioneering achievement would not be able to relay the delicate qualities of the human voice.

There are experiments that reveal that conversation held in the vicinity of a burning candle can be picked up. The light of the candle can be detected with a light-sensitive sensor and reproduced by electronic amplification. In the first third of the 19th century it had already been noticed that jets of water or wreaths of smoke react sensitively towards sound.

In 1858 LeConte, during a concert, saw that the gas-lighting in the hall altered its shape according to the beat of the music. And then, having become aware of this phenomenon, he even noticed the effect of a cello solo trill on the nearby flames. The British physicist John Tyndall (1820-1893), in 1867, noticed characteristic, repeatable distortions in the shapes of the flames with particular sounds, as for example shrill piping and hissing sounds. It soon became clear that the flame could serve as an amplifier, whilst the relatively low energy of a sound wave brought about substantially greater energy changes in the flame.

About ten years later, sound was converted into electrical signals for the first time by means of the carbon microphone. With this technique, the overtones of speech and especially of the consonants were not reproduced. Therefore Graham Bell, after inventing the telephone, experimented with the influence of sound on beams of light. In 1880 he succeeded in modulating sound waves on a light-beam with an apparatus he called a 'Photophone.' By means of a telephone receiver connected to a light-sensitive crystal he could change the light-beam back into sound at another place.

In a letter to his father he wrote: *"It's the greatest invention I have ever made; greater than the telephone!"* By 1886 he had gone so far as to use a flame as a loudspeaker, whilst previously he had influenced the gas of a flame with sound. Later it was discovered that electrical arcs also reacted to sound and are able to resound. At that time, there was intensive research into the transmission of sound with light. (In 1902, in Berlin, E. Ruhmer carried out experiments with a light-telephone set over more than seven kilometres.)

It could already be seen that developments in radio technology would lead to more useful alternatives. (See P. J. Rousselot, '*Principes de Phonétique Expérimentale* [Principles of Experimental Phonetics],' H. Welter, Paris, 2 Vols., Vol. 1, 1897-1901, Vol. 2, 1901-1908; Otto von Essen, '*Lehrbuch der Allgemeinen und Angewandten Phonetik* [Textbook of General and Applied Phonetics],' Berlin 1966, 4. Auflage [4th Edition].)

In the years 1916 and 1917, shortly before the condenser and piezo-microphone with much better quality were discovered, Rudolf Steiner spoke about the sound-affected flame in five different places (see also below). In 1932 H. Zickendraht noticed that flames also reacted to alternating electromagnetic fields (Helv. Phys. Acta, 14, 1941, S. 195). A perfect loudspeaker was formulated in the 1960s from this research ('Musical Flames'*; W. R. Babcock *et al.*, 'Nature,' Vol. 216, No. 5116, 18 November 1967, pp. 676-678). There a flame that has no chosen direction of reflection gives rise to a system that has an especially good reproduction of higher frequencies accompanied by nuances of speech and consonants close to the original.

With modern technology it is possible to transform sound into light-modulation. Avoiding the detour of electromagnetism, information can be carried by a glass-fibre cable and by means of light-sensitive material changed back again into sound.

Dr. Paul Eugen Schiller, motivated by Rudolf Steiner's suggested task (Folio 10), researched and described in detail for years the influence of the voice and music on sensitive flames. He carried out exacting experiments with sound at various pitches, volumes and timbres. New apparatus had to be invented for these delicate measurements which Dr. Schiller himself constructed and patented.** With this he could record extremely short momentary exposures of flames. These showed that a flame influenced by sound has a very complicated structure that reveals many vortices. In the course of his work in this field he proposed installing a microphone using light and temperature detectors (see '*Akustische Zeitschrift* [Journal for Acoustics],' Jg. 3 [3rd Yr.], Heft [Issue] 1, 1938, S. 45).

These experiments on sound-affected flames by Dr. Paul Eugen Schiller were carried further by P. E. M. Schneider and colleagues at the *Max-Planck-Institut für Strömungsforschung* [Max Planck Institute for Flow Research]. The results of this research into flow-processes showed for the first time the conditions under which sound could best be amplified and at the same time the disturbing noises of the burning gases repressed. Further descriptions concerning the comprehensive nature of these results can be found in the following publications: P. E. M. Schneider: '*Experimentelle Untersuchungen von Schallbeeinflußten Diffusionsflammen* [Experimental Investigation into Diffusion-Flames Influenced by Sound],' *Bericht* [Report] 12/1969, Göttingen. Similarly: '*Schallverstärkung und Geräuschminderung mit Hilfe des Mitnahmeprinzipes bei Beeinflußten Rhythmischen Wirbelströmungen, Dargestellt am Beispiel Sensibler Flammen* [Sound Amplification and Noise Reduction by Means of the 'Transmission Principle' Influencing Rhythmical Vortex Streaming, as Seen in the Example of Sensitive Flames],' *Bericht* [Report] 10/1975, October 1975, Göttingen. Andreas Heertsch: '*Wirbelbildung an rechteckigen Düsen und -umbildung in Sekundärwirbel* [Vortex Formation in Rectangular Nozzles and Transformation into Secondary Vortices],' *Bericht* [Report] 34/1976, December 1976, Göttingen.

---

* See also The Journal of the Acoustical Society of America (JASA), Melville, NY, Vol. 43, Issue 6, June 1968, pp. 1465-1466; Journal of the Audio Engineering Society (JAES), New York, Vol. 17, No. 3, June 1969, pp. 312-314. Available for purchase from webpage: http://www.aes.org/e-lib/browse.cfm?elib=1581.

** See '*Stroboskop zum subjektiven Beobachten rasch verlaufender Vorgänge* [Stroboscope for the Personal Observation of Fast-Moving Phenomena],' *Deutsches Reichspatentamt Patentschrift* [German State Patent Office Patent Specification] No. 621 085 dated July 5, 1932; Further development of the apparatus described in Patent Specification No. 621 085 is given in Patent Specification No. 642 209 with the same title dated 28 September 1933.

Report from Paul Eugen Schiller of July 5, 1984

Research into sound-sensitive flames

In Folio 10 a-b suggestions for research into flames are reported from conversations with Rudolf Steiner.

Influenced by remarks made in a series of lectures, Dr. P. E. Schiller proceeded with 'singing flames,' already described by John Tyndall in 1869. As well as the familiar transformations of such flames visible to the naked eye, it was also possible to observe the appearance of spiral forms and record them photographically.

It should be noted that flames of this kind only respond with spiral forms to the incident sound-wave. These spiral forms depend above all on the speed of the out-streaming gases and are determined by the direction from which the sound comes and that the pressure-wave appears at the only sensitive place of the flame (just above the jet opening). Demonstrating the 'shape' of the flame is possible to a limited extent only.

The uninterrupted in-streaming notes and vowels are recorded with a home-built exposure device. With the spatial dilution of the flames, this device could only deal with 100 images per second. Thus research into speech, that is, words and sentences, was not possible, also when specific and interesting forms arose from the uninterrupted vowels spoken.

This and other related research was published as follows: '*Die Naturwissenschaften* [The Natural Sciences],' H. [Issue] 16, 18.04.1930/S. 362: '*Die Empfindliche Flamme als Analysator* [The Sensitive Flame as Analyser]'; '*Das Goetheanum* [The Goetheanum],' 1930/59: '*Musik und die Lehre vom Schall* [Music and the Theory of Sound]'; '*Zeitschrift für Techn. Physik* [Journal for Technical Physics],' 1934/294: '*Gerät zur Untersuchung und Demonstration von Schwingungfiguren auf Membranen* [Equipment for Research and Demonstration of Wave-Figures on Membranes]'; '*Das Goetheanum* [The Goetheanum],' 1935/84: '*Die Chladni'schen Klangfiguren* [The Chladni Sound-Figures]'; '*Akustische Zeitschrift* [Journal for Acoustics],' 1937/11: '*Untersuchungen an Neuen Schalldüsen* [Researches on New Sound Nozzles]'; '*Zeitschrift für Techn. Physik* [Journal for Technical Physics],' 1937/332: '*Stroboskop für Aperiodische Vorgänge* [Stroboscope for Aperiodic Phenomena]'; '*Akustische Zeitschrift* [Journal for Acoustics],' 1938/36: '*Untersuchungen an der freien, schallempfindlichen Flamme* [Research into the Free Sound-Sensitive Flame]' (See *Beilagen* [Supplements]).

Over the years one asks the question again: What did Rudolf Steiner have in mind when he spoke of *"the effect of speech on a flame"*? In what sense did he use the words 'coherer' and 'curves'? New details have emerged in the new editions of the lectures of Rudolf Steiner and the available notes of many personalities.

Dr. G. Wachsmuth describes, in his book '*Die Geburt der Geisteswissenschaft* [The Birth of Spiritual Science],' (1941/S. 498) (See English translation: 'The Life and Work of Rudolf Steiner', Whittier Books, New York, 2nd ed. 1955, pp. 470-471) the circumstances which led to the conversation mentioned above and the answer given: *"At that time I could present Rudolf Steiner with several questions from the realm of physics and technology with which we were deeply concerned and sought new solutions. It was after the transition from wireless telegraphy to radio, and wireless sets had only served special purposes up to then, and compared with today were of very primitive construction. With the advance of technology, radio gradually reached private houses and began to exert its far-reaching influence on the daily life of man. I had such a primitive object with interchangeable coils where I lived, and when I asked Rudolf Steiner whether I should also build one for him, he had nothing against it. Still, it was not to be put in his studio. The problem with which we were now concerned was that the transmission of speech or the word, that is to say, the highest and noblest expression of the human being, was served by an apparatus using electricity and magnetism, i.e. forces and mechanical means which remained quite foreign to the finest life-processes of human speech. In a conversation that I, in company with Dr. von Dechend, had with Rudolf Steiner about this, we posed the question whether it was possible to find a more sensitive reagent for the spiritual and physical forces lying in the forms of human speech. After a moment of reflection he said: For that you must work with the sensitive flame. In this and further conversations he gave us a deep insight into the unique position taken up by the element of warmth in the transitional region between soul-life and the physical in nature. He described how heat processes in the human body are bound up with inner soul-spiritual activities, the organic connections between consciousness and temperature, and also the formative processes which the organs of speech exercise on the exhaled air warmed through the activity of speaking. He reminded us of Tyndall's discovery where the fine alterations in freely burning gas flames caused by noises, sounds and words had been observed in the same places and then advised us to concentrate our thoughts and experiments in this direction."*

In a note of the April 24, 1960, Dr. Wachsmuth wrote that Rudolf Steiner had also spoken of another possibility with a *"freely moving flame"*; and further Rudolf Steiner described to Dr. Wachsmuth how the apparatus was constructed in the Tibetan Mysteries *"which could carry out movements similar to eurythmy (etheric larynx). This, however, was unsuited for today, and, indeed, it was harmful"* (Note from 11.05.1961).

Dr. E. Pfeiffer remembered, in a letter of the December 14, 1959, that Rudolf Steiner instead of the word 'coherer' had also used the word 'detector.' Furthermore, he reported on the 6th of March 1960, that Rudolf Steiner remarked: *"Theoretically one could observe that when someone speaks the etheric body of the listener mimes the vibrations of the speech of the speaker. If one makes a eurythmical movement, the etheric body of the other mimes this movement in resonance. One must now investigate how far, for example, an 'I'-movement can be transmitted to a machine by means of resonance so that a lever arm, for example, of this machine mimes the 'I'-movement."*

Folio 11 has a further reference on work with a flame.

10.28.1916 in GA 171, 1964, Vierzehnter Vortrag [Lecture XIV], S. 297: The old clairvoyance of former times gave human beings the possibility of beholding their connection with the spiritual world. This ability died away more and more in the fifth cultural epoch. Therefore they sought *"by surrogation to gain the connection within the spiritual world. Concerning this surrogation, for which accounts are available, the enlightened world of today, of course, cannot find sufficient scorn, mockery and laughter…"*

People often attempted to pave the way by external means:

"Let us say such a man who attempted to gain sight of the spiritual world and did not have the strong power to call up in himself in order to win this vision purely spiritually. Such a man would then take certain substances, burn them and from the mixing of quite specific burning substances bring definite movements into the smoke produced which he evoked by working to quite definite traditional rules…from the particular substances which he burnt he used the smoke into which he made incantations, the smoke took on quite special forms. If he could have approached the spiritual world in a purely spiritual way he would not have needed to use the smoke…with such magical formulae, if uttered in the correct manner the smoke can immediately take on definite forms; if the formulae were correct, so that not only the smoke took on definite forms but these forms allowed the spiritual being, that could not only approach him spiritually, to come into his sphere…the relevant spiritual beings of an elementary nature could enter into these shapes, into these smoke-forms…we see that it is a surrogate, a clinging to that which one cannot grasp purely spiritually, through physical matter." (S. 298f)

S. 302: Rudolf Steiner mentioned that one spoke of the 'illnesses' of metals and reported on the experiments of the English physicist John Tyndall. Tyndall established that columns of smoke, jets of water and flames reacted to sounds and speech ('On Sound,' 1st edition, 1867, Lecture VI, p. 250: *"The sensitiveness of this vein* is now astounding; it rivals that of the ear itself."*) The influence of music on a gas flame was mentioned (p. 231).

Rudolf Steiner criticised this (S. 306): *"There you see how the same characteristics which have been developed for the living would enter into the non-living by another door!"* One ascribes the capacity of becoming ill to the non-living and of having sensation and memory. This shows once more how thinking no longer conforms to the wealth of facts.

10.30.1916 in GA 171, 1964, Sechzehnter Vortrag [Lecture XVI], S. 349: *"…certain secrets must be won out of free human activity and have spread for the first time in our fifth post-Atlantean epoch…and how, what I pointed out to you yesterday, that certain people now already see how smoke that unfolds becomes sensitive, and images sound, just as flames themselves image sound; here lies the beginning of a new knowledge which must come in the course of time…but certain things today are only misused by human beings. Just the most important things which must still emerge from our fifth post-Atlantean epoch, must emerge slowly because today they would be severely misused by humanity.…"*

11.12.1916 in GA 172, 1984, Lecture IV, p. 82f: *"Today machines are designed. Obviously these machines are something objective; but this will not always be the case. In future a connection will arise between what human beings are and that which they produce, that which they create. This connection will become more and more intimate. It will first arise in those spheres where a closer connection between person-and-person is established, as for example in dealing with chemical substances for the preparation of medicines. Today one still believes when something consists of sulphur and oxygen, and some other substance hydrogen or whatever, that what arises as the product consists*

---

* Refers to a liquid vein: sensitive water-jet.

only of those effects that come from the single substances. To a high degree this is correct for today; the course of world development goes in another direction…

The attitude [of the factory manager] will pass into the factory and be borne into the way and manner of how the machines work. The human being will grow together with what is externally objective. Everything that we touch will in time bear in itself the impression of the human being." (p. 83)

A little further on (pp. 83-84): *"…Think of someone in the future, a really good person with truly high ideals, what will he be capable of? He will construct machines and determine signs or signals that can only be carried out by persons who are minded like him, who are also well-disposed. All ill-disposed people will call forth a quite different vibration and the machine won't work! Today people already have a slight idea of this. I have not for nothing given you the indications about this, how certain people see flames dance under the influence of particular sounds. If one researched further in this direction then one would find the way to what I have just indicated; one could also say, find the way back to olden times where an alchemist who only wanted to put gold into his purse, achieved nothing with the very processes that another, who did not want to put gold into his purse, who would perform a sacrament to the honour of the gods and health of humanity, achieved something. So long as what emerges from their occupation is borne to some extent by the aura of human emotions, in the pleasure involved, it is impervious to the kind of influence described above. In the same degree that what is produced by human occupation could no longer be produced with particular enthusiasm, because this is a necessary condition, in the same degree will that what flows and streams from human beings be able to become motor force."*

02.27.1917 in GA 175, 1989, Lecture 4, p. 39: *"The alchemist of old…had in mind, that through his imaginations something was not merely presented but actually happened. Let us say: he produced smoke; then he had the imagination or uttered it so that he tried to bring such a power into this imagination that the substance of the smoke actually took on forms. He sought the kind of concepts that have the power to influence the external reality of nature, not merely to remain in human egoism, but to intervene in nature. Why? Because he still had the idea of the Mystery of Golgotha, that what happened there, what intervened in the course of nature on Earth, was likewise a fact just as the natural process is a fact of nature."*

03.13.1917 in GA 175, Lecture 6, p. 61f: *"You know, concerning so-called wireless telegraphy, that electrical waves become excited and that these waves are transmitted without wire. At certain places appliances are set up—coherers they are called—that because of their special arrangement offer the possibility, just in the station, of picking up the electrical waves and setting the coherer apparatus in motion. This rests quite simply on the set-up, I would say the exact forming of the filings, the metal filings in the coherer that shake down again after the passage of the wave. Just think now: the secrets of the Universe, the extra-mundane Universe, at this particular time, pass right through the Earth, as I have indicated. Only a device for intercepting is needed…a coherer, so to speak, is required for that which comes from the Universe. The ancient Greek Pythia, their priestesses were trained to make use of such coherers and by this means became exposed to what descended from the Universe and could reveal the secrets of the Universe."*

The above refers to technical equipment of the future whereby a novel, close connection between human and machine will be achieved. The use of certain substances was indicated; smoke and flames as the means of expression for spiritual impulses, especially for the formative force active in human speech.

How did Rudolf Steiner describe this formative force? In an early lecture he used 'real' images, so for example: *"Imagine for once that you could make the waves in the air quite rigid for a moment: then my words would fall down…like oyster shells…and you could see the shapes of my words in the hardened air."* (03.04.1907 in GA 96, 2001, p. 223.)

Later Rudolf Steiner could demand more of his listeners and employ spiritually-related images; describing the sources in particular from which the forms and gestures flow. In May of 1923 he said: *"…Where we form the word, we press out the air into certain gestures. Those who can look at the 'sensible-supersensible,' what comes out of the human mouth, sees gestures which are formed in the air: those are the words."* (05.18.1923 in GA 276, 2003, p. 184.) The forms and gestures that are spoken of here are the deeds of the human ether-body. *"…What we utter draws a certain form in the air, only one does not see it but one must assume it is there and think how it could be established by scientific means without drawing."* (06.24.1924 in GA 279, 2005, pp. 30, 240.) In speaking, we create in the air images of the etheric activity of our ether-body.

In Folio 10 a-b the task is described of setting up a transmitter, which is also a receiver, which would reproduce faithfully the personal nuances of the human voice and by means of which the reception of a broadcast can be limited to a chosen circle of listeners. Such an instrument must be so constructed that it can serve the speech-creating activity of the ether-body.

This task cannot be solved by what is known today of coding and decoding, created by the intellect. It seems to me that it cannot be solved so long as the person concerned has not developed the moral attitude, e.g. described in the lecture of 11.12.1916 (see above, page 88) and acquired the powers necessary for the new, intimate connection between human and machine. Put another way: As long as he has not succeeded in technical matters *'in placing the spiritual-etheric in the service of outer practical life.'* (11.25.1917 in GA 178, 2004, p. 178.)

Paul Eugen Schiller

*

Coherers

Wave recorders were invented in 1890 by the French physicist Édouard Branly (1844-1940). The original type for all later receiver sets was possible for the first time after identifying the electromagnetic waves predicted by Hertz. The apparatus was made from a glass tube sealed off with two metal plugs between which there is metal powder or filings and a battery whose poles are connected to each end of the tube, like a galvanometer or current detector. Whilst a very high resistance is offered by the iron granules under normal battery voltage, they become suddenly conducting and pass current as soon as they meet with electrical waves of high frequency aerial voltage. The galvanometer indicates the current. As soon as the tube is shaken, the metal powder returns again to itsoriginal high resistance and the current disappears. Alexander Stepanovich Popov (1859-1906) in 1895 received with a coherer, whose aerial hung in a balloon, the signals from a transmitter at a distance of 250 metres.

Dr. Ehrenfried Pfeiffer was reminded (letter of the 12.14.1959), that Rudolf Steiner has used the word 'detector' instead of 'coherer.'

*

I have indeed given out the task of studying the rhythms of magnetism in the Earth

Concerning Folio 8 (observation of Dr. Kühn and Dr. Schiller's letter to Dr. von Siemens) it is known that Dr. Paul Eugen Schiller worked on this theme. Sadly, no more details can be found concerning further experiments in *Der Kommende Tag* [The Coming Day] and elsewhere.

*

Some observations concerning the rhythms of Earth-magnetism

It has been known for more than 200 years that the intensity of the Earth's magnetic field, as well as the direction in which the compass needle is pointing, is constantly undergoing slight variations.

Measurements over several days show a 24-hour process with a large regular daily course and a somewhat smaller irregular nightly course. The western declination of a magnetic needle towards the north pole takes place in Europe between 6 and 8 am continuously, with a maximum at 9 am and falls quickly to a minimum at 2 pm. After that the needle moves quickly and then more slowly back to a constant mean position, and remains approximately in this position until the next morning. The total intensity, after a relatively quiet course in the night, declines continuously from 6 am to a minimum at 11 am and climbs again until 5 pm. The magnetic field strength then takes up the high and constant night value.

The form of these daily rhythms of the Earth's magnetic field changes in the course of the months. The form of the curve in winter is more irregular with shallow waves when the field is high; thus it compares more with the night-character of the daily course. In summer, on the contrary, the development is more regular with the greatest variations from April until August and two small insignificant maxima at the equinoxes. For this reason one speaks of a semi-annual double wave.

There are also rhythms of shorter duration but having greater disturbances, the so-called magnetic storms. Measurements over a longer period show that the frequency of these outbreaks declines in the mornings until reaching a minimum at midday and increasing in the afternoon until maximum between 5 and 11 pm. Throughout the year, magnetic storms increase around Easter and Michaelmas; around midsummer and Christmas they are most unlikely. It has been discovered that magnetic storms are the result of powerful outbursts of ultraviolet light in outer space.

The analysis of year-long series of figures showed further that distinct diurnal and annual rhythms are superimposed with something further. Quite early on, in 1839, periods with the duration of a Moon-day (the time that elapses until the Moon is again at the same place in the heavens) had been found. It can be very clearly seen that, in contrast to the approximately 30 times stronger daily variation and, after eliminating all other known variables, there is a double-wave: for a latitude 50° north the

91

horizontal intensity was found to be *"at maxima when the Moon is on the horizon and minima when at its upper or lower culmination."* (Alfred Nippoldt, '*Erdmagnetismus, Erdstrom und Polarlicht* [Earth Magnetism, Earth Current and Polar Light],' 3. Aufl. [3rd Ed.], Berlin, Leipzig 1921.) The vertical intensity has its minima and maxima correspondingly three hours earlier. This effect too appears stronger in summer than in winter. S. Chapman showed that this magnetic double-wave was connected with the corresponding double-wave of atmospheric pressure, the tide wave of the atmosphere, which Johann Wolfgang von Goethe had already described.

In addition to this, Moon influence on planetary rhythms has also been discovered. In Nippoldt's book there is a list that shows what share of the daily variation in the maximum amplitude is attributed to the influence of the planets: Mercury +11%, Venus −10%, Mars − 4%, Jupiter −19%, Saturn −2%. Greater variations in the planetary effects have been confirmed when Venus, Earth, and Jupiter happen to lie in a straight line.

There are other rhythms of the Earth's magnetic field of 11, 22 and 60 years dependent on the number of sunspots.

With all these rhythms of the Earth's magnetic field there are slight changes in the course of centuries. Since Gauss began measuring, it decreases from year-to-year.

Further references to magnetism may be found in the Collected Edition:

10.01.1911, GA 130: Magnetism and the harmony of the spheres, fallen sound-ether and magnetism.
06.10.1913, GA 150: Magnetism and destructive powers.
10.02.1916, GA 171: Magnetism and electricity in the human being.

The conductivity of the Earth

Telegraphy connects two stations by one cable. On account of the good conductivity of electric current by the Earth, the second pole, that is the return for both telegraph stations, could be realised when the electrodes were sunk into underground water. In this connection it was established that terrestrial currents undergo strong variations in summer (weaker in winter), the daily rhythm being regular. Further it was found that the expected variation of this Earth current at the same time caused an alteration in the magnetic field at the relevant place. (cf. L. Stemer, 'On Earth Currents and Magnetic Variations' in Terrestrial Magnetism and Atmospheric Electricity, Vol. 13, No. 2, June 1908, p. 57.)

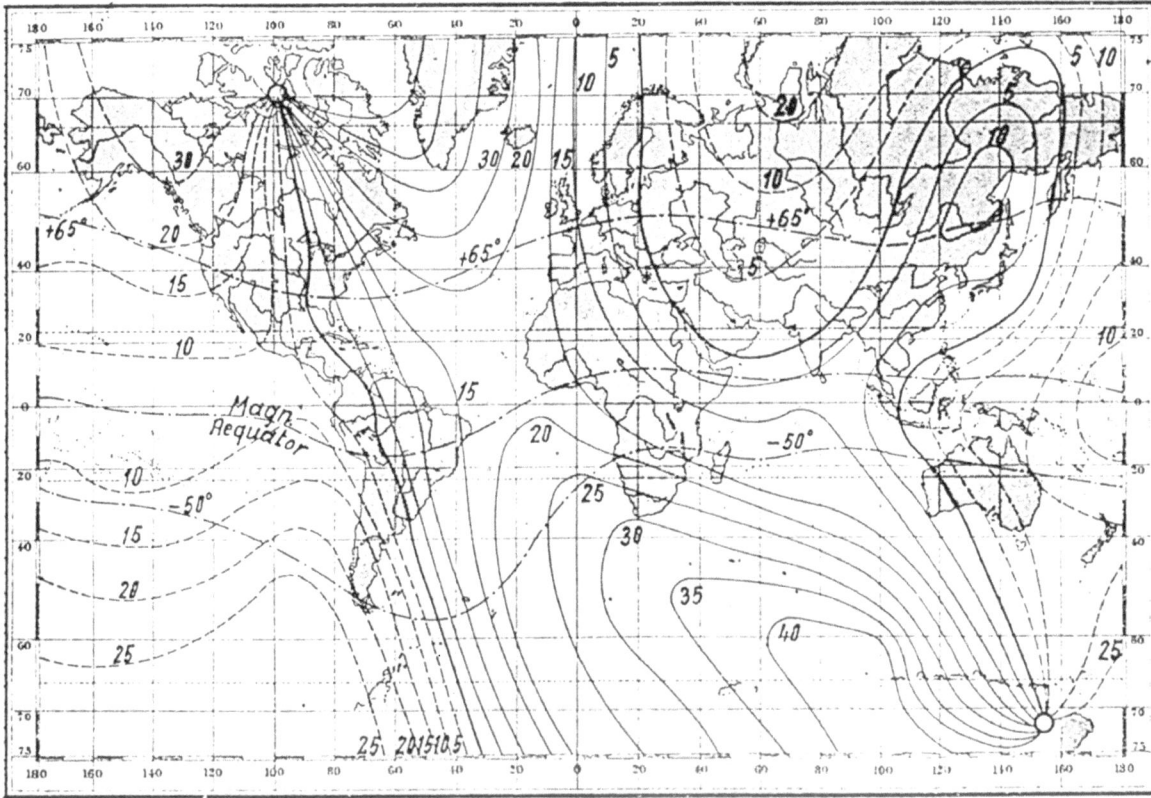

Figure 1: Magnetic field of the Earth at the beginning of the 20th century. The lines show equal declination (deviation of the magnetic needle from true north). Note the remarks of Rudolf Steiner e.g. in GA 178, concerning the snake-like line of the places where the magnetic needle points to the true north pole.

Dr. Guenther Wachsmuth quotes in his book, 'The Etheric Formative Forces in Cosmos, Earth and Man' (p. 74), again from the then standard work of Nippoldt (S. 128-129): *"We are most backward of all in the investigation of the terrestrial current; yet we do know, at least, that it is composed of combined magnetic and atmospheric electrical influences…the energy, however, of all these variations does not derive from the Sun, but from the energy-store of the Earth's rotation."*

In 'Beiträge [Supplements]' No. 95/96, Ostern [Easter] 1987: 'Der Zwölf-Farbenkreis [The Twelve-Colour Circle],' Mr. Hans Bucheim in Einsingen has taken year-long measurements of Earth currents.

Comments for Folio 11

None

Comments for Folio 12

The article by Mr. W. Pelikan mentioned in Folio 12 closes, after discussing the experimental results, with a further task from Rudolf Steiner:

"In connection with this work Dr. Steiner gave out a short experimental work, which sadly could not be carried out. He specified that perennial plants with small stems (we thought of fuchsias and perhaps roses) be fertilised with a solution of quicksilver. One would then ascertain abnormal crack-formations in the cambium."

The fundamentals of this then were briefly stated by Mr. Pelikan in Folio 12 b and referred to in the article mentioned ('*Gäa Sophia* [Gaia Sophia],' Bd. [Vol.] I, 1926, S. 140ff):

"Mineral substance is a process that has come to rest in a consolidated state in which the etheric formative forces are no longer active. Iron, copper, quicksilver are only the end-product of an iron-, copper-, quicksilver-process. Just the study of these processes which are etheric in their operation, gives rise to the understanding of the significance and activity of the metals in Earth, cosmos and human being. The dead, mineral-like metal is the process that has died away. How can one call it to life in order to pursue its activity? A path is there that can be found whereby the metal can be taken up from the life-processes of the plant. For the plant is a being that in its activity and structure tears itself away from the rigid physical system of death towards the life-rich forms of the etheric realm. On the other hand its external physical structure is an image of the etheric formative forces that constitute its nature. When one allows metals to be taken up by the plant in various ways and then follows up how they are changed in its being, the plant virtually makes the characteristic formative activities in the animated metal-processes physically visible. The material copper-salt, for example, disappears, the rigidified shape of a once-active formative force, which may be described as the copper-process. The structure again goes on into formative activity that can reveal itself physically in the most varied plant formation. Such effects are found characteristically with lead, tin, copper, quicksilver and phosphorus. These trials may be described at another time. Only the effects of quicksilver on the plant are described here.

Preliminary experiments already produced odd changes of form in different plants. For example, Nasturtium growing in air mixed with some mercury vapour, acquired strange tremulous wavy leaves and stems. Above all it was with Calendula that something altogether extraordinary was to be found. They sprouted new pedicles out of the angles of the sepals that are in a circle round the capitulum, on which very small leaves grow; each normal sized capitulum had 10 to 12 little capitulums round it! In order to understand such effects better, Dr. Rudolf Steiner suggested researching how quicksilver alters the rhythm of assimilation in the plant."

After a description of the experiments with quicksilver the article closed with a further research proposition: *"Dr. Steiner suggested that one should investigate how silver and lead salts affect the rhythm of assimilation; one would then see how silver and lead work polar to one another...."* The results of such a research series would establish this polarity which works as follows: *"...every time in the course of potentisation the effect for silver changes upwards, the change for lead tends downwards."*

Comments for Folio 13

None

Comments for Folio 14

You must also learn to use the day and night rhythms in the preparation of medicines:

See also what was said about morning and evening forces in the remarks about Folio 2 as well as in GA 178.

I am having experiments done in Stuttgart - sadly the people there are not progressing fast enough:

Rudolf Steiner's annoyance over the activities at that time as well as numerous references to method are recorded in the three Natural Scientific Courses (e.g. GA 323, Lecture XVIII 01.18.21, Lecture XVI 01.16.21). In addition there are more details to be found in the meetings of the '*Dreißigerkreises* [Circle of Thirty]' (GA 259).

From Dr. Ernst Lehrs' autobiography, '*Gelebte Erwartung* [A Life of Inner Expectancy]' (S. 195):

"*As a student of mathematics and physics I was naturally very interested in the department of the Institute concerned with this and related subjects. Thus I was impressed by the time and energy given to the work in hand but alarmed to notice what was lacking from the ideal. Obviously work was carried out with concepts derived from normal practice without noticing that it stood at the beginning of a new path and, initially, where this would have been appropriate, fell back on old established methods. There was inflation and, with the boundless funds that came with it, the physics and chemistry laboratory was quickly fitted out with a fair amount of traditional equipment. So it happened that when Rudolf Steiner visited this laboratory he was prompted to say that rather than so much apparatus he would have wished to see the place full of ideas.*"

Comments for Folio 15

At the end of the Astronomy Course (GA 323) in January 1921, Rudolf Steiner hoped that from the content of this course there would above all be a stimulation for research. He added a series of examples showing how the more mathematically described facts could also be done experimentally and verified. The following example from the course (Lecture XVIII on 18.01.1921) is closely connected with the notes to this folio of Walter Johannes Stein: "*...or when you attempt, by heating certain substances, to obtain lines of propagation for the warming – here from within towards the outside (radially), there from the periphery towards the inside; ...everywhere you will see how what is presented here for example over the opposition between Sun and Earth can be pursued experimentally.*"

From the notebook of Paul Eugen Schiller for the 2nd of July 1984 (see pp. 33ff.), he describes how such experiments were in fact put in hand:

"Folio 15: Propagation of warmth. The speed of heat propagation was investigated, a) in the direction of the centre of the Earth, b) with respect to the opposite direction. No difference could be established."

The realities of quantum theory will appear as the result of measurement...

On the 12th of March 1920, Rudolf Steiner extended the equation of heat conduction with an imaginary coefficient ($\sqrt{-1}$). During 1926, in a slightly modified form the same equation appeared again in the so-called wave equation of quantum mechanics. [See Notes, No. 49 for this lecture in the 'Warmth Course,' second edition 1988; reprinted 2005, on page 190 in both editions, Tr.]

Comments for Folio 16

Concerning the indications given in this folio Professor Dr. F. Halla (Brussels) gave a detailed report in '*Mathematisch-Physikalische Korrespondenz* [Mathematical-Physical Correspondence]' No. 11 (Michaeli [Michaelmas] 1957), S. 5f., entitled '*Einige Bemerkungen über das Potenzieren* [Some Observations about Potentising]':

"The distribution, for example the dissolving of a solid substance in liquid or the mixing of two solutions with different concentrations, can occur in two ways:

1. As a spontaneous process (the system remains self-contained): Diffusion.
2. External forces affect the system (shaking, stirring, centrifugal motion, etc.): Convection.
For diffusion it is characteristic that in the equations the dependence on time in this process is expressed not by time 't' itself, but the figure '$\sqrt{}$ t' appears.

In potentisation one has to do with the distribution of the stock solution into a larger volume (with the decimal potency it is 10 times greater). As a result of shaking (succussion), as well as diffusion, there is convection which then predominates.
The purpose of potentising is twofold:

a)   To introduce a new and greater volume as far as the boundary surface of the substance held in undiluted solution. Thereby enters what can be described from the spiritual-scientific point of view as the effect of light in the first place: a radiating activity that is not lost in the infinite but at a certain boundary is 'reflected' and, changed in quality, returns to its starting point. The diluted solution is only a model in miniature of such a process. Here the new surface attained in the substance becomes 'reflected' and comes back etherised towards the centre.

b) Because of the dilution of the dissolved substance the physical effect is simply weakened.

Regarding point a) it should be noted, between 1916 and 1918 in Vienna, Köstlergasse, from a chance remark of Rudolf Steiner, that diffusion consists not in the movement of physical particles but in the spreading out of qualities (such as the blue colour of copper sulphate). Consider too that from every point by volume through diffusion and evaporation there is a corresponding amount by weight of copper sulphate to be won back, and so, if one takes this statement seriously, accept that supersensibly something takes place that has only an image, a reflection, in space. That which holds together the separate visibly perceptible qualities of the substance in solution: the 'real nature of the copper sulphate'—is consequently not to be found at all in the world of the senses. Materialism consists in this: that one quality amongst many, for example weight, is given priority over the other. In this way the admittance of the 'Spirit of Gravity' is assured.

The difficulties that arise with the idea of a continuous spreading out of qualities are perhaps reduced when it is considered as a spreading out of wave-paths or movements which finally change to standing waves. With this description one and the same quality could just as well take on a positive or a negative sign. The view of diffusion as a superimposition of wave-paths has already appeared in current literature. In this respect our research (with H. Castelliz) was not completed but it would be well worth the trouble of being taken up again.

Regarding b) it is worth noting that by means of a single dilution with a correspondingly large amount of solvent the very same concentration can be reached as by repeated potentisations; this however lacks the repeated etherising effect.

For the practice of potentisation it follows that the etherisation of the dissolved substance cannot be attained by inadequate shaking (succussion). The process of convection can be accomplished by diffusion but only when there are sufficiently long pauses between the individual potentisations in order to allow diffusion to be completed. For practical reasons it is usually not possible. A difference might well arise whether one shakes or leaves it to diffusion to equalise the concentration. In the first case something of the human will takes part in the solution, in the latter, more the cosmic influence comes into operation." (07.11.1957)

Concerning current concepts in reciprocal lattices see also F. Halla, '*Raum und Gegenraum* [Space and Counter-Space],' *Mathematisch-Physikalische Korrespondenz* [Mathematical-Physical Correspondence], No. 4 (1955), and George Adams, '*Das Reziproke Gitter und die Röntgenanalyse der Kristalle* [The Reciprocal Lattice and the X-ray Analysis of Crystals],' op. cit., No. 12 (1957).

Comments for Folio 17

None

Comments for Folio 18

For the research work of Dr. Franz Thomastik and the indications from Rudolf Steiner see the article from the *Mathematisch-Astronomischen Sektion am Goetheanum* [Mathematical-Astronomical Section at the Goetheanum] 1968 by Ludwig Kremlin entitled '*Tonqualitäten und Bildgestaltungen durch Planetenwirksamkeit im Kolophonium* [Sound Qualities and Images Caused by Planetary Activity in Rosin (*Colophonium*)].'

Comments for Folio 19

The suggestions to Jan Stuten in 1915 for the development of an art of the play of light were closely connected with the indications given to Dr. Ehrenfried Pfeiffer for stage lighting. At the beginning of the century the attempt was made, by means of 'light pianos' and 'light organs,' to stage a moving projection of colour by performing music. One would make the audible in music visible with this newly created art: the so-called 'optophony.' Soon the cinema eliminated this artistic impulse and the idea fell into oblivion. In the 1960s Dr. Hans Jenny carried out experiments once more with stage lighting arrangements on the Goetheanum stage, in Dornach.

See also Wolfgang Veit, '*Bewegte Bilder. Der Zyklus 'Metamorphosen der Furcht' von Jan Stuten* [Moving Pictures. The Series 'Metamorphosis of Fear' by Jan Stuten],' Stuttgart 1993.

Comments for Folio 20

The formula $x^{2/3} + y^{2/3} + z^{2/3} = a^{2/3}$ is the three-dimensional formula of an astroid in Cartesian coordinates. Viewed in the plane, this curve is the geometrical position of the circumference of a circle with radius $= r$, which in its turn rolls on the inside of the circumference of a circle 4 or 4/3 times larger. The astroid, a special case of the hypotrochoid (roll-curve), has the special characteristic that the intersection of *every* tangent with the coordinate axes always has the constant distance a.

In researching the etheric world other authors (G. Adams, O. Whicher, L. Edwards, N. Thomas, et al.) use the so-called path curves, the egg, for example, initiates spiral forms.

For the Strader Machine see Heft [Issue] 107, Michaeli [Michaelmas] 1991 of the '*Beiträge zur Rudolf Steiner Gesamtausgabe* [Supplements to the Collected Edition of Rudolf Steiner],' (*Skizzen von Rudolf Steiner und Darstellungen von Oskar Schmiedel, Hans Kühn u. a.*) [Sketches by Rudolf Steiner and diagrams by Oskar Schmiedel, Hans Kühn, *et al.*].

See also Hans Kühn, '*Dreigliederungszeit* [The Time of the Threefold Commonwealth],' Dornach 1978, S. 113ff.

Comments for Folio 21

Rudolf Steiner's article *'Die Atomistik und ihre Widerlegung* [Atomism and its Refutation]' GA 38, from the year 1890 is reprinted in *'Beiträge zur Rudolf Steiner Gesamtausgabe* [Supplements to the Collected Edition of Rudolf Steiner],' No. 63, Michaeli [Michaelmas] 1978. English translation published in 'Atomism and its Refutation,' The Mercury Press, Spring Valley, New York, 1975. See also webpage: http://wn.rsarchive.org/Articles/AtmRef_index.html.

A facsimile reproduction of the original handwritten *'Beantwortung von 6 Fragen* [Answers to Six Questions]' is in the Appendix to the *'Geisteswissenschaftliche Impulse zur Entwicklung der Physik, Erster Naturwissenschaftlicher Kurs: Licht, Farbe, Ton-Masse, Elektrizität, Magnetismus (Lichtkurs)* [Spiritual-Scientific Impulses for the Development of Physics, First Natural Scientific Course: Light, Colour, Sound-Mass, Electricity, Magnetism (The Light Course)*],' in German edition only (4. Auflage [4th Edition], Gesamtausgabe Dornach [Collected Edition Dornach] 2000, S. 192-195), GA 320.

English translation of the 'Answers to Six Questions' first published in 'Atomism and its Refutation,' The Mercury Press, Spring Valley, New York, 1975. See also webpage: http://wn.rsarchive.org/Articles/AtmRef_index.html.

Comments for Folio 22

Supplements to Folio 22 d

GA 1, 'Goethe the Scientist' (1950), Chap. XVI, Part 2 'The Primal Phenomenon (*Urphänomen*),' p. 224 – **One of the most beautiful tasks of my life:**
"But here it cannot be my task to deduce from Goethe's principle the phenomena in connection with the theory of colour which were unknown in Goethe's time. If I should ever be so fortunate as to possess the leisure and means needed for writing a theory of colour, in Goethe's sense but completely on the level of the achievements of modern science, only in such a way could the task indicated be accomplished. I should consider that as belonging among the most beautiful tasks of my life…"

GA 324a, 'The Fourth Dimension' (2001), Part II Questions and Answers, 12.29.1922, p. 159 – **Tasks allotted to mathematical physicists:**
paraphrased as: *"… The problem to be solved is how the realm-of-touch, when expressed in mathematical formula, compares with the optical or realm-of-sight."* See also 02.28.1923, GA 257; 03.17.1921, GA 324; and 01.01.1923, GA 326.

---

* 'The Light Course', translated by George Adams and first published in English in 1977 in 2 volumes is also available on-line at webpage: http://wn.rsarchive.org/Lectures/LightCrse/LitCrs_index.html. The latest edition of 'The Light Course,' translated by Raoul Cansino, Anthroposophic Press, Great Barrington, MA, 2001, is downloadable on-line in pdf format from: http://steinerbooks.org/research/archive/light_course/light_course.pdf.

Further Allocation of Tasks for Natural Scientists
Given by Rudolf Steiner

Collected by Stephan H. R. Clerc

There follows further proposals of Rudolf Steiner which may be found in the secondary anthroposophical literature.

Sensitive crystallisation as a reagent for the formative forces in substances

Dr. Ehrenfried Pfeiffer reported in an address on the February 27, 1955 in Stuttgart how, on questioning Rudolf Steiner in the period from October 1920 until Spring 1921, the following proposals concerning reagents for the etheric were made:

"In order to find this reagent for the etheric world one should attempt to observe crystallisation processes with the addition of plant material and blood, then study the changes in these crystallisation processes. 'What you will discover from this, I cannot yet tell, you will be surprised how much will be found.' That is all that Rudolf Steiner said on this subject. …when I tried to ask him about the experimental set-up, he always replied: 'You must find the research set-up yourself.' …Dr. Steiner said once, on another occasion: 'In these matters you must allow the elemental beings to help. They will explain to you what you yourself do not know. But these elemental beings must feel at home in your laboratory. You must spiritually prepare such an atmosphere so that these elemental beings co-operate.'"

Dr. Ehrenfried Pfeiffer, in research with copper chloride crystals, found, almost by chance, a method which successfully indicated the formative forces in plants as well as the influences by night and day in crystal formations.

Experiments in the growth of plants as the starting point for potency research

As a further reagent for the etheric forces, Rudolf Steiner, in connection with the search for a remedy against the animal epidemic, proposed to the Chief of the Biological Department of the Scientific Research Institute of *Der Kommende Tag* [The Coming Day], Lilly Kolisko, experiments in plant growth. See also her report to Rudolf Steiner of the 30th of November 1923 at the end of this issue on page 105.

At that time an epidemic of foot-and-mouth disease raged in South Germany that did not spare the estates of *Der Kommende Tag* [The Coming Day] at Guldes-Mühle. In May 1920 from the Biological Department (first under the name 'Epidemic Department') a 'Physiological-Biological Research Institute' was founded in order to discover the correct method of preparation and dosage of the remedy. Lilly Kolisko wrote about this later:

"Asked about the question of dose Dr. Steiner replied: 'Germinate grains of seed in different dilutions of the remedy. You will obtain a curve that reflects the vital processes in the body of the cow.'" (See L. Kolisko, 'Physiologischer und Physikalischer Nachweis der Wirksamkeit kleinster Entitäten (1923-1959) [Physiological and physical proof of the effectiveness of the smallest entities (1923-1959)],'*

Herausgegeben durch die Arbeitsgemeinschaft anthroposophischer Ärzte [Published by the Working Association of Anthroposophical Medical Doctors], Stuttgart, 1960, I. Kapitel [Chapter I], *Was ist eine "kleinste Entität"?* [What is a "Smallest Entity"?], S. 3-4). See also E. and L. Kolisko, 'Agriculture of Tomorrow,'** Kolisko Archive, Stroud, 1st ed. 1946, pp. 81-218; 2nd edition 1978; 1982, Published by Kolisko Archive Publications, Bournemouth. See Part II – "Smallest Entities" in Agriculture; Nutrition; Capillary Dynamolysis, pp. 56-158.

With this experiment, Lilly Kolisko succeeded in establishing that the influence of etheric formative forces proceeded from potentised substances up to the 30th decimal potency.

An extension of this series of experiments is described in 'Mitteilungen des Biologischen Instituts am Goetheanum [Reports of the Biological Institute at the Goetheanum]', Nr. 1, Stuttgart 1934:

"The study of the effects of potentisation can be combined with the study of formative forces that lie hidden in matter. I am indebted to Dr. Rudolf Steiner also for the encouragement of this study. In the year 1923 he requested me to study the 'formative forces' in different plants. …Rudolf Steiner's suggestion of allowing plant saps to drip on to filter-paper was carried out." (S. 13)

Moon and planetary activities in earthly substances – the beginnings of rhythm research

For Dr. Pfeiffer, L. Kolisko and others (see Folio 8 for example) these trials resulted in the first experiments in the field of rhythm research: Lilly Kolisko investigated the function of the spleen under the influence of irregular meal times and her results published under the title '*Milzfunktion und Plättchenfrage* [Function of the Spleen and the Platelet Question]' in Stuttgart, 1921 and Dornach, 1922. Working closely with Rudolf Steiner, she then studied the influence of the Moon and planetary rhythms on plant growth and carried on this work independently over decades. With the *Steigbildmethode* [rising picture method]*** (capillary dynamolysis) developed further by herself, she further researched metallic salt solutions of the various planetary metals and compared the pictures which arose in connection with the corresponding planets in their constellations. The outcome of this rhythm research she published at regular intervals. The results are used in bio-dynamic agriculture and pharmacy but also in pedagogy and matters of hygiene.

The founding of research institutes at the Goetheanum before and after the Christmas Conference

This Physiological-Biological Department coming from the Epidemic Department already mentioned had a room with table, chair and a matchbox, which Rudolf Steiner considered the ideal situation for founding a laboratory, on the occasion of the Christmas Conference 1923 was definitely separated from the 'Biological Research Institute' and re-named 'Biological Institute at the Goetheanum.'

In 1924 because of the liquidation of *Der Kommende Tag A.G.* [The Coming Day plc] as a result of the inflation many other lines of research were completely broken off and it was only rarely, for example in the Goetheanum or in America, taken up again.

---

* See also her earlier 1932 paper translated into English as: 'A Physiological Proof of the Activity of Smallest Entities,' under: 'Homeopathy – Research and Theory,' in 'Mercury,' Journal of the Anthroposophical Therapy and Hygiene Association (A.T.H.A.), Spring Valley, N.Y., Number 11, 1991, pp. 1-27. See footnote on page 31.

** The 1st (1946) edition of this book is available for download in five parts in pdf format from webpage: http://www.soilandhealth.org/01aglibrary/01aglibwelcome.html.

*** Also known as the filter-paper chromatographic rising picture method.

The origin of the founding of a research laboratory at the Goetheanum in the summer of 1921 on the initiative of Dr. Guenther Wachsmuth and Dr. Ehrenfried Pfeiffer is described by Dr. Wachsmuth in his book 'The Life and Work of Rudolf Steiner' as follows (pp. 420-421):

"…quite understandably, as a result of working together, a place was sought where experiments could be carried out in order to test what had before only existed in thought. When I think back on the first beginnings many a humorous memory arises; for the birth of the laboratory took place in a primitive cellar with the only advantages of gas and water supply and was otherwise deserted and empty. At our request Rudolf Steiner had allowed us, for the time being, to occupy this space in the basement of the Glasshouse, where above, the coloured glass windows were ground. We began in the most primitive way in establishing the laboratory by putting together borrowed tables and chairs with the addition of essential glass, retorts, Bunsen burners, etc. The research equipment indicated a view towards rhythm and life and so clearly in my memory there stands as one of the first instruments a large Torricelli barometer. On account of its awkwardness it soon served no longer for measuring air pressure but its vacuum and quicksilver was readily available for other experiments."

What exactly was done in this laboratory is described by Dr. Alla Selawry in her book, 'Ehrenfried Pfeiffer – A Pioneer in Spiritual Research and Practice – A Contribution to his Biography,' Mercury Press, Spring Valley, New York, 1992. There she describes on pages 98-100 the research tasks given by Rudolf Steiner on which Dr. Pfeiffer had worked, these being in addition to the tasks indicated in The Schiller File: for example, he researched the connection between the poisonous nature of the flowers of the nightshade family and other flowers or how far plant growth was influenced by sound waves or cosmic rays which in the laboratory was mirrored by metal surfaces. In connection with breeding questions Rudolf Steiner has recommended:

"For example with a seed of wild couch grass carry out meditatively and experience inwardly in exact 'sensory fantasy' to develop it in the way suited to its origin. At the same time the archetype of the plant arises as it will in the course of breeding. When these thoughts are carried through in a sufficiently active manner, then the ether-organism of the plant is shown the way to its transformation."

Just as with this activity of thinking the attempt is made to obtain certain forms in growing crystals.

The electric process takes place in a radial direction from outside towards the conductor

Dr. Ernst Lehrs, who was not directly involved with the research programme of *Der Kommende Tag* [The Coming Day], writes in his book '*Gelebte Erwartung* [A Life of Inner Expectancy],' J. Ch. Mellinger Verlag, Stuttgart 1979 (S. 227), about a relatively unknown task. The conversation took place in February 1923 following an assembly of delegates at Gustav-Siegle-Haus* in Stuttgart. It concerned at first the experiments done by Lehrs just for his doctorate (Distribution of alternating current in an electrical conductor, skin effect):

"As a result of this Rudolf Steiner took a notebook and a thick carpenter's pencil from his coat pocket, drew a circle on the paper representing the cross-section and shaded it along the inner edge, indicating the layer along which the current takes place. Was that what was meant, he asked and then began to explain to me what in reality took place. The concept of 'current' had no meaning at all.

---

* Now the *Philharmonie Gustav-Siegle-Haus* [Philharmonic Concert Hall Gustav Siegle House].

In reality nothing occurred in the direction of the conductor. The whole electrical process took place much more in a radial direction from outside toward the conductor and into it. The higher the frequency, the less it can penetrate and even the DC voltage remains somewhat free in the middle, people just do not notice it. He then added that I should prove this experimentally and could then unsaddle the accepted theory of electricity."

In the Introduction to his book 'Man or Matter'* (Third edition, revised and enlarged, 1985), Dr. Lehrs describes on page 15 the same conversation again in a similar manner:

"Judge of my astonishment when he at once took out of his pocket a notebook and a huge carpenter's pencil, made a sketch and proceeded to speak of the problem as one fully conversant with it, and in such a way that he gave me the starting point for an entirely new conception of electricity. It was instantly borne in on me that if electricity came to be understood in this sense, results would follow which in the end would lead to a quite new technique in the use of it."

In conclusion, Dr. Lehrs relates in the first-named book (S. 228):

"Further references made by Rudolf Steiner lead me to understand that he had the intention of creating the appropriate department at the Goetheanum where impulses within the meaning of the newly founded Free High School for Spiritual Science could be inaugurated. Like so much else, nothing came of it."

Concerning this task, see also the closing words of the discussion** with Rudolf Steiner on the 08.08.1921, GA 320, and the article by Rudolf Cantz, '*Das elektrische Anschlußkabel* [The Electric Connecting Cable],' *Elemente der Naturwissenschaft* [Elements of Natural Science], 1971, Nr. 14, S. 31-36.

Addendum:

Below is a letter to Rudolf Steiner from Lilly Kolisko (cf. p. 101). The supplements mentioned there, with the exception of the 'reports,' that appear in the *Chemisches Zentralblatt*,*** are not to be found in the Archive. – A detailed description of the work of Lilly Kolisko by Dr. Gisbert Husemann entitled '*Lili Kolisko. Werk und Wesen* (1889-1976) [Lili Kolisko – Her Life and Work (1889-1976)]' is published in '*Beiträge zu einer Erweiterung der Heilkunst nach geisteswissenschaftlichen Erkenntnissen* [Contributions to an Extension of the Art of Healing Based on Insights Gained by Spiritual Science],' hg. von der Medizinischen Sektion am Goetheanum und der Gesellschaft Anthroposophischer Ärzte [Published by the Medical Section at the Goetheanum and the Society of Anthroposophical Medical Doctors], 31. Jg. [31st Yr.], Heft [Issue] 2, März/ April 1978, S. 37-55. This biography was translated by Dr. David Heaf from the original German article and published in '*Archetype*,' Science Group of the Anthroposophical Society in Great Britain, London, Issue No. 7, September 2001, pp. 31-48.

---

* 1st (1950) edition is downloadable on-line in pdf format from: http://static.scribd.com/docs/dqxki7e3lja99.pdf.

** See 'The Light Course,' Anthroposophic Press, Great Barrington, MA, 2001, Discussion Statement, pp. 172-185 + Notes, pp. 195-196. Downloadable on-line in pdf format from: http://steinerbooks.org/research/archive/light_course/light_course.pdf.

*** Chemical abstract journal published by the *Deutschen Chemischen Gesellschaft* [German Chemical Society], Berlin.

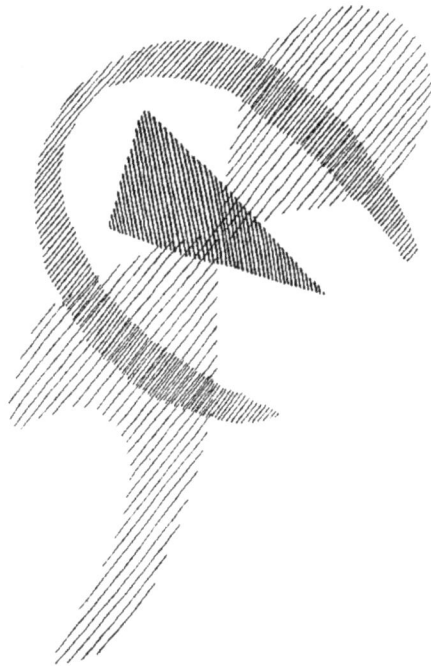

„*DER KOMMENDE TAG*"

Wissenschaftliches
Forschungsinstitut

Biologische Abteilung

„THE COMING DAY"

Scientific
Research Institute

Biological Department

Stuttgart, November 30, 1923
Kanonenweg 44

Most respected Dr. Steiner,

Since Herr Doktor is hardly likely to come to Stuttgart before Christmas, may I be allowed to give a short report about my recent research?

On your last visit here in October you proposed the foremost task of obtaining curves where the intensive activity of light caused the weight-curve to show the opposite picture of the growth-curve. It should show that the light worked against weight, gravity. It causes me endless joy to be able to tell you that a good part of this task appears to be solved. Intensive sunlight could not be provided and for the time being I have carried out my research with electric light. I let the light burn day and night in order to increase the intensity of the light-effect. The experiment was carried out in the darkroom. On a large table stood 63 jars (three water vessels 60th potency with iron sulphate 1 gram to 100 ccm stock solution). Above the table a large wooden framework was erected which bore six light-bulbs of 100 watts, equally spaced. The darkroom has a high window opening on to the staircase allowing the passage of air. The six lamps remained switched on day and night and at the same time kept the little room at a temperature of 22°C. Already after a few days it could be seen that the little plants had grown more quickly than they would have done in just daylight. After eight days the plants in electric light were as large as they would have been in 14 days. The second leaf appeared quite clearly. The plants appeared healthy and were a lively green, but one had the decided impression that they were stretched and slender. The breadth of the leaf was decidedly narrower than in normal daylight. After 14 days the plants were measured and I enclose herewith a photograph of the growth-curve (Supplement No. 1). The minima lie at the 13th, 24th, 34th, 42nd, 55th and 57th potencies respectively. The second leaf was shooting considerably beyond the first leaf, with the node at normal height. Further it is striking that the curve for the second shows strong variations, the first leaf only minor. The leaf growth exceeded that of the root growth.

When one compares this curve with the iron-curve of the previous year, already published, one sees that the leaf growth is twice as large. The maximum heights were 17 cm, against 34 cm with electric light. Because of this the relationship of leaf growth to root growth changed. The previous year we established leaf to root = 1:2, this time the relationship became approximately leaf to root = 1.4:1.

The weight-curve (Supplement No. 2) shows the minima: suggested by the 12th, then the 24th, 37th, 42nd, 39th, 57th and 60th potencies respectively. In the root the 14th, 21st, 38th, 52nd, 55th and 60th potencies respectively. The minima have somewhat shifted compared to the growth-curve, although a direct reversal has not taken place. Compare this, however, with the weight-curve of the previous year, then there is a quite surprising result.

Iron experiment 1922 in daylight   Weight of root : leaf = 1 : 2

Iron experiment 1923 in electric light Weight of root : leaf = 1 : 4

The root has therefore become twice as light even though the growth in length has increased. The weight of the leaves for the daylight experiment reached a maximum of 500 mg, with electric light a maximum of 600 mg. Against this must be placed the fact that the growth in length was nearly 100%, the weight about 20%. One must therefore establish also for the leaves a decrease of the special weight.

This first experiment encouraged me to undertake a second, involving 150 flower-pots. At the same time three experiments were set up. The 60th potency of copper sulphate in daylight as usual. (I chose just this metal because Herr Doktor wanted a repeat of the copper experiment to the 60th potency for publication.) The 60th potency of copper sulphate in the darkroom with electric light as described above. Then I divided the darkroom so that a very small space could be kept completely dark. There I placed the copper sulphate with 30th potency, leaving no space for more. For these three experiments were potentised at the same time and as far as possible had the same room temperature and differed only in the manner of illumination and non-illumination. I began with the assumption that if the light works against gravity, the darkness must work in a similar way, which means the little plant must become heavier than if it were grown in daylight. After eight days the three experiments were photographed and after 14 days measured. The light and darkness experiment on one day, and the following day the usual daylight experiment, there was one day when the work was not accomplished.

Supplement No. 3 shows the curve for the daylight experiment and is outstandingly fine. The 1st through 30th potencies show exactly the same curve-form as the published copper-curve. 1. Minimum 15th potency, then the depressions with the 25th to the 29th potencies, they appear as a repetition of the first part of the curve. First rise, then a minimum at the 42nd and 51st potencies followed by a further rise. It is interesting that the space between the first two minima (15th through 16th potencies) is the same length as that between the second two minima (42nd-51st). Thus the second part of the curve represents a repetition of the first but to an intensified degree. The minima are pronounced, but the maxima are also larger. The curves are formed beautifully into three sections. The first up to the 24th potency, the second to the 42nd potency and then follows the third, the end of which cannot be seen. This threefolding is again reflected at the point of intersection.

It is worth noting that for potencies 1 through 24 the second leaf (pointed) lies under the first, then until the 37th potency lies above the first leaf, from 37th to 52nd potencies again below, and from 52nd to 60th, again above.

For the entire experiment the root is for the most part longer than the leaf.

Supplement No. 4 shows the curves of the experiment in electric light. The first minimum is at the 14th potency, the second at the 22nd, then comes a depression at the 26th; maximum 28th potency, the fourth at the 52nd. The first leaf has a gentle curve, the second a very lively one, somewhat like the other light experiment with iron sulphate. Because of this the finer curve-path is obscured. Regarding the curve in daylight it may be noted that: The point of intersection is roughly at the same height. The first leaf lies roughly at the height in the daylight curve, the second leaf shoots out over it. The root has become somewhat smaller. The relationship now shifts to the benefit of the leaves. The length of leaf surpasses that of the root.

Supplement No. 5 shows the curve of the experiment in darkness. 1. Minimum with the 11th potency, a second with the 21st. Depression with the 28th and 29th potencies. The point of intersection lies significantly higher, likewise the first leaf is considerably lengthened. It is also still longer than the first leaf in the light experiment. The second leaf is _reversed as in the light experiment_, lying under the first leaf and shows in any case a lively curve. The root for the first 20 potencies is held back and then seems to want to become longer. It is regrettable that this curve was also not drawn for the 60th potency, but for various reasons it was impossible. If one makes the attempt to draw the light-curve and the dark-curve for the two leaves together then there is an interesting result (Supplement No. 6). Partly, both curves make diametrically opposed movements and partly they run parallel.

Supplement No. 7 shows that the weight-curve for the day experiment roughly approximates to the measurement-curve.

Supplement No. 8 shows that the weight-curve of the light experiment shows the maximum weight in the root at the 22nd and 35th potencies even at the points where the minima lie in the measurement-curve. The proposed task seems to be solved here where the weight shows a maximum and the measurement is at a minimum. For the maxima of the measurement-curve the reversal is not so easily seen, although there are many interesting details to study in the curves. I want to bring out the main points in order not to make the report too long.

Supplement No. 9 shows the weight-curve of the experiment in darkness. Maximum weight of the root occurred at the 11th potency then a smaller maximum occurred at the 21st and 23rd potencies respectively just at the places where the minima lie on the measurement-curve. My assumption that plants which grow in the dark will have the greatest weight was not confirmed. Perhaps my assumption was incorrect or experimental arrangement unsatisfactory. The plants were diseased and looked like stubble.

The experiment with gold chloride which Herr Doktor saw take place last October also produced beautiful curves.

I have continued with the capillary analysis experiments and tried to obtain pictures with a combination of potassium iodide and mercury nitrate with respectively mercury chloride and also coloured quicksilver.

Perhaps it will be possible when I come to Dornach at Christmas to present Herr Doktor with the gold-curves and capillary analysis pictures? I would be most grateful to receive your good advice for the continuation of the work.

At present I still have 30 jars watered in daylight and electric light in order to have the big water-curve ready to place before you at Christmas time.

Finally, please allow me to include a copy of a report that appeared on the 5th of September in the 'Chemisches Zentralblatt.' It deals with the very interesting experiments on high dilutions by a Russian.* Dr. Theberath, a member of the association,** will send a *précis* of the work on the smallest entities to the editor. Perhaps we should meet the author?

I ask to be excused for such a long report and remain with the greatest respect,

Yours sincerely,
Lilly Kolisko

---

* Prof. N. P. Krawkow, Director of the Pharmacology Laboratory of the Military Medical Academy of Petersburg, Russia.
** The Association of German Chemists [*Des Vereins Deutscher Chemiker*].

CBd. [Vol.] III, Heft [Issue] Nr. 10, 5th September 1923, Teil [Section] E. Biochemie [Biochemistry] 4. Tierphysiologie [Animal Physiology], S. 697

N. P. Krawkow,

Über die Grenzen der Empfindlichkeit des lebenden Protoplasmas [Beyond the boundary of sensibility of living protoplasm],

(cf. **G. L. Schkawera**, *Über die verschiedenen Stadien der Giftwirkung auf isolierte Organe* [Concerning the various stages of the action of poison on isolated organs], *Ztschr. f. d. ges. exp. Medizin (Zeitschrift für die gesamte experimentelle Medizin)* [Journal for General Experimental Medicine], Berlin, Bd. [Vol.] 28, S. 305-323, 1922; abstracted in *Chemisches Zentralblatt*, Berlin, Bd. [Vol.] III, Heft [Issue] Nr. 13, September 27, 1922, Teil [Part] 4. Tierphysiologie [Animal Physiology], S. 896)

Poisons with blood vessel action indicate that with stronger dilution a neutral point is reached where they are ineffective, but, with increasing dilution (up to 10^{-32}) show a new activity. The action of such minimal doses is very much clearer after previous stronger action for example with *adrenalin* or *histamine*, similarly when the solutions are heated in the incubator to 40°C and cooled again. All pharmacological doses of poisons causing constricted vessels such as adrenalin, histamine, *nicotine, cocaine, strychnine*, etc, increase with minimal concentration, normal strengthening of dose, with *chloroform, Ä.,** hedonal*, etc. reduces the effects. Between the degrees of dilution and the intensity of the action, there is often an inconsistency in these minimal doses so that the activity grows with increasing dilution. Herein lies the essential difference between the action of minimal poison doses and the characteristic action of pharmacological doses. In the enormous dilutions the action of the poisons lose their specific character: all poisons begin to release a similar action, quite disconnected from their pharmacological and chemical nature. The following were investigated: alkaloids, narcotics in the aliphatic series, salts of heavy metals, colloids of metal salt solutions and especially $CuSO_4$, $BP(NO_2)_2$, Fe_2Cl_6, $AgNO_3$, $HgCl_4$, $PtCl_4$, $UO_2(SO_4)$, *colloidal Hg*** solutions, 'infusions' with Ringer-Locke solution from *Cu, Ag, Ni, Al, Au, Pt, Rah*, and finally *radium emanations*. They work partly intensifying, partly diminishing. From all the investigations it became quite clear that living protoplasm is a remarkably sensitive reagent for such minimal doses and dilutions which provisionally are accessible to chemical and physic-chemical analysis, but, above all, the condition of substance in such enormous dilutions the usual customary thinking fails. These effects are in many cases of a non-material nature, which perhaps lie in the realm of 'electrical energy.' (*Ztschr. f. d. ges. exp. Medizin (Zeitschrift für die gesamte experimentelle Medizin)* [Journal for General Experimental Medicine], Berlin, Bd. [Vol.] 34, 1923, S. 279-306. Petersburg, Russia, *Mil.-med. Akad., Pharmakol. Lab. (Militär-medizinische Akademie, Pharmakologie Labor)* [Military Medical Academy, Pharmacology Laboratory]) Wolff (abstractor).

---

* *Ä. = Äther* [ether]. Also known as diethyl ether or ethyl ether $(C_2H_5)_2O$.

** Hg is the chemical symbol for mercury, being derived from the element's Latin name *Hydrargyrum* meaning 'liquid silver.'

CHEMISCHES ZENTRALBLATT

CBd. [Vol.] III, Heft [Issue] Nr. 13, 27th September 1922, Teil [Section] E. Biochemie [Biochemistry] 4. Tierphysiologie [Animal Physiology], S. 896. **G. L. Schkawera,**

Über die verschiedenen Stadien der Giftwirkung auf isolierte Organe [Concerning the various stages of the action of poison on isolated organs]

Many poisons show three stages in their action on isolated hearts and blood vessels of warm and cold-blooded animals: 1. Penetration of the poison into the tissue, 2. Saturation, and 3. Expulsion of the poison from the tissue. These stages are distinguished from one another by their intensity, and, with other poisons by their mode of action. The intensity of the reaction in the vessels at the expulsion stage is characteristic for each poison and appears only at certain concentrations and is in many cases stronger than during the first two stages. The expulsion stage is an active period for the working of the poison. The reaction of the vessels to cocaine and strychnine at the expulsion stage is more pronounced at body temperature than at room temperature. The reaction of the vessels to the passage of a poison in the repulsion stage of long duration is stronger than that of shorter duration. The latter reaction can be weakened by reducing the concentration of the poison. At the stage of saturation of the tissue with a poison the reaction can be altered, weakened or strengthened with another poison. One out of two poisons in a mixture, for example, after saturation with one of the poisons produces a different reaction than without the previous saturation. *(Ztschr. f. d. ges. exp. Medizin (Zeitschrift für die gesamte experimentelle Medizin)* [Journal for General Experimental Medicine], Berlin, Bd. [Vol.] 28, 1922, S. 305-323. 30/6.* [18/3.**] Petersburg, Russia, *Pharmakol. Lab. d. Militär-Akad. (Pharmakologie Labor des Militär-Akademie)* [Pharmacology Laboratory of the Military Academy]) Lewin (abstractor).

---

* Date of the publication.
** Date the work was presented at a meeting of a Society or Academy.

APPENDIX

Towards a History and Sociology of the
Anthroposophical Research Institutes in the 1920s

Towards a History and Sociology of the Anthroposophical Research Institutes in the 1920s

Updated reprint, with minor corrections, courtesy of Dr. David J. Heaf, from 'Archetype: Newsletter Articles Supplement,' Science Group of the Anthroposophical Society in Great Britain, London, Issue No. 5, September 1999, pp. 48-60. See also webpage: http://www.science.anth.org.uk/history.htm.

Christoph Podak

This article first appeared in the monthly journal 'Der Europäer [The European]' (Jg. 3 [3rd Yr.], Nr. 9/10, July/August 1999, pp. 30-36, see web article: http://www.perseus.ch/PDF-Dateien/forschungsinstitute.pdf *) and was originally intended as part of Issue No. 122 of Beiträge zur Rudolf Steiner Gesamtausgabe – Aufgaben-stellungen von Rudolf Steiner für wissenschaftliche Forschungen: Die vier Ätherarten / Elektrizität / Veredelung von Torffasern / Holzbehandlung / Radio / Wärme-Leitung / Erdmagnetismus / Pflanzenwachstum [Supplements to Rudolf Steiner's Complete Works – Suggested topics for scientific research work – Comments from Rudolf Steiner on the four kinds of ether, electricity, refinement of peat fibres, wood treatment, radio, thermal conduction, Earth magnetism, plant growth. Rudolf Steiner Verlag, Dornach. Publication expected 1999], but was not included. Rudolf Steiner gave many indications and suggestions for scientific research, often including experimental details. Many of these were during his lectures, which are now largely published, but many more were given in personal conversation with scientists. Paul Eugen Schiller (1900-1992), former leader of the Physics Laboratory at the Goetheanum, Dornach, Switzerland, collected together these suggestions so as to make them available as research material for the Natural Science Section at the Goetheanum School of Spiritual Science. This collection, often referred to as the 'Schiller File,' is included in Issue No. 122 together with a commentary and relevant references (mostly of German works).*

"Two tasks:
To personalize the machine;
to personalize science."

Simone Weil

The history of the 'Schiller File' reflects at once the history of the research institutes of '*Der Kommende Tag* [The Coming Day]' Company in Stuttgart and of the laboratories at the Goetheanum in Dornach, as well as of those still continuing efforts to do justice to Rudolf Steiner's intended programme for the development of an 'etheric technology.' A further aspect is that these initiatives are closely connected with the history of the anthroposophical movement itself. The task is to sketch these connections and their historical-institutional context or at least to describe these in a concise way.[1] But because part of this story concerns what those individuals involved wished to achieve and actually achieved, a report on the main milestones and results of these efforts must include an attempt to reconstruct a 'sociology of the circle around Steiner.'[2] This in turn means an unavoidable confrontation with the problems surrounding attempts at anthroposophical community-building, so that a History and Sociology of the Anthroposophical Research Institutes in the Twenties and of their leading personalities has a single aim, seen in the one case more from the simple facts, in the other more from the point of view of the motives, the interpersonal relations and the effectiveness of the research in the outer world.

In view of the still inadequate state of the source material, I shall first attempt to describe what can so far be stated with certainty i.e. what has been thoroughly researched so far. At some later date it might then be possible to shed a more wide-ranging and revealing light on those times and to venture a more comprehensive interpretation based thereon.[3] This will inevitably require a partial revision of the views which have so far been held or emphasized in the relevant literature, and of what later commentators have often merely copied from one another without a concern for overall consistency between the available records. This essay aims to provide some indications for such a revision and also to at least suggest some of the fundamental questions which are necessary to establish specific connections to the present situation.

Two contemporaneous research institutes

The 'Akten des Stuttgarter Forschungsinstitutes [records of the research institute in Stuttgart]' (referred to in Folio 2 of the Schiller File – see page 7), have not been found and are sadly missed. Were these extant, they would most probably offer decisive information on who exactly was working in the various departments, at what times and on what projects. The scanty and still unpublished records relating to this institute which are so far in the possession of the 'Rudolf Steiner-Nachlassverwaltung [Administration of the Estate of Rudolf Steiner]' and at the Goetheanum Archive reveal nothing fundamentally new, in fact scarcely anything which cannot in principle be found elsewhere.[4]

Nonetheless, it is possible to state, on the evidence currently available, that the Stuttgart Institute came about as a result of the initiative of the scientists themselves and that it was founded in about mid-March 1920 in connection with Rudolf Steiner's Second Natural Scientific Course (GA 321) and was most probably deliberately timed to coincide with the formation of the enterprise of Der Kommende Tag A.G. [The Coming Day plc].[5] However, its existence was a brief one, ending abruptly in the course of 1924, when, on 24th July of that year and in the light of the apparently inescapable financial situation, the general shareholders' meeting voted in favour of the plan for a gradual liquidation of the institute, including a splitting up of the various research areas.

The Biological Department under the direction of Lili Kolisko had already, at Rudolf Steiner's request, been contractually attached to the Goetheanum under the new name of the 'Biological Institute at the Goetheanum, Stuttgart.'[6] In the face of this move, it became impossible for the other departments to continue, especially as an appeal to Dornach for a similar take-over fell on deaf ears.[7] The argument has therefore been advanced that the decisive factor for the sudden liquidation was not so much – as has been often stated – the devastating inflation and the inability of the Company to continue to finance its thus far unprofitable institutes and employees, as rather a lack of interest on the part of the majority of the members of the Anthroposophical Society in such exoteric goings-on, in this so-called 'new way.'[8]

It seems that very few of the employees were subsequently able to continue working independently. Only Rudolf E. Maier and Hans Buchheim were able to find in Einsingen [9] a suitable place to work, where they could carry on their particular studies in an intensive manner. We also know of Hermann von Dechend that he was able to continue working on his own for a while in the rooms at Kanonenweg 44/2 in Stuttgart.

On the other hand, in the spring of 1926, the young engineer Paul Eugen Schiller (1900-1992), who had joined the Stuttgart Institute in 1923, was apparently able to move part of the equipment from Stuttgart to Dornach, where he founded a Physics Laboratory (the 'Physics Section of the Natural Scientific Research Laboratory at the Goetheanum') in the two small corner towers of the so-called '*Heizhaus* [boiler house].'[10] However, it is not clear whether he initially worked alone or whether he already had one or more colleagues. We know for certain that others did join him later.[11] It would be even more important to discover to what extent there were at that time two parallel research institutes operating around the Goetheanum and in what way these collaborated. For it is certainly a fact that Dr. Guenther Wachsmuth (1893-1963, leader of the Natural Science Section from 1924 onwards) and Dr. Ehrenfried E. Pfeiffer (1899-1961) had established their own improvised laboratory in Dornach at roughly the same time as the institute in Stuttgart and must be considered as the pioneers of the research into the formative forces and the significance of rhythmical processes.[12]

This part of the whole history in particular remains still to be written. At any rate, what has until now been the standard description of this time – Guenther Wachsmuth's own account – refers exclusively to his own role and to the circumstances in Dornach and fails to mention by name a number of important researchers and intimate pupils of Rudolf Steiner.[13]

Even more importantly, perhaps, there are in relation to Wachsmuth's own work (cf. his basic texts: '*The Etheric Formative Forces in Cosmos, Earth and Man*' [Anthroposophical Publishing Co., London, 1932; photocopy available from Borderland Sciences Research Foundation (BSRF), Eureka, California. See webpage: http://www.borderlands.com/ethericphysics.htm; facsimile edition available from Sacred Science Library, Idyllwild, California, 2003. See website: http://www.sacredscience.com] and 'The Etheric World in Science, Art and Religion' [translation available only in typescript from Rudolf Steiner House library, London]) serious objections from two sources, which have unfortunately been given insufficient attention so far.

Firstly, in a letter Ehrenfried Pfeiffer wrote to Marie Steiner in 1948 we find him making the following corrections, in part biographical, in part substantial:

"Nonetheless, I had tried for a long time to support Wachsmuth. One of the reasons why I left Dornach and made no effort to return was that I knew that, had I done so, I would have had to resume the struggle with Wachsmuth. I was afraid of coming off worst and merely wearing myself down without achieving anything of value. The best I felt able to do under the circumstances was to adopt the same tactic you report that [Günther] Schubert employed: that of remaining silent; and, at least as regards the scientific work, of putting my own work and my own views to one side. There are serious differences of opinion between us, for example in relation to the [Wachsmuth's] book on the etheric formative forces, in which in my opinion Wachsmuth should have stated that Dr. Steiner's original indication as to the archetypal etheric forms (triangle – light-ether; half-Moon – chemical-ether, etc.) was in fact taken from the book by the Indian Râma Prasâd entitled 'Nature's Finer Forces,' which Dr. Steiner, in my presence, had recommended Wachsmuth to study.* Today Wachsmuth stands there as the creator of the theory of formative forces. What Wachsmuth wrote in the 'Lebensgang [My Path of Life],'** or whatever the book about Dr. Steiner is called which appeared several years ago [1941; 2. Aufl. [2nd Ed.] 1951], is, in my

opinion, misleading in many places, in particular regarding Dr. Steiner's scientific indications. These things, too, ought one day to be put right." [14]

Secondly, the Swiss doctor Ernst Marti (1903-1985), author of the sadly unfinished second standard work on the etheric, pointed during the 60s to a central error in Wachsmuth's book, considered for decades to be the reference work on the etheric. According to Marti, Wachsmuth had failed to make a distinction between the 'general' etheric and the specific realm of the etheric formative forces.[15]

Researchers employed in Stuttgart

We know for certain that altogether between 9 and 11 co-workers were employed on a full-time basis in Stuttgart between 1920 and 1924, receiving their salary from *Der Kommende Tag* [The Coming Day].[16] Those in leading positions were:

- the engineer Dr. Alexander Strakosch (1879-1958), administrative director of the scientific institute until replaced in this role at the latest in February 1923 by the medical researcher Dr. Eugen Kolisko (1893-1939);
- Dr. Rudolf Ernst Maier (1886-1943), director of the Physics Department and for a time a member of the Board of Trustees of *Der Kommende Tag* [The Coming Day];
- Frau Lili Kolisko (1889-1976), director of the Biological Department—which developed out of the former 'Epidemic Department'—until 1923/4.

As assistants or co-workers, we find, in addition to P. E. Schiller:

- Dr. Hermann von Dechend (1883-1956);
- Dipl. Ing.* Wilhelm Pelikan, engineer (1893-1981);
- Dipl. Ing. Henri Smits, engineer (?-1969), who joined the Fibre Department of the Stuttgart Research Institute on 1st April 1921;
- Dr. Hans Theberath (1891-1971).
   [* Dipl. Ing. corresponds to 'Dip. Eng.,' signifying an academically qualified engineer. Tr.]

Co-workers whose names do not appear in the Schiller File were:

- Dipl. Ing. Karl Lehofer, engineer, (1897-1946), who joined the Fibre Department of the Stuttgart Research Institute in October 1921;
- Dr. Johann Simon Streicher (1887-1971), summoned to Stuttgart by Rudolf Steiner circa 1920 to work on the development of plant-based paints and dyes.

In addition there was:

- Hans Buchheim (1899-1987), assistant to R. E. Maier, at first in Stuttgart, then in Einsingen.

---

* Note: there appears to be an apparent contradiction between this statement by Pfeiffer and that given in Folio 5 a-b on page 12 where Schiller states that 'Rudolf Steiner warned expressly about the book by Râma Prasâd. It includes examples, which could be dangerous for modern humanity.'

** Published in English translation as: 'The Life and Work of Rudolf Steiner,' Whittier Books, Inc., New York, second edition, supplemented and expanded, of the volume published in 1941, 1955; Garber Communications, Incorporated, Blauvelt, N.Y., 2nd edition, June 1988.

Also mentioned in the Schiller File is Dr. Walter Johannes Stein (1891-1957),[17] who kept a close eye on all the research work, as did Dr. Ernst Lehrs (1894-1979). [Please note also the boxed quotation from W. Stein below.]

Researchers employed in Stuttgart

It has not been possible to elicit with any certainty how exactly what was referred to in certain documents relating to the issuing of shares as '*Der Kommende Tag A.G.* [The Coming Day plc], Scientific Research Institute Stuttgart' was organised, or what the exact number and the structure of the individual departments was. Most documents refer to two departments—a Physics Department and a Biological Department—as, for example, in the only document to have been discovered so far in which the aims of the departments was spelled out in some detail.[18] Yet there were clearly other departments: a Chemistry Department and a Colour Department. The Fibre Department mentioned only in internal records was possibly part of the Chemistry Department. On the other hand, two records only[19] refer—and then by name only—to a fifth, Technology Department.[20]

"*These experiments were demonstrated by Dr. Steiner during his Second Natural Scientific Course, which was held at the Free Waldorf School in Stuttgart from 1st to 14th March 1920. They show that it is possible, by virtue of placing certain solutions in front of the prism, to exclude the effects of three of the etheric forces: warmth, chemical and light. They therefore demonstrate that these forces can be distinguished from one another purely empirically-phenomenologically, though all are imponderable. Efforts to isolate from the spectrum also the fourth etheric force indicated by Dr. Steiner—the life-ether—are being pursued at the Stuttgart research institute of Der Kommende Tag A.G.* [The Coming Day plc]. *Once these experiments have produced the expected results, we will have demonstrated the fourfold nature of the etheric as consisting of warmth, light, chemical and life-ethers. It will then be necessary to develop a physics of the etheric. This will of necessity proceed in such a manner as to show that physical matter is the 'ponderable' stuff of three-dimensional space, which exerts pressure, is subject to centrifugal forces and to which the concept of potential can be applied, whereas the imponderable etheric exerts a force of suction,* is subject to universal cosmic forces and resists the application of the concept of potential.*"

From: Walter Johannes Stein, *'Vorstellung,' 'Begriff' und 'Urteil' in der Lehre Rudolf Steiners, in: Änigmatisches aus Kunst und Wissenschaft – Anthroposophische Hochschulkurse der Freien Hochschule für Geisteswissenschaft* ['Idea,' 'Concept' and 'Judgement' in the Teachings of Rudolf Steiner, in: The Enigmatical in Art and Science – Anthroposophical High School Course of the Free High School for Spiritual Science] (Goetheanum in Dornach vom [from] 26.9. bis [to] 10.16.1920), Bd. [Vol.] 1, Verlag der Kommende Tag A-G, Stuttgart 1922.

* i.e. where there is the etheric, space is 'emptier than empty.' It contains 'negative materiality' (modern physics so far lacks this concept) and therefore 'sucks.' The result of this suction is that a *being* makes its appearance. Something that has the nature of *being* appears within the phenomenal world. This can be thought of in the same way as the process which takes place when a tone sounds in space i.e. 'appears' as a result of the shaping of the air by an instrument. The '*being*' of the sound (the qualitative element) appears within the wave form of the air.

As regards the rooms used, we know that part of the initial research institute began its life in the basement of the first temporary buildings of the Waldorf School at Kanonenweg 44 (now Haußmannstraße). Later on, the institute was able to move into its own rooms at 44/2 Kanonenweg. Unfortunately, no photographs appear to exist of these premises; there do exist photos of the administration building of the school, in which at the start Lili Kolisko was able to make use of a simple room. The scanty records also reveal the following:

"New laboratories were set up for the chemical, physico-chemical and technical research. A new building has been erected for the physical experiments and for the Biological Department and will be occupied during the course of this summer [1922]." [21]

Practical results of the scientific research work (1920-1924)

It is well known that Rudolf Steiner referred on numerous occasions to the exemplary nature of Frau Lili Kolisko's work and that he was completely satisfied with the progress of her research. That her paper on the spleen was quite literally boycotted by her colleagues provoked Rudolf Steiner to issue a stern reprimand on various occasions. Rudolf E. Maier's work was also mentioned in a positive light. Other than this, however, little emerged from the Stuttgart institute which offered the promise of fulfilling within a useful period of time the hopes which had initially been placed in it. Little was forthcoming of the published material which Rudolf Steiner insistently requested. It is in this light that we can perhaps interpret Steiner's ironic comment that it appeared as if the employees of the institute were merely *'going for a stroll.'* And we can perhaps view in the same light the recorded discussions in the so-called *'Dreißigerkreis* [Circle of Thirty]'[22] and the memoirs of Ernst Lehrs, Alexander Strakosch and *Der Kommende Tag* [The Coming Day] director, Emil Leinhas, the main motif of which is the failure to break free of a certain stodgy, uncreative conservatism and formalism and to find new, radical and adventurous lines of approach. The opportunity of making a decisive breakthrough had not been seized with both hands before the venture had been overwhelmed by the financial problems which had prevented further progress.

It is also evident that 'formalities' and 'social obligations' played a significant role in preventing a number of the tasks Rudolf Steiner set the researchers from being properly understood or acted upon. The following quotations—relating to P. E. Schiller—are symptomatic of this disabling formality:

"Mr. Schiller told me that he still regrets not having asked Rudolf Steiner any further questions on this point, but that such a failure [to ask important questions] was not uncommon at the time – out of awe of Dr. Steiner!" [23]

"Unfortunately, I have been prevented for some considerable time from carrying out my practical work in the laboratory because of my preoccupation with matters relating to the society. There is now some hope that this situation will change at Michaelmas. I would be very happy if I could return to the laboratory and resume the investigations already begun." [24]

However, it is not yet possible to identify with any clarity what precisely was achieved during the four relevant years, nor exactly what experiments were carried out. We must therefore withhold any final evaluation of the social-psychological context and its problems and attempt to shed some further light on aspects of the situation subsequent to what has almost universally been judged the failure of the Stuttgart initiative.

A sketch of an anthroposophically-inspired research into formative forces and rhythmical processes

That the objections of Ehrenfried Pfeiffer and Ernst Marti quoted above have not yet been taken onboard in many quarters has contributed to the fact that there is still no consistent anthroposophical teaching on the ethers and etheric formative forces. A further problem is that the work of exceptionally gifted scientists and inventors such as Ehrenfried Pfeiffer (who as far back as the 1950s—as well as much other valuable work—invented a process for composting agricultural and industrial wastes) or Hugo Erbe (1895-1965, who worked on specialised preparations for agriculture and on the breeding of novel varieties of grain) has only recently been accorded its due respect. Their important writings still tend to be subjected to an almost *samizdat-like* treatment as regards publication. The work of George Adams (formerly George Adams Kaufmann; 1894-1963), who must also be considered as one of the pioneers of research into the etheric, has in part received the same lack of attention as that of Pfeiffer or Erbe. The books of the internationally famous doctor and founder of *'Cymatics,'* [25] Hans Jenny (1904-1972), are almost all out-of-print.*
Furthermore, only recently—on the occasion of the centenary of his birth—did it become apparent that in the work of Paul Schatz (1898-1979) a form of etheric technology ('inversion kinematics') has existed for decades, is used throughout the world in industry and is only waiting for further development. For further information on the industrial applications of inversion technology see webpage: http://www.inversionmixers.com/inversioninformation.html.

Again and again one comes across the remarkable phenomenon that in the time following on those years of the '20s the various exponents of anthroposophical research were preoccupied with their own particular fields and thus rarely joined together in the kind of team-work which is common in so-called 'mainstream' science and which often seems like a *sine qua non* of success. Numerous anecdotes reveal the existence of a considerable degree of indifference towards other, even closely related, endeavours of scientists working in non-anthroposophical institutions.

Notwithstanding all provisos, people of our own generation find this attitude incomprehensible. They look back to the time of their grandparents, to what the Schiller File reveals, to what the 'first-generation' scientists and researchers have bequeathed as their testament. They are also very much aware of what is going on in the 'non-anthroposophical' world, of the research questions of the '20s which in the meantime have become the subject of serious study or the fact that the concept of 'ether' (under the names 'orgone,'** *'ch'i,'* *** *'prana,'* *'vril,'* 'morphogenetic fields,' etc.) has become increasingly widely used. [26] In many other respects, too, [27] the need for a clearly differentiated

---

* Newly republished (hard cover) deluxe edition containing both volumes of Dr. Hans Jenny's groundbreaking books entitled "Cymatics: A Study of Wave Phenomena & Vibration," published by MACROmedia Press, Newmarket, NH, July 2001, ISBN 1-888-13807-6. See website: http://www.cymaticsource.com/.
** Term coined by Dr. Wilhelm Reich in the late 1930's to represent his discovery of the 'universal life energy.'
*** *Ch'i* (or *qi*) is a Chinese word used to describe the natural energy of the Universe.
**** *Prana* is a Sanskrit word meaning 'breath.' It refers to a vital life-sustaining force in living beings.
***** The word *'vril'* was coined by Sir Edward G. D. Bulwer-Lytton to describe a mysterious life-force.
****** Term coined by Dr. Rupert Sheldrake in 1981 to represent the fields of consciousness of different species.

understanding of and convincing evidence for the existence of the formative forces and rhythmical processes which underlie the natural world has become more and more pressing. The year just past—1998— is the very one which emerges from the 'calculation' Rudolf Steiner made at the end of 1923:

"But all these efforts are, from an anthroposophical point of view, fundamentally parts of a greater whole, a scientific whole which is urgently needed in our time—as urgently as at all possible. And if the work in our research institute proceeds as it has done so far, then it will take perhaps 50 or 75 years to reach the point which actually needs to be reached: that the many parts join to become a whole. [28] *This greater whole will then be enormously significant not only for a path of knowledge, but for the whole of practical life.*

People today have no idea of the enormous impact these things can have on everyday practical life, on the production of useful materials and objects and especially on therapeutic methods and products and the like.

Now you may say that human progress has always been slow and that it will be the same in this field also. But it may well be that with the brittleness and liability to fracture of our current civilisation we would not manage in those 50 or 75 years to make the necessary connections in order to achieve what it is absolutely essential we do achieve. And so I may perhaps express it—not as a wish, not even as a possibility, but as—I might say, I might refer to it only as an illusion: that it would really be possible to achieve in only five or ten years what will take 50 or 75 years if we continue to work at the speed at which we are forced to work, the speed at which we are able to proceed through the dedication of such workers as Frau Dr. Kolisko. And I am convinced that if we were able to provide the necessary apparatus, the necessary institutes, to find however many co-workers it would require who could collaborate in greater numbers in the true spirit of the work—that we would be able to achieve in five or ten years what otherwise would take 50 or 75. We would need only around 50 to 75 million [Swiss] francs. We could perhaps then get the necessary results in a tenth of the time. As I said, I put this forward not as a wish, not as a possibility, but only as an 'illusion'—but as a very 'real' illusion. If we had the 75 million [Swiss] francs, we would really be able to achieve what is absolutely necessary. This is something which could at least be considered." [29]

The author of this article would like to take up this 'illusion' and, in conclusion, firstly ask his readers to assist him in further 'pathfinding' by making available any hitherto unseen relevant material, and, secondly, encourage them to take up the practical impulses mentioned in the articles. However, we recognize that the success of any such endeavours still depends on the creation of the necessary supportive framework…. [30]

Notes

The introductory quotation from Simone Weil is taken from her book: *'La Pesanteur et La Grâce'* ('Gravity and Grace,' Arthur Wills (Translator), Gustave Thibon (Introduction), University of Nebraska Press, 1997. ISBN: 0803298005 p/b.; 'Gravity and Grace,' Emma Crawford and Mario von der Ruhr (Translators), Gustave Thibon (Introduction and Postscript), Routledge Classics, London, 2002. ISBN 0-415-29000-7 h/b. See Chapter entitled 'The Mysticism of Work,' p. 179.)

(Where English versions of documents are traceable, full bibliographic data are given. In other cases titles are translated. The abbreviation 'GA' followed by a number refers to the volume in Rudolf Steiner's collected works published by Rudolf Steiner Verlag, Dornach, Switzerland.)

1. Please refer to the bibliography of *Beiträge zur Rudolf Steiner Gesamtausgabe* [Supplements to the Collected Edition of Rudolf Steiner], Issue No. 122 (Rudolf Steiner Verlag, Dornach, Summer 2000) listed under the heading: '*Anthroposophische Naturwissenschaft und Forschungsinstitute von Der Kommende Tag A.G. und am Goetheanum* [Anthroposophical Natural Science and the Research Institutes of *Der Kommende Tag A.G.* [The Coming Day plc] and at the Goetheanum],' which contains a complete list of all the documents so far recovered in which there are details of the context of the research and of the specific work undertaken.

2. Refers to the title and scope of enquiry of the essay under the same title by Walter Johannes Stein, published in: '*Versuche zu einer Soziologie des Wissens* [Essays on a Sociology of Knowledge],' Max Scheler (ed.), Duncke, Munich/Leipzig 1924, pp. 376-388.

3. A planned publication in the series: '*Rudolf Steiner-Studien* [Studies in the Work of Rudolf Steiner],' (Rudolf Steiner Verlag, Dornach), will contain all the existing documents relating to the research institutes. Brief biographies of all the researchers and further information on their unpublished works will also be given.

4. See Note 1.

5. Rudolf Steiner's Second Natural Scientific Course, published in English as the 'Warmth Course' (Mercury Press, Spring Valley, New York, second edition 1988; reprinted 2005; also available on-line at webpage: http://wn.rsarchive.org/Science/WrmCrs_index.html), is published in German under the title '*Geisteswissenschaftliche Impulse zur Entwicklung der Physik, Zweiter Naturwissenschaftlicher Kurs: Die Wärme auf der Grenze positiver und negativer Materialität (Wärmekurs)* [Spiritual-Scientific Impulses for the Development of Physics, Second Natural Scientific Course: Heat at the Border between Positive and Negative Materiality (Warmth Course)],' (14 lectures, Stuttgart, 1 – March 14, 1920, Rudolf Steiner Verlag, Dornach, 1982). A. Strakosch refers in his memoirs—presumably mistakenly—to a meeting of the Board of Trustees of *Der Kommende Tag A.G.* [The Coming Day plc] which took place in the spring of 1921 and at which he and R. Maier (who *"first had the idea for a research institute"*) were supposedly appointed joint directors.

6. In 1936 Lili Kolisko moved her institute to England, where she continued till the end of her life the work she had begun in 1920.

7. There are reliable reports that Albert Steffen and Guenther Wachsmuth, both significant decision-makers after Rudolf Steiner's death, showed no interest in supporting the continuation of the work of the Stuttgart institute. We have no such reports concerning the other members of the *Vorstand* [The Executive Council], in particular Dr. Ita Wegman (1876-1943) and Dr. Elisabeth Vreede (1879-1943).

It is interesting to compare the fate of Dipl. Ing. Joachim Schultz (1902-1953), revealed in his own notebooks from the time. The above-mentioned request dated March 5, 1924 and signed by eight individuals can be found in the '*KommTag-Mappe* [Kommenden Tag File],' Nr. 28, of the

Rudolf Steiner-Nachlassverwaltung [Administration of the Estate of Rudolf Steiner] under the heading: '*Wissenschaftliches Forschungsinstitut und biologische Abteilung* [Institute for Scientific Research and Department for Biology].' This small collection of only a few documents reveals some more fragments of the picture relating to the transition period of 1924.

8. The term '*new way*' was used predominantly by the many members who were fundamentally nostalgic for the old 'theosophical' era of the General Anthroposophical Society, which had supposedly been characterised by a refusal to challenge the dominant scientific worldview or to carry the impulses of spiritual science into practical daily life. Note also Rudolf Steiner's references to an '*inner opposition*' or to the '*curule chairs*' concerning the affairs in Stuttgart.

9. For information concerning the experiments in Einsingen see Stephan Clerc's '*Kommentaren zur Schiller Mappe* [Comments on the Schiller File, p. 37]' and the bibliography to this, which are due to be published in the '*Beiträge zur Rudolf Steiner Gesamtausgabe* [Supplements to the Collected Edition of Rudolf Steiner],' (Issue No. 122). See also the note on the title page of this article on page 113.

10. We learn from a recently received copy of a letter with reminiscences written by Hertha von Dechend (1892-1971, wife of Hermann von Dechend, *née* Schepp), how it was that P. E. Schiller managed to move his work to Dornach in spite of the rejection of the appeal from Stuttgart mentioned earlier. The former assistant to Hermann von Dechend had succeeded in securing funding from "*an anthroposophical industrialist.*" Another surprising revelation concerns the fact that, as leader of the Natural Science Section at the Goetheanum, Guenther Wachsmuth had apparently originally invited Hermann von Dechend to move to Dornach, but that "*at the last moment,*" Wachsmuth had written to withdraw this offer and had asked Dechend to destroy the letter.

11. Known co-workers are: Dr. Otto Eckstein (1894-1944, chemist, who moved in 1926 to work in the chemistry/biology laboratories at the Goetheanum); Frieda Bessenich (1892-1969, who as a result of her friendship with Ehrenfried Pfeiffer moved to Dornach in 1938 and who took over the Blood Crystallisation Department when Pfeiffer emigrated to the U.S.A.); Dr. Heinz Castelliz (dates unknown. Castelliz and P. E. Schiller published an essay on gas jets for use with sensitive flames (*Akustisch Zeitschrift* [Journal for Acoustics], Jg. 2 [2nd Yr.], January 1937, pp. 11-17)); and Wilhelm Wolf (1905-1984, mechanic by training, who produced the first hand-assembled model of the later patented revolving mirror stroboscope and was also involved in the experiments on the so-called 'sensitive flame').

12. Precise details can be found in the books by G. Wachsmuth and A. Selawry/E. Pfeiffer (cf. Bibliography, [see Note 1] and the biography: *Ein Leben für den Geist: Ehrenfried Pfeiffer (1899-1961)* [A Life for the Spirit: Ehrenfried Pfeiffer (1899-1961)], edited by Thomas Meyer, Perseus Verlag, Basel, 1999; 2. Aufl. [2nd Ed.] 2000; 3. Aufl. [3rd Ed.] 2003, ISBN 3-907564-31-6). It is uncertain from which date formal designations were introduced for the various 'departments' of the Natural Science Section at the Goetheanum.

13. All this can be seen as a reflection of the extent to which the expulsion (now generally acknowledged to have been illegitimate) from the General Anthroposophical Society in 1935 of

Eugen Kolisko and many others found its way—even retrospectively in this case—into the 'official histories of anthroposophical research.' It was perhaps due to his 'omnipresence' that the physicist and mathematician W. J. Stein's place in the Schiller File was nonetheless secured, despite the fact that he had already emigrated to England at the time the Schiller File was put together.

According to Ernst Lehrs, W. J. Stein's crucial question about the nature of warmth was the instigation for Rudolf Steiner's Second Natural Scientific Course (see Note 5). W. J. Stein remains a figure of key importance for the understanding of many of the issues raised by the Schiller File.

14. Extract from a letter dated March 8, 1948, Spring Valley, New York, published in: Marie Steiner, '*Briefe und Dokumente* [Letters and Documents],' *Rudolf Steiner-Nachlassverwaltung* [Administration of the Estate of Rudolf Steiner], Dornach 1981, pp. 268-269. Details of the book referred to by Marie Steiner: Râma Prasâd: 'Nature's Finer Forces: The Science of Breath and the Philosophy of the *Tattvas*,' (Theosophical Publishing Society, London, second and revised edition 1894. Available on-line at webpage: http://www.hermetics.org/prasad.html); The Society of Metaphysicians Ltd, Hastings, East Sussex, Reprint April 1986. See website: http://www.metaphysicians.org.uk/; Samata Books, Chennai, India, Reprint December 1998. See website: http://www.samatabooks.com/; R A Kessinger Publishing Company, Whitefish, Montana/U.S.A., Reprint March 1997. See website: http://www.kessingerpub.com; Health Research Books, Pomeroy, WA, Reprint February 2003. See website: http://www.healthresearchbooks.com/; facsimile of third and revised edition 1897 available from Sacred Science Library, Idyllwild, California. See website: http://www.sacred-science.com.

15. First described in Ernst Marti's essay '*Über die notwendige Unterscheidung der ätherischen Bildekräfte von den Ätherarten* [Concerning the Necessary Distinction Between the Etheric Formative Forces and the Ethers],' *Beiträge zu einer Erweiterung der Heilkunst nach geisteswissenschaftlichen Erkenntnissen* [Contributions to an Extension of the Art of Healing Based on Insights Gained by Spiritual Science], *Arbeitsgemeinschaft anthroposophischer Ärzte* [Working Association of Anthroposophical Medical Doctors], Stuttgart, Vol. 13, Issue No. 1 (January/February 1960) available in English as: 'Concerning the Necessary Distinction Between the Etheric Formative Forces and the Ethers' in: Ernst Marti, 'The Four Ethers,' Schaumburg Publications, Roselle, Illinois, 1984. Guenther Wachsmuth's empty response entitled "*Zur Richtigstellung* [Towards a Rectification]" can be found on p. 78 of Vol.13, Issue No. 2 (March/April 1960) of the same journal.

16. Sources: *Rudolf Steiner Das Schicksalsjahr 1923 in der Geschichte der Anthroposophischen Gesellschaft (Vom Goetheanumbrand zur Weihnachtstagung, Ansprachen – Versammlungen – Dokumente, Januar bis Dezember 1923)* [1923: Year of Destiny for Rudolf Steiner in the History of the Anthroposophical Society (from the Goetheanum Fire to the Christmas Conference, addresses – meetings – documents, January to December 1923)], GA 259, Dornach 1991, not yet available in English. Also the letter referred to above from the scientists in Stuttgart to the Goetheanum, cf. Note 7.

17. It may be assumed that the other personalities mentioned in the Schiller File did not have a direct connection with *Der Kommende Tag* [The Coming Day] laboratories. The titles of 'Dr.' etc., refer in some cases to a later period and should therefore be seen in that context.

18. From the '*Anlage zum Prospekt über M. 35,000,000. – neue Aktien der Firma Der Kommende Tag, Aktiengesellschaft zur Förderung wirtschaftlicher und geistiger Werte, Stuttgart* [Investment Prospectus concerning M. 35,000,000. – new shares of the firm *Der Kommende Tag, Aktiengesellschaft* [The Coming Day plc] for the promotion of economic and spiritual values, Stuttgart].' This advertisement for the sale of shares in *Der Kommende Tag A.G.* [The Coming Day plc] is reproduced in the Appendix of the book by Kühn (Hans Kühn, '*Dreigliederungszeit – Rudolf Steiners Kampf für die Gesellschaftsordnung der Zukunft* [The Time of the Threefold Commonwealth – Rudolf Steiner's Struggle for the Social Order of the Future]', Philosophisch-Anthroposophischer Verlag am Goetheanum, Dornach 1978, Chap. IX, '*Der Kommende Tag* [The Coming Day]', pp. 101-124.).

19. In the brief '*Mitteilungen des Bundes für freies Geistesleben* [Reports of the Union for the Free Spiritual Life]', *Anthroposophie* [Anthroposophy], Vol. 4, Number 25 (1922), p. 6, and in a whole-page *Der Kommende Tag* [The Coming Day] advertisement two issues later (Number 27 (1923), p. 8), Leinhas refers to a physics/scientific research institute concerned with optical experiments and research into plant colours and peat fibres. Kühn (see Note 18) places the latter two within the Physics Institute.

20. This is noteworthy insofar as there is the possibility that work was carried out here on the so-called 'Strader machines,' about which—significantly—almost nothing meaningful can be established (cf. The Schiller File, Folio 20, page 26). The same is true of a team going by the name of '*Rhythmus und Maschine* [Rhythm and Machine]' in the Stuttgart of the 1920s.

It is difficult to decide how best to describe the Strader idea—as 'invention,' 'motor,' 'machine,' 'device,' 'appliance' or even 'mechanism.' An unsuccessful attempt was made in issue number 107 (Michaeli [Michaelmas] 1991) of the Beiträge zur Rudolf Steiner Gesamtausgabe [Supplements to the Collected Edition of Rudolf Steiner], (Rudolf Steiner Verlag, Dornach), to solve the important questions about the Strader 'machines.'

Hans Kühn (see also Note 18) called it the most important task of that time. The closing sentence of his article in 'Mitteilungen aus der anthroposophischen Arbeit in Deutschland [Reports from the Anthroposophical Work in Germany]', Vol. 25, Number 4 (1971), pp. 291-293, can hardly be overstressed: "If we pull together this train of thoughts, we are justified in describing the Strader machine as the energy source of the future, which Rudolf Steiner said:…would have to be invented within the next 20 years, otherwise the Ahrimanic 'double' of this machine would appear and be used for purely destructive purposes." Exactly when and where Rudolf Steiner said this is unfortunately not recorded.

There is firm evidence that P. E. Schiller, H. von Dechend, as well as the factory owner Dr. Carl Unger, had been entrusted with the development of a rotating disc to be used in the production of the mistletoe preparation. However, the suggestion that the famous Austrian forester and authority on vortices, Viktor Schauberger (1885-1958), was consulted on this, cannot be confirmed, despite efforts to secure relevant information from his descendants.

See also Paul Schatz's 'Memorandum' of May 28, 1969 (unpublished, archived at the *Paul Schatz Gesellschaft* [Paul Schatz Society], c/o Eva-Maria Blank-Schatz, Unterer Zielweg 117, CH - 4143 Dornach, Switzerland), which outlines a more 'gentle' procedure involving forces of levitation and which still awaits serious investigation. See also webpage: http://www.paul-schatz.ch/en/paulschatz.htm.

21. From '*Der Kommende Tag, Aktiengesellschaft zur Förderung wirtschaftlicher und geistiger Werte, Stuttgart – Bericht über das zweite Geschäftsjahr 1921* [*Der Kommende Tag, Aktiengesellschaft* [The Coming Day plc] for the promotion of economic and spiritual values, Stuttgart – Report of the second financial year 1921],' May 1922 (cf. Note 18).

22. Viz. GA 259, cf. Note 16.

23. Letter to the author from Joachim Bramsch, 01.27.1997.

24. Letter of 09.15.1964 from Paul Eugen Schiller to Joachim Bramsch. In passing it may be mentioned that the possession of a doctorate represented an essential 'seal of approval' in anthroposophical circles of the time. This can be seen in the way the work of such outstandingly innovative persons as Lili Kolisko (occasionally addressed as '*Frau Doktor Kolisko*' on account of her husband's doctoral title) or Paul Schatz was generally appraised, leaving aside for the moment any prejudice relating to either gender or (specifically Jewish) race.

25. Rudolf Steiner referred in various lectures to the so-called 'Chladni sound-figures' and to certain formative forces which are thereby made visible. (GA 101, Stuttgart 09.13.1907 [Occult Signs and Symbols, Anthroposophic Press, Third Printing 1980, p. 11]; GA 102, Berlin 03.16.1908 [The Influence of Spiritual Beings Upon Man, Anthroposophic Press, 1982, p. 80] and GA 123, Berne 09.03.1910 [The Gospel of St. Matthew, Rudolf Steiner Press, 1985, p. 59].) Hans Jenny's study of form is implicitly linked to these ideas.

Similarly, references in various of Steiner's lectures can be linked to the 'ice-crystallisation method' (see H. Heinze: *Einiges über künstliche Eisblumen, in: Ehrenfried Pfeiffer: Kristalle* [Concerning artificial ice-flowers, in: Ehrenfried Pfeiffer: Crystals] (*Bericht aus den Arbeiten des Naturwissenschaftlichen Forschungslaboratoriums am Goetheanum, Sonderdruck aus der Gäa Sophia* [Report of the Work of the Natural Scientific Research Laboratory at the Goetheanum, Special Edition from Gaia Sophia], Orient-Occident-Verlag, Stuttgart/Den Haag/London, 1930, pp. 25-31) developed by Dr. Hans Heinze and Ehrenfried Pfeiffer, which nobody after Joachim Schultz (see Note 7) appears to have concerned themselves with, or to Johanna Zinke's study of the forms generated in the air by speech (see for instance Johanna Zinke: *Luftlautformen, Beiträge zur einer Erweiterung der Heilkunst nach geisteswissenschaftlichen Erkenntnissen, Sonderdruck* [Forms of Sound in Air, Contributions to an Extension of the Art of Healing Based on Insights Gained by Spiritual Science, Special Edition], 29(1), 1976 & 31(3), 1978, Gerabronn, Germany, o.J. [without date]; and *Die schöpferische Kraft der Laute* [The Creative Power of Sound], in: *Die Christengemeinschaft* [The Christian Community], 56(1), January 1984, pp. 18-29).).

26. This debate must also include the work and the discoveries of Wilhelm Reich (1897-1957). A critical comparison of his and Rudolf Steiner's concepts of the 'super- and sub-natural worlds' has not yet been attempted.

Revision to Note 26: Trevor James Constable (1925-) made an attempt to integrate the ideas of Reich with those of Steiner and the American radionics pioneer Dr. Ruth B. Drown (circa 1891/2-1962/3) in his book 'The Cosmic Pulse of Life: The Revolutionary Biological Power Behind UFOs,' Merlin Press, Tustin, California, 1976; Neville Spearman Limited, Sudbury, Suffolk, 1977; 'Sky Creatures: Living UFO's,' Pocket Book Library, Simon and Schuster, New York, 1978; Borderland Sciences Research Foundation, Garberville, California, Revised and enlarged edition 1990. See also the book by W. Edward Mann and Edward Hoffman entitled 'The Man Who Dreamed of Tomorrow: A Conceptual Biography of Wilhelm Reich,' J. P. Tarcher, Inc., Los Angeles, California, First Edition 1980; Crucible, Wellingborough, Northamptonshire, 1990. See Chapter 6 Orgone: The All-Embracing Life Energy, pp. 168-171.

In 1975 two University of Birmingham scientists Dr. Dennis R. Milner and Edward Smart, published empirical evidence of the existence of etheric forces in their book 'The Loom of Creation: *A study of the purpose and the forces that weave the pattern of existence*,' Neville Spearman Limited, London, First published in Great Britain in 1975; Harper & Row, New York, 1st U.S. edition 1976.

27. As an example, Highfrequency Active Auroral Research Program (HAARP) might be mentioned by name: this is the acronym for an enormous military project due to commence in 1998/9 with potentially devastating ecological consequences. This project bears a close relationship to the research orientation of the '20s in the field of Earth magnetism and also to certain indications of Rudolf Steiner about the so-called 'Third Force'—a clear reference to the work of the inventor Nikola Tesla, whose patented ideas form the basis for HAARP (see for instance: 'Angels Don't Play this HAARP: Advances in Tesla Technology,' by N. Begich & J. Manning, Earthpulse Press, Anchorage, 1st Edition 1995, and also the official website for HAARP: http://www.haarp.alaska.edu/).

Recommended reading (in addition to various biographies and recent publications about HAARP): Karl-Heinrich Meyer-Uhlenried, '*Rudolf Steiners dreifacher Atombegriff – Die geistigen Hintergründe des Atoms* [Rudolf Steiner's Threefold Concept of the Atom – The Spiritual Background of the Atom],' lecture manuscript, Burchau, Germany 1997.

In general, the fruits of Tesla's discoveries (as also those of the non-anthroposophical pioneers of etheric technology already mentioned), have only been recognised and applied in recent years, thus revealing the extent to which they represent the antitype of what was being worked towards in Stuttgart.

28. Author's italics.
29. On the financial preconditions for anthroposophical research, continuation of the foundation meeting of 12.31.1923, 10am, Meeting of the Members of the General Anthroposophical Society, presentations and discussions. In: Rudolf Steiner: 'The Christmas Conference for the Foundation of the General Anthroposophical Society 1923/1924,' (GA 260), Anthroposophic Press, Hudson, New York, 1990, page 210.
30. *"Those who are familiar with the history of the anthroposophical initiatives will be aware that the largest part of what constitutes 'practical' anthroposophy today can be traced back to the experiments and initiatives of those early years. We draw spiritual nourishment even today from what was begun then. The money invested at that time in research has proved to be the most worthwhile*

investment of the last 70 years. Without it there would be today no anthroposophical medicine, no picture-forming techniques of investigation (…). If one thinks of the millennium, if one remembers Rudolf Steiner's words…then it is by no means absurd to imagine that we might aim to make such a drastic change over the next decade in the way the resources of the Society are used that by the year 2000 about a third of all the financial resources would be invested in genuine research. …" From: Christoph Lindenberg, '*Wird genügend geforscht?* [Is enough research being done?],' *Mitteilungen aus der anthroposophischen Arbeit in Deutschland* [Reports from the Anthroposophical Work in Germany], Number 173 (1990), pp. 179-183.

Translated from the original German by Paul Carline.

Christoph Podak,
Gellertstrasse 135,
CH - 4052 Basel,
Switzerland.
E-mail: ch.podak@bluewin.ch

Lili Kolisko with her daughter Eugenie
© Andrew Clunies-Ross

INDEXES

Name Index with Biographies

Adams, George [formerly Kaufmann, George Adams von] (1894-1963) [Austro-Hungarian born German scientist who read chemistry at Christ's College Cambridge. Mathematician, translator and interpreter of Rudolf Steiner. In a seminal essay entitled 'Physical and Ethereal Spaces,'* first published in 1933, Adams enunciated the concept of 'ethereal' or 'negative-Euclidean' space where life processes take place through his pioneering research into projective geometry. Later in 1947 Adams together with Michael Wilson (1901-1985) founded The Goethean Science Foundation in Clent, Stourbridge, Worcestershire, West Midlands], 75 (footnote), 97, 98, 99 (footnote), (Appendix, 119)

Aisenpreis, Ernst (1884-1949) [German born architect, who became Chief Architect for both Goetheanum buildings in Dornach, Switzerland], 34

Aquinas, St. Thomas (ca. 1225-1274) [Italian philosopher and theologian, known as *Doctor Angelicus* [Angelic Doctor], *Doctor Universalis* [Universal Doctor]], 30

Babcock, W. R., 85

Barber, D. R., 44

Beckh, Prof. Dr. Hermann (1875-1937) [German orientalist, University lecturer, indologist, linguist, musicologist, in fact a universal scholar who was co-founder of the Christian Community], 50

Becquerel, Antoine Henri (1852-1908) [French physicist who shared one half of the Nobel Prize for Physics in 1903 *"in recognition of the extraordinary services he has rendered by his discovery of spontaneous radioactivity"*], 44

Begich, Dr. Nicholas (Nick) [Alaskan born author and lecturer on the influence of technology on society. Begich is the publisher and co-owner of Earthpulse Press. See webpage: http://www.earthpulse.com/src/category.asp?catid=13. Since 2004 he has served as Executive Director of The Lay Institute on Technology, Inc. See website: http://www.layinstitute.org/], (Appendix, 126)

Bell, Alexander Graham (1847-1922) [Scottish scientist, inventor and innovator. Best known for his invention of the telephone in 1876], 84

Béraud, Georges Henry [Béraud developed a process for the manufacture of peat-thread for the textile industry which became known as the Béraudine method], 63

Bessenich-Schmitz, Frieda (1892-1969) [Dutch biologist and leader of the Biomedical Department at the Goetheanum], (Appendix, 122)

Blank-Schatz, Eva-Maria [daughter of Paul Schatz and Board Member of the Paul Schatz Foundation], (Appendix, 125)

Bourquin-Troesch, Marie [wife of Paul Eugen Schiller], (202)

Bramsch, Dipl. Ing. Joachim (?-2005) [engineer and Waldorf School mathematics and physics teacher], 70-71, 73, 79, 81, 82, (Appendix, 125)

Branly, Dr. Eugène Édouard Désiré (1844-1940) [French physicist and inventor of the coherer in 1890], 90

Bruce, Dr. Charles Edward Rhodes (1902-1979) [Scottish mathematician, physicist and electrical engineer], 83

Brugmans, Sebald Justinus (1763-1819) [Dutch physician, botanist and chemist], 44

Buchheim, Hans (1899-1987) [assistant to Dr. R. E. Maier in Stuttgart and later in Einsingen], 40, 59, 61, 69, (Appendix, 114, 116)

Bulwer-Lytton, Sir Edward George (1803-1873) [famous Victorian novelist, playwright, politician and occultist. Coined the word *'vril'* which featured in his book entitled 'The Coming Race' first published in 1871 and reprinted as 'Vril: Power of the Coming Race'], (Appendix, 119 (footnote))

---

* First published under the German title '*Von dem ätherischen Raume* [On Ethereal Space]' in the periodical *Natura: eine Zeitschrift zur Erweiterung der Heilkunst nach geisteswissenschaftlicher Menschenkunde* [*Natura:* Journal for the Extension of the Art of Healing Through a Spiritual-Scientific Knowledge of the Human Being], Dornach, Switzerland, 6. Jahrgang [6th Year], Heft 5/6 [Issue 5/6], Februar/März [February/March] 1933, S. 143-184; Studien und Versuche [Studies and Experiments], Eine anthroposophische Schriftenreihe Band 6 [An Anthroposophical Series of Publications Vol. 6], Verlag Freies Geistesleben GmbH [Free Spiritual Life Publishing Ltd], Stuttgart, 1964; 1981; English edition first published in two parts in Anthroposophy: A Quarterly Review of Spiritual Science, London, Vol. 8, No. 3, Michaelmas 1933, pp. 235-271 and Vol. 8, No. 4, Christmas 1933, pp. 364-392; Reprinted under the title 'Physical and Ethereal Spaces,' Rudolf Steiner Press, London, 1965; 1978.

Bunsen, Prof. Robert Wilhelm Eberhard (1811-1899) [German experimental chemist, teacher and inventor. The gas burner that bears his name is usually attributed as his invention, but the Bunsen burner design was invented by Michael Faraday. Bunsen merely introduced it in 1855 and popularised its use], 103

Cantz, Dr. Rudolf (?-1996), 104
Carline, Paul (1944-) [former Waldorf School teacher, now writer and translator], (Appendix, 127)
Cassini, Giovanni Dominico (1625-1712) [French astronomer who in 1680 found the curve that bears his name (Cassini oval) whilst attempting to describe the movement of the Earth relative to the Sun], 40
Castelliz, Dr. Heinz, 97, (Appendix, 122)
Chapman, Sydney (1888-1970) [British mathematician, astronomer and geophysicist], 92
Clerc, Dr. Stephan H. R. [Swiss scientist], 2, 4, 37, 101, (Appendix, 122)
Cloos, Walther (1900-1985) [German pharmacist who worked at Weleda AG], 54 (footnote), 70 (footnote)
Clunies-Ross, Andrew [grandson of Lilly Kolisko, celloist, publisher and founder of the 'Kolisko Archive.' See website: http://www.talbot-2.demon.co.uk/], (Appendix, 127)
Constable, Trevor James (1925-) [New Zealand born American author, aviation historian and pioneering investigator into the etheric], (Appendix, 126)

Dechend
    Dr. Hermann von (1883-1956) [physicist], 16, 18, 71-72, 87, (Appendix, 115-116, 122, 124)
    Hertha von (née Schepp) (1892-1971) [wife of Hermann von Dechend], (Appendix, 122)
Dewar, Sir James (1842-1923) [Scottish-born chemist and physicist who invented the Dewar flask in 1892 to aid him in his research with the liquefication of gases at very low temperatures. The Dewar flask is a double-walled vessel with a vacuum between the walls to reduce the transfer of heat], 77
Dibbern, Albert, 57
Didier, Pascale [author], 47
Dreher, Dr. Eugen (1841-1900) [German natural philosopher, lecturer at the Martin-Luther-University Halle-Wittenberg. In the 1870's Dreher conducted many experiments into the three spectra found in light], 37
Drown, Dr. Ruth Beymer (circa 1891/2-1962/3) [American licensed chiropractor and radionics pioneer], (Appendix, 126)

Eckardtstein, Baroness Imme von (1871-1930) [French-born German artist and costume maker], 46
Eckstein, Dr. E. Otto (1894-1944) [German-born substance and remedy researcher], 46, (Appendix, 122)
Edwards, Lawrence (1912-2004) [Waldorf School teacher of mathematics and pioneering researcher into the rhythmical planetary influences on plant buds], 44, 98
Einstein, Albert (1879-1955) [German-American physicist who developed the special theory of relativity in 1905 and the general theory of relativity between 1907-1915. Winner of the Nobel Prize for Physics in 1921 *"for his services to Theoretical Physics, and especially for his discovery of the law of the photoelectric effect"*], 40
Erbe, Hugo (1895-1965) [biodynamic farmer], (Appendix, 119)
Erman, Prof. Paul (1764-1851) [German physicist], 51
Erne, Ruth [Swiss peat fibre textile researcher. Runs a studio [Atelier] *TÜVA Torffaser-Verarbeitung* [TÜVA (meaning 'tuft of grass') Peat Fibre Processing] for spinning, weaving and colouring peat fibres in Hettenschwil, Switzerland. See the on-line article by the German medical and environmental journalist Hans Krautstein published in '*Schrot & Korn: das Naturkostportal* [Grist & Grain: the Natural Food Portal],' Heft [Issue] 10, Oktober 1997 entitled '*Torfprodukte – Heilende Kräfte aus dem Moor* [Peat Products – Healing Forces from the Bog]' on webpage: http://www.schrotundkorn.de/1997/sk971007.htm], 63
Essen, Otto von (1898-1983) [German phoneticist and speech scientist], 84

Faraday, Michael (1791-1867) [British inventor, pioneering natural philosopher and discoverer of the *Faraday effect or Faraday rotation* in 1845 representing the first experimental evidence that light and magnetism are related], 41, 44, 83
Fiechter, Nik (1914-1998) [physician], 83
Franklin, Benjamin (1706-1790) [American scientist, inventor, statesman, printer and philosopher], 14
Fraunhofer, Joseph von (1787-1826) [Bavarian glass & instrument maker and optician physicist, rediscovered the presence of dark lines in the solar spectrum in 1813, now known as *Fraunhofer lines* and inventor of a spectroscope in 1814], 24

Gassiot, John Peter (1797-1877) [English merchant, electro-chemist and scientific writer], 83

Gauss, Carl Friedrich (1777-1855) [German mathematician], 92

Geissler, Johann Heinrich (1815-1879) [German glassblower and inventor], 83

Goethe, Johann Wolfgang von (1749-1832) [German poet, dramatist, novelist, pioneering natural scientist, traveller, amateur musician, author of Faust and the founder of morphology], 3, 27, 37, 92, 99

Hagemann, Dr. Ernst (1913-2003) [musicologist, compiler and commentator of texts from Rudolf Steiner's spiritual science], 202

Hahn, Mr. G., 17, 22

Halla, Prof. Dr. Franz (1884-1971) [physical chemist], 23, 96-97

Halske, Johann Georg (1814-1890) [German master mechanic who together with Werner von Siemens founded Siemens & Halske in Berlin in October 1847], 76

Hamilton, Sir William Rowan (1805-1865) [Irish mathematician, physicist and astronomer. Hamilton spent years trying to discover a three-dimensional number system. He was only successful when he ventured into four-dimensions and discovered *quaternions* on 16 October 1843. Hamiltonian quaternions are a non-commutative (meaning that multiplication is not symmetric, i.e. $ij \neq ji$, $ij = - ji$, etc.) extension of complex numbers and a more general class of hypercomplex numbers. Each quaternion consists of four composants ($q = a + bi + cj + dk$) and has one arbitrary scalar number (e.g. a) and three vector numbers (arbitrary scalar and hyper-imaginary, e.g. bi, cj and dk) representing one real dimension and three imaginary dimensions. A quaternion with zero scalar is entirely hyperimaginary and is historically called a pure quaternion. Hamilton introduced the term *quaternions* in his first paper on the subject read before a meeting of the Royal Irish Academy on 13 November 1843], 40 (footnote)

Hansdingl, A., 62

Harrison, Charles George (1855-?) [British theosophist and author of 'The Transcendental Universe,' first published in 1894], 50

Hauschka, Dr. Rudolf (1891-1969) [Viennese chemist, nutritionist and natural scientist], 34, 58, 62

Heaf, Dr. David J. (1947-) [biochemist, Newsletter & 'Archetype' editor for the Science Group of the Anthroposophical Society in Great Britain and since 1995 UK co-ordinator of *Ifgene* (International Forum for Genetic Engineering)—see website: http://www.ifgene.org], 104, (Appendix, 113)

Heertsch, Dr. Andreas [physicist and physician], 35, 85, 201, 202

Heinze, Dr. Hans (1899-1997) [German engineer, farmer and journalist], (Appendix, 125)

Helmholtz, Hermann Ludwig Ferdinand von (1821-1894) [German physiologist, physicist and inventor of the ophthalmoscope], 27

Herberg, Dr. Ing., 27

Hertz, Heinrich Rudolph (1857-1894) [German physicist and mechanician. In 1888 he was the first to demonstrate the existence of electromagnetic radiation by building an apparatus for producing Ultra High Frequency (UHF) radio waves. The SI* unit of Hertz for frequency (cycles/second) is named in his honour], 90

Hess, Viktor Franz (1883-1964) [Austrian-American physicist and discoverer of cosmic radiation], 51

Hoffman, Dr Edward (1951-) [American licensed clinical psychologist and author], (Appendix, 126)

Husemann

Dr. med.** Friedwart [German internist and son of Gisbert Husemann], 31 (footnote)

Dr. med. Gisbert (1907-1997) [German physician, researcher, writer, Goetheanist and father of Friedwart Husemann], 31 (footnote), 104

Jenny, Dr. Hans (1904-1972) [Swiss physician, animal artist, natural scientist and researcher into the life-patterns of the etheric. Founded the Basel Institute for Wave Phenomena Research and pioneered the science of Cymatics [*Kymatik*]***], 98, (Appendix, 119 (text and footnote), 125)

---

* SI is abbreviated from the French language name *Le Système international d'unités* [The International System of Units] of the modern metric system.

** German doctoral degree in medicine.

*** Term coined by Dr. Hans Jenny derived from the Greek word 'to kyma' meaning 'the wave' and 'ta kymatika' meaning 'matters pertaining to waves, wave matters.'

Jurgens, Harold [American translator], 31 (footnote)

Kauffungen, Dr. Fritz [Swiss chemist], 4, 21-22

Kaufmann, George Adams von [see under Adams, George], (Appendix, 119)

Keely, John Ernst Worrell (1827-1898) [American carpenter, musician and inventor], 11-12, 48

Keyserlingk, Count Carl Wilhelm von (1869-1928) [German officer and agriculturalist. See webpage: http://www. anthromedia.com/articles/agriculture/beginning_developments/paths_leading_to_rudolf_steiners_lecture_ course_on_agriculture/], 12

Kirchner-Bockholt, Dr. Margarete (1894-1973) [German-born physician, curative eurythmist and leader of the Medical Section at the Goetheanum], 34

Kloss, Johannes (1937-) [German engineer and founder in 1971 of the Swedish company *Älma Torvtextil* [Älma Peat Textile] in Rydöbruk, Sweden. See his bilingual (German and Swedish) website: http://www.naturtextilien.se/ and also webpages: http://www.peatlandsni.gov.uk/history/int_uses.htm and http://www.eco-world.de/scripts/ basics/eco-world/service/produkte/basics.prg?a_no=55. Kloss has his peat fibre manufactured into products by Thomas Kleiner in Sebexen (approximately 60 miles south east of Hannover), Germany. See his website [Natural Hair Bed]: http://www.naturhaar-betten.de/. *Turfpost* [Peat Office] at *Instituut Breidablick Sociaal-Therapeutische Gemeenschap* [Institute Breidablick Social Therapeutic Community] in Midden Beemster (approximately 15 miles north of Amsterdam), The Netherlands, import *Älma Torvtextil* peat fibre for manufacturing peat products and have documentation available in English. The Eriophorum Foundation [*Stichting Eriophorum*] for the promotion of developmental research, technology and application of peat fibre is located at the same Institute address. They publish a report on the results of a study on 'The healthful effects of peat fibre products.' See the Dutch website: http://www.breidablick.nl], 62

Kolisko

Dr. med. Eugen (1893-1939) [Austrian-born physician, medical researcher and Waldorf School teacher. Lecturer in medicine, zoology, chemistry and history both in Europe and America. Husband of Lilly Kolisko. Moved to England in 1936],* 44, 57 (footnote), 102, (Appendix, 116, 123)

Frau Lilly [or *Lili*] Noha (1889-1976) [Austrian-born nurse, natural scientist, pioneering rhythm researcher and wife of Eugen Kolisko. Moved to England in 1936],** 3-4, 12 (footnote), 31, 43-44, 57 (footnote), 101-102, 104, 108, (Appendix, 114, 116, 118, 120-121, 125, 127)

Krawkow, Prof. Nikolai Pavlovich (1865-1924) [Russian Pharmacologist. Director of the Pharmacology Laboratory of the Military Medical Academy of Petersburg, Russia. Known as an idealist and mystical clairvoyant!],*** 108 (footnote), 109

Kremlin, Ludwig, 98

Kühl, Johannes (1953-) [physicist and leader of the Natural Science Section at the Goetheanum for the last 9 years], 1, 4, 202

Kühn, Dr. Hans (1889-1977), 61, 68, 71, 91, 98, (Appendix, 124)

Kugler, Dr. Walter (1948-) [curator of the Rudolf Steiner Archive in Switzerland], 2, 4, 31

Kürschner, Prof. Joseph (1853-1902) [German publisher of '*Deutsche National-Litteratur* [German National Literature]'], 37 (footnote)

---

* See his biography by Lilly Kolisko entitled '*Eugen Kolisko, ein Lebensbild* [Eugen Kolisko, a Life Portrait],' Entworfen von L. Kolisko zugleich Ein Stück Geschichte der Anthroposophischen Gesellschaft [Drafted by L. Kolisko and at the Same Time a Piece of History of the Anthroposophical Society], Als Manuskript gedruckt für die Mitglieder [Printed as a Manuscript for the Members], Hohenloher Druck- und Verlagshaus [Hohenloher Press and Publishing House] Gerabronn-Crailsheim, Germany, 1961.

** See her biography by Dr. med. Gisbert Husemann entitled 'Lili Kolisko – Her Life and Work 1889-1976,' Translated by Dr. David J. Heaf from the original German article, '*Archetype*,' Science Group of the Anthroposophical Society in Great Britain, London, Issue No. 7, September 2001, pp. 31-48. See the Addendum on page 104.

*** See his biography by Prof. O. Steppuhn of Moscow entitled '*Zum Andenken an Prof. N. P. Krawkow* [In memory of Prof. N. P. Krawkow],' Münchener Medizinische Wochenschrift (MMW) [Münich Medical Weekly Journal], Münich, 72. Jahrgang. [72nd Year], Heft [Issue] Nr. 27, 3. Juli [3rd July] 1925, S. 1117-1118.

---

* Doktor *rerum naturalium* [doctor of natural sciences].

** Pelikan, Wilhelm and Unger, Georg, '*Die Wirkung potenzierter Substanzen. Pflanzenwachstums-Versuche mit statistischer Auswertung,*' Philosophisch-Anthroposophischer Verlag am Goetheanum, Dornach, Switzerland, 1965; Translated into English and published as: 'The Activity of Potentized Substances. Experiments on Plant Growth and Statistical Evaluation,' The British Homœopathic Journal, London, Vol. LX, No. 4, October 1971, pp. 233-266.

Pfeiffer, Dr. Ehrenfried E. (1899-1961) [gifted German-American chemist, inventor and pioneering spiritual researcher], 10-13, 18, 20-21, 25-26, 34, 43-44, 46-49, 62, 87, 91, 98, 101-103, (Appendix, 115, 116 (footnote), 119, 122, 125)

Piper, Dr. Kurt (1875-1952) [editor, physician and poet], 51

Plato, Bodo von [historian, philosopher and member of the Executive Council (*Vorstand*) at the Goetheanum], (202)

Pliny the Elder [Gaius Plinius Cecilius Secundus] (circa A.D. 23-A.D. 79) [Roman officer and encyclopedist], 63

Plücker, Julius (1801-1868) [German mathematician and physicist], 83

Podak, Christoph O. [Swiss researcher and writer], 1, (Appendix, 113, 127)

Popov, Prof. Alexander Stepanovich (1859-1906) [Russian physicist and radio engineer], 91

Proskauer, Heinrich Oskar (1913-2000) [German actor, lecturer and researcher into Goethe's scientific works. Founding director of the Goethe Colour Studio in Dornach, Switzerland, in 1970], 46

Pyle, William Scott (1888-1938) [American artist and researcher into the production of new plant-based paints ('Anthea Paints'). Early research was performed in the *Anthea Institut für Rudolf Steiner Pflanzenfarbenforschung* [Anthea Institute for Rudolf Steiner Plant Colour Research], Dornach, Switzerland. From 1960 this research was continued in the *Pflanzen-Farben-Labor am Goetheanum* [Plant Colour (Pigment) Laboratory at the Goetheanum] in the Art Section's research department. In January 2005, the Plant Colour (Pigment) Laboratory at the Goetheanum was refounded by the laboratory co-workers as '*Anthro-Color Pflanzenfarben – Verein zur Förderung des Pflanzenfarben-Impuls von Rudolf Steiner* [Anthro-Color Plant Colours – Association for the Development of Rudolf Steiner's Plant Colour Impulse].' See webpage: http://paintingschool-goetheanum.ch/en/plantcolour.php. Plant colour paints and pigments are now available from Hans Stockmar GmbH* & Co. KG** in Kaltenkirchen, Germany. See webpage: http://www.stockmar.de/index.php?language=en. Other manufacturers' include: *Sehestedter Naturfarben* [Sehestedt's Natural Colours], Sehestedt, Germany, webpage: http://www.chito.com/english/about/ and *Heidelberger Naturfarben* [Heidelberg's Natural Colours] GmbH & Co. KG, Heidelberg, Germany, webpage: http://www.naturfarben.de/English.25.0.html], 46

Pyle-Waller, Maria Elisabeth Mieta (*née* Waller) (1883-1954) [Dutch-American eurythmist, actress, artist and husband of William Scott Pyle], 46

Râma Prasâd Kasyapa, Pandit [Indian theosophist and Sanskrit scholar. President of The Meerut Theosophical Society, Uttar Pradesh. Commencing in November 1887 a series of nine essays on *tantric* philosophy that he wrote were published in volumes IX and X of '*The Theosophist*,' entitled 'Nature's Finer Forces.' For this he won the Society's Gold Medal. In 1889 he was persuaded to revise the original essays and add new ones (bringing the total number to fifteen) together with a full translation of a small book containing the ninth chapter of an ancient Sanskrit Upanishad work called the '*Sivagama* [The Teaching of Siva]' on which the essays are mainly based. This was first published as 'The Science of Breath and the Philosophy of the Tatwas' in 1890. See the first edition on-line at webpage: http://www.rexresearch.com/prana/essays.htm or download in pdf format from: http://www.hermetics.org/pdf/NaturesFinerForcesTheScienceofBreathRamaPrasad.pdf. The second and revised edition published in 1894 is also available on-line at webpage: http://www.hermetics.org/prasad.html], 11-12, 49-50, (Appendix, 115, 123)

Rebmann, Dr. Hans (1912-1999) [mathematician, physicist and Waldorf School teacher], 35

Reich, Dr. Wilhelm (1897-1957) [Austrian-American physician, psychiatrist, psychotherapist, natural scientist and the father of orgone energy], (Appendix, 119 (footnote), 125-126)

Reipert, Dipl.-Ing. Hans (1895-1981) [engineer, eurythmist and educationalist], 70 (footnote)

Rosenthal, Werner (1898-1961), 10

Rousselot, L'Abbé Jean-Pierre (1846-1924) [French inventor and creator of experimental phonetics], 84

Ruhmer, Ernst Walter (1878-1913) [German experimental physicist], 84

Sabarth, Dr. Erica [or Erika] [assistant to Dr. Ehrenfried Pfeiffer and co-inventor with him of the copper chloride crystallisation method], 46

---

* GmbH = *Gesellschaft mit beschränkter Haftung* [Company with limited liability equivalent to limited in the UK].

** KG = *Kommanditgesellschaft* [Limited partnership].

---

* Inversion products are available from *KulturatA® e.V.* (*eingetragener Verein* [Registered Association]), Wuppertal, Germany. See webpage: http://kulturata.inversis.de/shop/.

* German doctoral degree in medicine and philosophy.

Subject Index

amorphic masses, 27
amorphous, 19
amplification
    electronic, 84
        sound, and noise reduction by means of the
        'transmission principle' influencing rhythmi-
        cal vortex streaming, as seen in the example of
        sensitive flames [*Schallverstärkung und Geräus-*
        chminderung mit Hilfe des Mitnahmeprinzipes
        bei Beeinflußten Rhythmischen Wirbelströmun-
        gen, Dargestellt am Beispiel Sensibler Flammen]
        (report), 85
amplified, the conditions under which sound could
    best be, 85
amplifier, flame, 84
analyser, 86
angels don't play this HAARP (book), (Appendix,
    126)
animals, 10, 13, 49
    machine- [Maschinentiere], 49
    warm and cold-blooded, 110
animation, 22, 58
annealing, 79
anode, 14, 51, 71, 74, 83
Anthea colours, 46
anthroposophical
    high school course of the free high school for
        spiritual science [*Hochschulkurse der Freien*
        Hochschule für Geisteswissenschaft, Anthroposo-
        phische], (Appendix, 117)
    initiatives, 46, (Appendix, 113, 126)
    medical doctors, 102, 104, (Appendix, 123)
    movement, (Appendix, 113)
    natural science and the research institutes of
        Der Kommende Tag A.G. [the coming day plc]
        and at the Goetheanum [*Naturwissenschaft*
        und Forschungsinstitute von Der Kommende
        Tag A.G. und am Goetheanum, Anthroposo-
        phische], (Appendix, 121)
    point of view, (Appendix, 120)
    research, official histories of, (Appendix, 123)
    research institute(s), 1, 3-4, 7-8, 30-31, 42-43, 57-
        59, 61, 65, 69, 71, 95, 101-102, (Appendix, 113-
        118, 120-122, 124), (201)
    society, 18-19, (Appendix, 113-114, 123) (202)
    society, general, (Appendix, 122, 126)
anthroposophy, vii, 3, 10, (Appendix, 126), (201, 202)
antithesis, 51, 71
antitype, (Appendix, 126)
apparatus, 1, 12, 16, 18, 41, 43, 48, 74, 77-79, 81, 84-
    85, 87, 89-90, 95, (Appendix, 120), (201)
appearance
    and suppleness, 67 (British patent)

and the spinning properties of the peat-fibre, 67
    (British patent)
    glossy, 68 (British patent)
    of cyanide compounds, 47
    of spiral forms, 86
    the results of this suction is that a *being* makes its,
        (Appendix, 117)
    whenever anode and cathode make their, 71
archetypal
    etheric forms, 45, (Appendix, 115)
    or formative forces active in the cosmos, seven
        etheric, 50
archetype
    (newsletter articles supplement), 104, (Appendix,
        113)
    of the plant, 103
architecture, 10
arcs, electrical, 84
arithmetical
    and rhythm-producing activity, 82
    expression of measure, 27
art, 46, 98, 104, (Appendix, 115, 117, 123, 125)
artificial
    generation of plants, 29
    ice-flowers, (Appendix, 125)
    materials, 57
    night, 43
    thread, 62
    wood, 62
asbestos, 59
ascending
    and descending stream in the plant, 58 (footnote)
    in peat the etheric has a descending tendency that
        must be changed into an, one, 58
ash, 45
ash-skeleton, 60
ashes
    by spreading out the, 9
    mineral, 45, 60
    mineralised, 8-9
    of plants, 45
    physical
        difference between mineral and plant, 45
        differences between plant and mineral, 45, 60
    plant, 8
    (weed-control), 45
assistant
    as a young and inexperienced, 72
    at the research laboratory in Stuttgart, 201
    Dr. P. E. Schiller
        was working as an, 16
        with his, 70
    former, to Hermann von Dechend, (Appendix, 122)

electron-proton, 63
electroscope, 11
electro-technology, 79
element
    of warmth, 87
    the qualitative, (Appendix, 117)
elemental *beings*, 58, 101
    Ahrimanic, 29
    co-operate, 101
    fettered, 58
    Luciferic, 29
    must feel at home in your laboratory, 101
    production of, 29
elements
    are the expression of certain meetings of forces, 27
    classical occidental, 50
    of natural science [*der Naturwissenschaft, Elemente*] (journal), 41, 104
    single, 13
    to heat, 24
    watery, 24
embryo
    cow, 31
    dog, 31
emotions, human, 89
empirical
    evidence of the existence of etheric forces, (Appendix, 126)
    material, 3
empty
    emptier than, (Appendix, 117)
    response, (Appendix, 123)
    space, 76
emulsifying agent, 60
emulsion(s), 67 (British patent)
    medium for, 21
    of resins, 67-68 (British patent)
    or resins, 68 (British patent)
energy
    ch'i, (Appendix, 119 (text and footnote))
    heat, 27
    kinetic, 23
    life, the all-embracing, (Appendix, 126)
    mechanical, 27
    morphogenetic fields, (Appendix, 119)
    of the universe, natural, (Appendix, 119 (footnote))
    orgone, (Appendix, 119, 126)
    potential, 23
    prana, (Appendix, 119 (text and footnote))
    source of the future, (Appendix, 124)
    structure, changes of the, 73
    vril, (Appendix, 119 (text and footnote))

engine
    hydro-pneumatic pulsating vacuo, 48
    steam, 48
engineering at the *Technischen Hochschule* [technical high school] in Stuttgart, diploma in, (201)
enormous
    dilutions, 109
    impact, (Appendix, 120)
    military project, (Appendix, 126)
    work, 42
enterprise
    of *Der Kommende Tag A.G.* [The Coming Day plc], (Appendix, 114)
    peat, 65
enthusiasm, 89
entities [*Entitäten*], 31 (footnote)
    smallest [*kleinster*], 31 (text and footnote), 102 (text and footnote), 108
entity, smallest [*Entität, kleinste*], 102
environment
    condition of warmth in our, 33
    heat must be drawn from another part of the, 33
    soul-spiritual, 25
epidemic
    animal, 101
    of foot-and-mouth disease, 101
epoch
    fifth cultural, 87
    fifth post-Atlantean, 88
equation
    in a slightly modified form the same, 96
    of heat conduction, 42, 96
    wave, 42, 96
equations, 96
    Maxwell, 41
equinoxes, 91
equipment, 46, 62, 78, 81, (Appendix, 115)
    for cooling, 75
    for research, 86
    for spinning and weaving, 62
    research, 103
    technical, 90
    traditional, 95
    vacuum, 78
error
    central, in Wachsmuth's book, (Appendix, 116)
    I [Theberath] am afraid of having made a cardinal, 69
errors, uncertainties and, 7
esotericism, foundations of (book), 33
esoteric science, an outline of (book), 3
essay, (Appendix, 114, 121-123)

-like 'cilia', hundreds of small sensitive, 49
measurements on a silver wire spiral and a, 69
hands
    discussions are in the, of P. E. Schiller, 34
    hold the, 19
    over the flame, 19
    the opportunity of making a decisive break-
        through had not been seized with both,
        (Appendix, 118)
harmful
    even to the following generations, quicksilver
        could prove, 12
    indeed it could be, 12
    indeed it was, 87
    the addition of poison is so small that it is not, 9
harmony
    of the spheres, 92
    of the universe, reverence for the, 29
harvest, 66
head, 19
    body similar to the, 53
    similar to the body, 53
healing
    contributions to an extension of the art of
        [Beiträge zu einer Erweiterung der, Heilkunst]
        (periodical), 104, (Appendix, 123, 125)
    effects of peat, 62
    indications about the use of magnets in the, of
        certain illnesses, 45, 81
health
    of humanity, 89
    my [Schiller's], is not as I would wish, 82
healthy
    clothing, 62
    fashion with J. R. von Mayer, 27
    or sick person, 19
    plant appeared, 105
hearts, action on isolated, 110
heat, 22-24, 27, 30, 33-35, 42, 49, 63
    at the border between positive and negative
        materiality [auf der Grenze positiver und nega-
        tiver Materialität, Die Wärme] (German title
        of the warmth course), (Appendix, 121)
    being of, 33, (202)
    -condition, 19
    conditions beyond the earth-organism point
        towards lower temperatures, 76
    conduction, 42, 71, 96
    conduction of, 9, 23, 35
    fabric would retain, 64
    nature of, 44
    on the nature of [Vom Wesen der, Wärme] (book),
        33, (202)

processes in the human body, 87
quality, research into, (201)
radiation and conduction of, 9
rays, invisible, 38 (notes from Rudolf Steiner)
reaction, 35
speed of, 96
trap, 38 (notes from Rudolf Steiner)
white, 45
heating, 34
    certain substances, 95
    degree of, 65
    electrical resistance, 34
    installation for, 75
    materials, 44
    measure the rate of, 22
    research on gas, 34
    the fibres after the soaking, 65
hemisphere [Halbkugel], (cover diagram, ii)
    antimony [Antimon halbkugel], (cover diagram,
        ii)
    copper hollow [Kupferne hohle Halbkugel],
        (cover diagram, ii)
historical-institutional context, (Appendix, 113)
history
    and sociology of the anthroposophical research
        institutes in the 1920s, towards a, (Appendix,
        113)
    in particular remains still to be written, whole,
        (Appendix, 115)
    of the anthroposophical initiatives, (Appendix, 126)
    of the anthroposophical movement, (Appendix,
        113)
    of the anthroposophical society, (Appendix, 123)
    of the production of peat fibre, 63
    of the research institutes of 'Der Kommende Tag
        [the coming day]' company in Stuttgart and of
        the laboratories at the Goetheanum in Dorn-
        ach, (Appendix, 113)
    of the 'Schiller file,' (Appendix, 113)
    of the theosophical movement, 71 (footnote)
    of this institute, 1
Hochfeld magnet laboratory [Hochfeld-Magnetlabor],
    41
hollow sphere, nickel [Hohlkugel, Nickel], (cover
    diagram, ii)
holy, ix
hops, 59
horizon, 92
horn, 61
horns, cow, 12
horse, 12, 27
    blankets, 63
    -chestnut [Æsculus hippocastanum], 41, 60

hot
    beds, 66
    plate, electric, 34
human *being*
    and mechanisation, 49
    composes his thoughts in salt (NaCl), 54
    develops as his own warmth towards his
        surroundings, 34
    everything that we touch will in time bear in itself
        the impression of the, 89
    head and limb polarity in the, 70
    inner nature of the, 12
    is and that which he produces, between what the,
        88
    magnetism and electricity in the, 92
    must be bound up with what happens within the,
        29
    must produce his 'inner' warmth himself, 33
    must start with the, 21
    produce universal forms that appear negative as
        the upper, becomes conscious of them, 56
    research into the reaction of the, 11
    significance and activity of the metals in earth,
        cosmos and, 94
    the highest and noblest expression of the, 87
    they work directly on the lower, 56
    will grow together with what is externally
        objective, 89
    with 80 stands in the middle, 12
human *beings*
    be able to become motor force, 89
    but certain things today are only misused by, 88
    could protect, 58
humanity
could be dangerous for modern, 12
    had another moral constitution, 11
    sacrament to the honour of the gods and health of,
        89
    today they would be severely misused by, 88
human voice
    delicate qualities of the, 84
    reproduce faithfully the personal nuances of the,
        90
    sensitive flame as a reagent for the, 84
humidity, air, 24
humorous
    light, 49
    memory, 103
humus, 20-21, 58
hunger, will is, 52
hydraulic press, 62
hygiene
    association, journal of the anthroposophical

therapy and (A.T.H.A.), 31 (footnote), 102
        (footnote)
    matters of, 102
hygrometers, 42
hyperbola, branch of a, 26
hyperfine structures, activation of spectra for the
    investigation of [*Hyperfeinstrukturen, Anregung
    von Spektren zur Untersuchung von*], 83
hyperimaginary numbers, 40 (text and footnote)
hypothesis, 41
hypotrochoid (roll-curve), 98

ice-crystallisation method, (Appendix, 125)
ice-crystals, 44
ice-flowers, (Appendix, 125)
idea, 29, 43, 89
    'concept' and 'judgement' in the teachings of
        Rudolf Steiner ['*Begriff' und 'Urteil' in der
        Lehre Rudolf Steiners, 'Vorstellung*'] (course
        publication), (Appendix, 117)
    exceptionally ingenious, 25
    fell into oblivion, 98
    for a research institute, (Appendix, 121)
    fundamental, 37
    is not just to show a few new lines in the
        spectrum, 81
    of a continuous spreading out of qualities, 97
    of the mystery of Golgotha, 89
    people today have no, (Appendix, 120)
    reject such an, 18
    Strader, (Appendix, 124)
    that everything rests on polarity in the inorganic
        world, 10
    that the activity of life-forces would be identifi-
        able through their vitalising affect on bacteria
        and flies, 49
    that through the discovery of such energies a new
        technology and social order could be created, 48
ideas
    additional, 60
    he [Steiner] would have wished to see the place
        full of, 95
    his [Steiner's] proposals are so new and so often
        at variance with contemporary, 81
    many erroneous and senseless, 34
    of Reich with those of Steiner, attempt to
        integrate the, (Appendix, 126)
    patented, (Appendix, 126)
    produced more, 60
    study of form is implicitly linked to these,
        (Appendix, 125)
ill
    -balanced, 31

163

and electric earth-currents, 69
and planetary processes, 30
double-wave, 92
field(s), 8, 41, 58, 64, 91-93
force(s), 8-9, 11, 37, 44
iron, 69
metal spheres, 8
needle, 91, 93
phenomena, 11, 23
pole, 44
storms, 91
variations, 92
magnetic field(s), 41, 58
    alteration in the, 92
    earth's, 69, 91-92
    of the earth, 93
        rotating, 8
    strength, 91
    strong, 41
    (Zeeman effect), 41
magnetic iron, 69
magnetism, 45, 81
    and destructive powers, 92
    and electricity, 92
    and the harmony of the spheres, 92
    diamagnetism for repulsion, 44
    earth, 92, (Appendix, 113, 125)
    electricity and, 41, 87
    fallen sound-ether and, 92
    formative forces that arise with, 44, 81
    high intensity of, 8
    hypothesis that fundamentally light cannot be
        influenced by, 41
    in the earth, 91
    in the healing of certain illnesses, 45
    is the counter-image of the chemical-ether, 45, 81
    light and, 41
    of metals, 44
    paramagnetism for attraction, 44
    references to, 92
    rhythms of earth-, 70, 91
    terrestrial, 18, 92
man
    and machine, 90
    -and-man, 88
    as a sensing being, 27
    as little as the activity of one, goes into that of
        another, 27
    astral vibrations of, 12
    connection of, 45, 87
    earth and man, 50, 93, (Appendix, 115)
    enters the earthly realm, 54
    evolution of earth and, 3

exists within the same lines of force, 28
far-reaching influence on the daily life of, 87
influence of spiritual *beings* upon, (Appendix,
    125)
intellectual fall of, into sin [*Intellektueller Sün-
    denfall*], vii, 1
moral side of, 11
or matter (book), 104
out of thankfulness to, 58
physiology of plant and, sub-nature and super-
    nature in the (booklet), 47-48
upper, 56
who attempted to gain sight of the spiritual world,
    88
who dreamed of tomorrow, the (book),
    (Appendix, 126)
would then take certain substances, 88
young, 4
manager(s)
    slight opposition which held sway among many,
    61
    the attitude [of the factory], 89
manna-sugar, 21
masses, amorphic, 27
master
    craftsman, (201)
    of my [Schiller's] time and strength, I am not
        always, 82
masters, 29
matchbox, 102
material
    and articles of clothing, 63
    astro-physical, 76
    compressible, 15, 59, 61
    copper-salt, 94
    empirical, 3
    fibre, 61
    fibrous, 67-68 (British patent)
    filling, 62
    filling and insulating, 63
    fluid and gaseous, 42
    for clothing, 64
    for natural protection from light and sun, 41
    for textiles, 59, 63
    light-sensitive, 85
    major part of the, 3
    non-, 27, 109
    one half of the cycle lies beyond the, 23
    plant, 46, 101
    private and confidential, 74-75
    production of a fibrous, 67 (British patent)
    production of substitute, 58
    published, (Appendix, 118)

side of man, 11
technology, 28
morality
altruistic, 11
experimenting on a higher stage of, 29
highest, 30
mortar, 21, 62
motion, 1
centrifugal, 96
Keely motor in, 11
mechanics of human, 30
planetary, 30
setting the coherer apparatus in, 89
wave, 11
motionless burning flame, 11
mountains, 14
mouth, human, 90
moved
according to the moon rhythms, 11
her [Lili Kolisko] institute to England, (Appendix, 121)
in 1926 to work in the chemistry/biology labora- tories, [Otto Eckstein], 122
to Dornach in 1938, [Ehrenfried Pfeiffer], 122
movements
corresponding to the course of the planets, 68
diametrically opposed, 107
in the animal body, 49
similar to eurythmy (etheric larynx), 12, 87
the mixing of quite specific burning substances bring definite, 88
verified, 19
wave, 29
which finally change to standing waves, 97
mucus, 31
mud, 62
mushroom-juice, 20
music
acoustics and, 25
add some, 19
and the theory of sound, 86
gas-lighting in the hall altered its shape according to the beat of the, 84
influence of, 88
on sensitive flames, 85
prerequisite for a quite special performance of, 25
stage a moving projection of colour by performing, 98
visible, 98
musical
flames, 85
instruments, 24
mysterious life-force, (Appendix, 119 (footnote))

Nachlassverwaltung [adminstration of the estate], 1, 4, (Appendix, 114, 121/122, 123)
narcotics, in the aliphatic series, 109
NATEL® (*Nationales Autotelefon* [national car tele- phone]), 63 (text and footnote)
nationalism, 29
natural energy of the universe, (Appendix, 119 (footnote))
natural science, 1, 3, 7, 13, 51, 75
and spiritual science [*und Geisteswissenschaft, Naturwissenschaft*] (book), (202)
anthroposophical, and the research institutes of *Der Kommende Tag A.G.* [the coming day plc], (Appendix, 121)
coming out of anthroposophy, 3
concepts, 27
elements of [*Elemente der Naturwissenschaft*] (journal), 41, 104
Goethean, 4
impulses arising from anthroposophy, 3
mathematics and, 3
path of anthroposophical schooling based on, 3
relationship of the various branches of, to astron- omy, the (third natural scientific course), 75 (text and footnote)
section, 1, 3-4, 7, 13, 20, 50, 79, (Appendix, 113, 115, 122), (201)
two pillars of anthroposophically-oriented, 37
natural scientific course(s), 3, 37 (text and footnote), 40, 75 (text and footnote), 95, 99, (Appendix, 114, 117, 121, 123)
natural scientist(s), 41, 101, (201)
natural world, (Appendix, 120)
nature, 44, 85
a living knowledge of [*Lebendiges Naturerkennen*], ix, 1
concepts that have the power to influence the external reality of, 89
element of warmth in the transitional region between soul-life and the physical in, 87
especially within the fluid and gaseous material, 42
how could we recognise the life-forces or forma- tive forces, which he [Steiner] named life- ether, in, 49
if there arises in, an effect such as heat, 33
image of the etheric formative forces that constitute its, 94
intervene in, 89
just as the natural process is a fact of, 89
new well-founded insight into the forces of, 81
non-material, 109
of *being*, (Appendix, 117)

null-sphere, 43
Nuremberg Rudolf Steiner school, 76, 79
nutrition, 102
    a holistic approach (book), 34
    the true basis of, sub-nature and super-nature in
        the physiology of plant and man (booklet),
        47-48

objections of Ehrenfried Pfeiffer and Ernst Marti,
    (Appendix, 119)
observation
    appropriate physical method of, 42
    experimental, 83
    is also being made at the apex of the spiral, 69
    Michael Faraday generalised this, 44
    ocular and photographic, 79
    of a coloured line or coloured band in the
        spectrum, 73
    of Dr. Kühn and Dr. Schiller's letter to Dr. von
        Siemens, 91
    of fast-moving phenomena, stroboscope for the
        personal [*rasch verlaufender Vorgänge, Stro-*
        boskop zum subjektiven Beobachten], (German
        patent), 85 (footnote)
    of the nature of peach-blossom (life-effect), 8
    personal, 74
observatory, astrophysical, 83
occult signs and symbols (book), (Appendix, 125)
occupation, 89
    human, 89
omnipresence, due to his [Eugen Kolisko's],
    (Appendix, 123)
optical, 16, 30
    brightener, 41
    experiments, (Appendix, 124)
    magneto-, 41
    or realm-of-sight, 99
optics, fundamentals of spectroscopy and, 76
optophony, 98
orchestra, 24
ore, radium [*radiumhaltig*], (cover diagram, ii)
organ
    in the middle of a space, 24
    into the earth, 25
    sunk into the earth, 25
organic
    and inorganic compounds, 10
    chemistry, 47
    connections between consciousness and
        temperature, 87
    processes of liver, kidneys, heart, and lungs, 19
    products, 28
    to inorganic chemistry, 46

transition where inorganic to, can be realised, 29
organisms
    should be used for detecting the effects, 48
    such as paramecium were suggested as reagents, 40
    the influence of daily and annual rhythms in, 42
organs
    eye, 17, 49, 83, 86, (Appendix, 117)
    heart, 10, 19
    kidneys, 19
    liver, 19
    lungs, 19
    of speech, 87
    skin, 34
    spleen, 102, (Appendix, 118)
    the action of poison on isolated, 110
orthodox
    science, 44
    timber chemistry, 21
oscillation, 11
    is the occasion for imitating the suffering, 27
    verification of the laws of, 10
oscillations
    frightful law of the harmonisation of the, 31
    harmonisation of certain, 30
    Keely motor and the future use of, 10
    new way of working with, 12
    through harmonised, 42
    tranformation of small, 47
    transposing the human pulse-rhythm into greater,
        12
outside
    activities do not pass from the centre to the, 76
    arise from, 30
    covered with planks both inside and, 62
    from inside towards the, 71
    from within towards the, 95
    mountains tower up by the force from, 14
    phosphorus (P) works thus from, 52
    the arrangement of the sphere in the plane, 9
    the electrical process takes place in a radial
        direction from, 103
    the whole electrical process took place much
        more in a radial direction from, 104
    towards the centre-point, run from the, 76
    two metal electrodes are brought inside and are
        lead, 83
oxygen
    and ozone, 60
    fibres are subsequently treated with, 67 (British
        patent)
    fibrous material
    being subsequently treated with, 68 (British
        patent)

is put on shelves and treated with, 68 (British
    patent)
mixture could be observed, 72
-ozone bath, 60
-producing substances, 67-68 (British patent)
sulphur and, 88
turns the earth into a life planet, 13

paper, 9, 103, (Appendix, 118)
    -making, 63
paramagnetism, 44
paramecium [small unicellular organism], 10, 40, 49
particle, 23
    transition from the wave to the, 23
particles
    diffusion consists not in the movement of physical,
        97
    electric, 63
patented, 60, 62, 85, (Appendix, 122, 126)
patent specification, 67 (British patent)
path
    curves, 98
    of knowledge, (Appendix, 120)
pattern of existence, (Appendix, 126)
peach-blossom [*Pfirsichblüt*]
    colour of the spectrum, 40
    poisonous and non-poisonous plant substances
        of, 9
    reagents for observing the nature of the, colour, 40
    reagents for the, colour, 40
    reagents for the observation of the nature of, (life-
        ether), 8
    the red and violet ends together produce the
        colour of, 8
peas, fodder, 59
peat, 15, 45, 57-59, 61-68, (Appendix, 113, 124)
    artificial wood made from, 62
    blocks the ascending and descending stream in
        the plant, 58 (footnote)
    -bog huts, 62
    bricks and panels, moulded, 62
    -bundles, 57 (footnote)
    clothes made from, 58
    dynamic-etheric influences must be removed
        from the, 59
    extraction and utilisation with special consider-
        ation for the available machines, equipment
        and their installation, including running costs,
        handbook of [*Torfgewinnung und Torfver-*
        wertung mit besonderer Berücksichtigung der
        erforderlichen Maschinen und Geräte nebst
        deren Anlage- und Betriebskosten, Handbuch
        der], 62

fibre department, 59
fibre laboratory, 66
fibre(s), 15, 45, 57-59, 61, 63, 65-67, (Appendix,
    113, 124)
    for loosening the soil, use, 58 (footnote)
    "great warmth-giving quality" of, 63
    hair, Düsseldorf, 63
    healing effects of, 62
    houses insulated with, 63
    in, the etheric has a descending tendency, 58
    is much better suited to the conservation of
        processes in matter, 58 (footnote)
    I [Smits] went from the implicit assumption that
        the, is dead, 58
    moorland, 57 (footnote)
    neither is the work on, progressing, 57
    one can make a compressible material out of, 59
    peculiarities of, fibre, 62/63
    plant fibres become, 58
    -powder, dried mixture of, 62
    process of manufacturing a textile fibre from, 62,
        67 (British patent)
    pulverised, 62
    refinement, several formulae for, 63
    refinement of, 57-58, 61, (Appendix, 113)
    some physical qualities of, 63
    suggestions about the use of, 64-65
    suggestions of Rudolf Steiner to Henri Smits for
        the refinement of, 61
    Swiss, 64
    -thread for the textile industry, manufacture of, 63
    utilisation, journal for bog culture and [*Torfverw-*
        ertung, Zeitschrift für Moorkultur und], 62
    widespread production of, 63
    wool, 63
pedagogy, 102
pedicles, new, 94
pencil, 72
    huge carpenter's, 104
    thick, 72
        carpenter's, 103
pendulum
    clock, 30
    movement of the, 23
penetration
    in order to also make it capable of, 64
    of natural rhythms, 42
    of the poison into the tissue, 110
people, 4, 7, 11, 18, 22, 73, 81, 88-89, 95, 104,
    (Appendix, 119-120), (202)
peptonisation, 21
perception
    of sound, 27

and technical research, (Appendix, 118)

physics

and biology, 3

and chemistry laboratory, 95

and spiritual science, 79

and technology, 86

department, (Appendix, 117)

institute, (Appendix, 124)

journal for [*Zeitschrift für Physik*] (periodical), 83

journal for technical [*Zeitschrift für Techn. Physik*] (periodical), 86

laboratory, 3, 18, 75, 79, (Appendix, 113, 115), (201)

modern, 23, (Appendix, 117)

Nobel prize in, 51

of the etheric, (Appendix, 117)

practical, 76

/scientific research institute, (Appendix, 124)

section at the Goetheanum, (Appendix, 122)

section of the scientific research laboratory, (Appendix, 115)

spiritual-scientific impulses for the development of [*Geisteswissenschaftliche Impulse zur Entwicklung der Physik*] [*Lichtkurs und Wärmekurs* (the light course and warmth course)], 99, (Appendix, 121)

student of mathematics and, 95

teacher of mathematics and, 76

physiological

and physical proof of the effectiveness of the smallest entities [*Physiologischer und Physikalischer Nachweis der Wirksamkeit kleinster Entitäten*] (paper), 31, 101/102

-biological department, 102

-biological research institute, 101

proof of the activity of smallest entities, a (paper), 31 (footnote), 102 (footnote)

physiology of plant and man, sub-nature and super-nature in the (booklet), 47-48

picture

-forming techniques of investigation, no, (Appendix, 127)

fragments of the, (Appendix, 122)

frames, 15, 59, 61, 64

in miniature of planetary motion, 30

method, rising (capillary dynamolysis), 102

of the growth-curve, 105

of the remarks of Rudolf Steiner, 28

pictures

capillary analysis, 108

moving, 98

which arose in connection with the corresponding planets in their constellations, 102

with a combination of potassium iodide (Kl) and mercury nitrate ($Hg(NO_3)_2$)…, 108

pigments

manufacture of, 46

plant, 9

pioneers

of etheric technology, (Appendix, 126)

of research into the etheric, (Appendix, 119)

of rhythm research, 43

of the research into the formative forces, (Appendix, 115)

pitches, 85

places

America, 11, 30, 102

Australia, (202)

Austria

Vienna [*Wien*], 24, 63, 97

boiler house [*Heizhaus*], 3, 70, (Appendix, 115), (201)

Brussels, 23, 96

Canada, (202)

England, 60, (Appendix, 121, 123), (202)

London, 62-63, (Appendix, 115)

Europe, 91

middle, 63

far east, (202)

Finland, 57 (footnote), 63

Sammatti, 63

France, 83

Barr, Alsace, 70 (footnote)

Grenoble, 41

Germany, 21, 44, 62

Berlin, 51, 57, 76, 84, (Appendix, 125)

Black Forest, 57 (footnote)

Bonn, 83

Burchau, (Appendix, 126)

Dorenwaid, Land Bayern, 65

Düsseldorf, 63

Einsingen bei Ulm, 40, 61-62, 93, (Appendix, 116, 122)

Erlangen, 76

Fulda, 44

Guldes-Mühle, 57-58, 101

Gustav-Siegle-Haus (now the *Philharmonie Gustav-Siegle-Haus* [philharmonic concert hall Gustav Siegle House]), Stuttgart, 103

Hamburg, 15, 57, 71

Haußmannstraße, Stuttgart, (Appendix, 118)

Kanonenweg, Stuttgart, 105, (Appendix, 115, 118)

Munich, iii, 46

Neckar river, 66

Neresheim, district of, 57

certain illnesses, 45
raised by Rudolf Steiner in 1920 and 1921, 48
regrets not having asked Rudolf Steiner any
further, (Appendix, 118)
research, of the '20s, (Appendix, 119)
the text of the actual, 27
three documented versions of answers to the
same, 47
to ask important, (Appendix, 118)
to clarify these, 34
we can discuss these, 83
without the teacher Rudolf Steiner at one's side
the way to the, 4
quicksilver, 12, 52, 94
alters the rhythm of assimilation in the plant, 94
and phosphorus (P), 94
coloured, 108
experiments with, 94
fertilised with a solution of, 94
on the plant, 94
-process, 94
was readily available for other experiments, 103

race, Jewish, (Appendix, 125)
radiation
and conduction of heat, 9
coming from above, 51
cosmic, 51
could also give undoubted protection against, 57
energy-rich short-wave, 63
from a source of heat, 35
heat-, 23
light-, 28
long-wave heat, 63
radio, (Appendix, 113)
broadcast Dr. Steiner's lecture by, 18
gradually reached private houses, 87
in the current use of, 18
technology, 84
transition from wireless telegraphy to, 87
transmission, 18, 84
-waves, 41
wireless telephony and, 18
radioactive, 45
decay, 20
isotopes, 19
radioactivity, 19, 45
radionics pioneer, (Appendix, 126)
radio waves, 41
radium
emanations, 109
ore [*radiumhaltig*], (cover diagram, ii)
rainwater, moistened with, 21

Ranunculus [*"little frog"* – Buttercup family], 20
rareification of matter on the sun, 76
ray
cathode, tube, 14
magnetic field orientated at right angles to the, 41
of light, 41
the light should, out on all sides, 26
x-, analysis of crystals, the reciprocal lattice and
the [*Röntgenanalyse der Kristalle, Das
Reziproke Gitter und die*], 97
x-, interference in the crystal, 23
rays
alpha-, 20
cause this process of decomposition, 9
cosmic electricity, 14
force-, 27
infrared, 38 (notes from Rudolf Steiner)
invisible heat, 38 (notes from Rudolf Steiner)
plant growth was influenced by sound waves or
cosmic, 103
ultraviolet, 38 (notes from Rudolf Steiner)
reagent, 65
for such minimal doses and dilutions, 109
for the etheric forces, 101
for the etheric formative forces, 10
for the etheric world, 101
for the spiritual and physical forces, 87
sensitive crystallisation as, 101
sensitive flame as a, 84
what we needed above all is a, 49
reagents
an eclipse of the sun affected her [Lilly Kolisko's],
44
bacteria, as, 49
especially suited as, 49
for observing the nature of the peach-blossom
colour, 40
for the etheric were made, 101
for the observation of the nature of peach-
blossom (life-ether), 8
for the peach-blossom colour, 40
organisms, 40, 42, 48
paramecium (caudatum), 10, 40, 49
physical-chemical methods and suitable processes
or, 37
realm
earthly, 54
etheric, 48, 58, 94
of acoustics, 48
of 'electrical energy,' 109
of physics and technology, 86
-of-sight, 99
of the etheric formative forces, (Appendix, 116)

-of-touch, 99

physical-sensible, 31

soul-, 9

realms, spiritual and material, 33

Realschule [secondary school], (201)

real suffering [*wesenhaften Quale*], 27

receiver, 90

sets, 90

telephone, 11, 84

recorders, wave, 90

reflected

and, changed in quality, 96

and comes back etherised towards the centre, 96

at the point of intersection, 106

in chemical action, 23

reflection

a, 97

direction of, 85

moment of, 87

of the extent, (Appendix, 122)

refraction of light, 28

refutation, atomism and its (booklet), 27, 99

relationship, 106-107

brought into, 71

of leaf growth to root growth, 106

of the various branches of natural science to astronomy, the (third natural scientific course), 75 (text and footnote)

things have to one another, 82

to the research orientation of the '20s, close, (Appendix, 126)

relativity, Einstein's theory of, 40

remedies

medicines like phenacetin ($C_{10}H_{13}NO_2$) are quite terrible, 22

pure shock, 22

these, are moreover not taken up by the astral body, 22

remedy, 22

against foot-and-mouth disease, 57

against the animal epidemic, 101

correct method of preparation and dosage of the, 101

different dilutions of the, 101

reports from the anthroposophical work in Germany [*Mitteilungen aus der Anthroposophischen Arbeit in Deutschland*], 70 (footnote), (Appendix, 124, 127)

reproduction

experimental, 76

of higher frequencies, 85

of sketches by Rudolf Steiner, 7

of the original handwritten '*Beantwortung von 6 Fragen* [answers to six questions],' a facsimile, 99

repulsion

diamagnetism for, 44

of antimony (Sb), 44

of bismuth (Bi) in the proximity of a magnet, 44

stage of long duration, 110

the ether is found on the sun with a negative sign and light effects and, 42

research

anthroposophical, 30-31, (Appendix, 113, 119, 122, 126)

anthroposophically-inspired, (Appendix, 119)

atomic, 51

being done?, Is enough [*geforscht?, Wird genügend*], (Appendix, 127)

chemical, physico-chemical and technical, (Appendix, 118)

equipment, 103

ether, 42

genuine, (Appendix, 127)

in the outer world, (Appendix, 114)

laboratory, 15-16, 37, 74, 76, 103, (Appendix, 115, 125), (201)

physics/scientific, (Appendix, 124)

potency, 101

rhythm, 37, 41, 43, 102

scientific, 1, 3, 5, 58, (Appendix, 113, 115, 117-118, 122, 124-125), (201)

stimulation for, 95

technical, (Appendix, 118)

workers, 61

research institutes, 30, (Appendix, 121)

anthroposophical, (Appendix, 113)

at the Goetheanum, 102

biological department (formerly the epidemic department), 101, 105, (Appendix, 114, 116-118)

biological institute at the Goetheanum, 43, 102, (Appendix, 114)

biological research institute, 102

epidemic department (became the biological department), 101-102, (Appendix, 116)

of *Der Kommende Tag* [the coming day], (Appendix, 113, 121)

physiological-biological department, 102

physiological-biological research institute, 101

two contemporaneous, (Appendix, 114)

two parallel, (Appendix, 115)

research on

electrical resistance heating, 34

gas heating, 34

the air breathed out through the nostrils, 31

181

cooled
    spectrum, 72
    vacuum, 16-17, 48, 70, 72, 74-75
cooling, 17, 33, 79
imposed rhythms, 69 (footnote)
nature, 47-48
sensibly, 37, 97
superimposition of red and violet, 40
supplements [*Beiträge*], 1, 27, 32, 40, 48, 86, 93, 98, 113, 121-122, 124, (202)
suppleness, 67 (British patent)
surface
    attained in the substance becomes 'reflected,' 96
    boundary, of the substance, 96
    of the sun, 17, 74, 76
    sun's, and interior, 75-76
    tension, 34
    unit in a unit of time, 22
surrogate, 88
surrogation, 87
symbols, occult signs and (book), (Appendix, 125)
synthetic colours, 46
system
    axis, 26
    entire, 71
    external forces affect the, 96
    nervous, 29
    of death, rigid physical, 94
    planetary, whole, 31
    remains self-contained, the, 96
    sense, 19
    that has an especially good reproduction of higher frequencies, 85

table, 102, 105
tangent, intersection of every, 98
task, 4, 15-18, 35, 37, 40, 45, 57-58, 61, 68-69, 71, 73, 76, 79, 81-82, 85, 90-91, 94, 99, 103-105, 107, (Appendix, 113, 124), (201)
tasks, 8, 35, 71
    allotted to mathematical physicists, 99
    and suggestions of Rudolf Steiner, 1
    could be taken up within the framework of the college of teachers, 10
    for experimental research, concrete, 7
    for natural scientific research, 5, (202)
    for natural scientists by Rudolf Steiner, 101
    for research, 4
    for the scientific research institute *Der Kommende Tag A.G.* [the coming day plc], 58
    given by Rudolf Steiner, 103, (202)
    group of, 84
    indicated in the Schiller file, 103

of my [Steiner's] life, the most beautiful, 99
of Rudolf Steiner, 7, 37
of the research institute, 57
of this institute, 3
one of the earliest, 46
one of the first, 71
our anthroposophically-oriented world conception will have significant, 43
placed before the Stuttgart research laboratory, 15
Rudolf Steiner had set for Dr. G. Wachsmuth and Dr. E. Pfeiffer, 12
Rudolf Steiner set the researchers, (Appendix, 118)
set by Rudolf Steiner, 10
two, (Appendix, 113)
unfulfilled, 4
tattvas [or *tatwas*], 50, (Appendix, 123)
teacher, (201)
    in the Waldorf school, 4
    of mathematics and physics, 76
    Rudolf Steiner, 4
team-work, (Appendix, 119)
Technischen Hochschule [technical high school] in Stuttgart, 1, (201)
technology, 14
    advance of, 87
    aim of, 41
    constructive, 48
    department, (Appendix, 117)
    electro-, 79
    etheric, (Appendix, 113, 119, 126)
    future, 42, 48
    godless, 30
    in the future, 42
    inversion, (Appendix, 119)
    modern, 65, 85
    moral, 28
    new, 48, 84
    new natural force into, 48
    of the future, 31/32, 49
    radio, 84
    realm of physics and, 86
    science and, 1
    Tesla, (Appendix, 126)
    use of the rhythmical in, 42
    vacuum, 21
telegraphy, 92
    wireless, 18, 87, 89
telephone
    Bell, after inventing the, 84
    greater than the, 84
    light-, 84
    national car (NATEL® (*Nationales Autotelefon*)),

63 (text and footnote)
    receiver, 11, 84
    wireless, 63
telephones, 62
telephony, wireless, 18
telescope, 15
temperature, 44
    above 37°C should be avoided, 59
    body, 22, 35, 110
    certain, 17
    condensation, 16
    constant, 15
    cycle, 44
    detectors, 85
    difference in, 17
    further raised to white heat, 45
    gas discharges dependent on pressure and, 83
    gradient, 17
    high, 35
    influence of, 22
    low, 79
    lower, 72
    of 22°C, 105
    organic connections between consciousness and, 87
    room, 16, 106, 110
    shifts, 35
    very low, 19
temperatures
    daily global, 44
    heat 'elements' to higher and higher, 24
    inlet and outlet, 16
    low, 35, 72, 74-76, 81
    lower, 76
tensile-strength, 60, 67-68 (British patent)
tension
    high-, 79
    surface, 34
term
    coined by Dr. Rupert Sheldrake, (Appendix, 119 (footnote))
    coined by Dr. Wilhelm Reich, (Appendix, 119 (footnote))
    'darkness' that implies a combination of the sub-physical forces, 82
    'light' is often used to imply a combination of the entire etheric forces, 82
    long-, permission, 79
    new way was used predominantly by the many members who were fundamentally nostalgic for the old 'theosophical' era of the general anthroposophical society, (Appendix, 122)
terrestrial, 8-9, 34

extra-, 8-9, 33, 35, 42, 51, 81
    current of warmth, 33
    origin, 51
    warmth, 81
current of warmth, 33
current(s), 92-93
magnetism, 18, 92
warmth, 42, 81
tests
    and corrections to the equipment, after, 78
    could not be continued, 75
    for the day and night effects, 68
    from Upper Swabia, 57
    in this series of, he [Steiner] saw the possibility of acquiring more knowledge of the formative forces, 75
    pilot, 40
    pre-treated water, 44
    should be recommended, 66
tetrahedral character, atom of, 27
textiles
    making, 59, 61
    raw material for, 59, 63
theorists, 41
theory
    commentary on Goethe's colour, 37 (footnote)
    of colour, Goethe's, 28, 99
    of electricity, unsaddle the accepted, 104
    of formative forces, [Wachsmuth] creator of the, (Appendix, 116)
    of relativity, Einstein's, 40
    of sound, music and the [*vom Schall, Musik und die Lehre*] (article), 86
    of the senses, 3
    realities of quantum, 22, 96
theosophical
    circles, 50
    era, old, (Appendix, 122)
    movement, history of the, 70 (footnote)
theosophy (book), 33
therapeutic
    methods and products and the like, (Appendix, 120)
    purposes, 63
thermometers, 42
thinking, 4
    activity of, 103
    bearer of, 52
    fails, usual customary, 109
    no longer conforms to the wealth of facts, 88
    particularly of the rotating magnetic field between the pole pieces, 8
'third force,' so-called, (Appendix, 126)

thought, 8, 74, (Appendix, 117)
    about it daily, 4
    forms, chemical, 29
    from Rudolf Steiner, I [Pelikan] had requested a
        leading, 19
    of as encouragement, 61
    of as having two ends but with one end, may not
        be, 71
    of crystallisation, 57
    of fuchsias and perhaps roses, 94
    test what had before only existed in, 103
    transference, 30
thoughts
    are carried through in a sufficiently active manner,
        103
    bearer of, 13
    brings the, 13
    concentrate our, 87
    if we pull together this train of, (Appendix, 124)
    in salt (NaCl), 54
    in the depositing of salt (NaCl), 54
    power of, 29
    that are fundamental to his [Steiner's] proposals,
        81
    turned again to peat fibre, 63
thread
    artificial, 62
    cord or, 60
    could only manufacture about 60 kg of, 63
    forming plants, 59
    peat-, 63
    spin-able, 61
    textile, 61, 63
    waxed, 60
    wire or, 11
threefold
    commonwealth, the time of the [Dreiglieder-
        ungszeit] (book), 61, 68, 71, 98, (Appendix,
        124)
    concept of the atom, Rudolf Steiner's [Atombeg-
        riff, Rudolf Steiners dreifacher] (lecture manu-
        script), (Appendix, 126)
    social order, 11
threefolding, 106
three-phase generator, 8
Tibetan
    mysteries, 11, 87
    mystery centres, 12
tide
    tree stem diameters fluctuate with, 44
    wave of the atmosphere, 92
tiles, decorative materials and, 63
timber chemistry, orthodox, 21

timbres, 85
time
    and energy, 95, (201)
    anthroposophical circles of the, (Appendix, 125)
    as a factor, 22
    a scientific whole which is urgently needed in our,
        (Appendix, 120)
    -body, 37
    Christmas, 108
    co-workers were employed on a full-, basis,
        (Appendix, 116)
    equations the dependence on, 96
    I am not always master of my [Schiller's], 82
    in Goethe's, 99
    money invested at that, (Appendix, 127)
    most important task of that, (Appendix, 124)
    new knowledge which must come in the course
        of, 88
    not uncommon at the, (Appendix, 118)
    of the threefold commonwealth [Dreiglieder-
        ungszeit] (book), 61, 68, 71, 98, (Appendix,
        124)
    own notebooks from the, (Appendix, 121)
    possibility did not arise again in my [Smits'] life-,
        61
    processes of space and, 50
    process is expressed not by, 96
    promise of fulfilling within a useful period of,
        (Appendix, 118)
    published for the first, 3
    school leaves me no, 4
    sowing, 66
    standard description of this, (Appendix, 115)
    that elapses until the moon is again at the same
        place in the heavens, 91
    the Schiller file was put together, (Appendix,
    123)
    unit of, 22
    various remarks to the co-workers at that, 3
    was not yet ripe for the etheric forces to become
        operative, 11
    was not yet ripe to make use of the power of the
        ether, 48
    we could perhaps then get the necessary results in
        a tenth of the, (Appendix, 120)
times
    former, 87
    olden, 89
tissue, 110
    firm, 52
    -fluidity, 52
    saturation of the, 110
tone, (Appendix, 117)

x-ray
    analysis, 97
    interference, 23

yarn(s), 61, 63, 67 (British patent)
yearbook of the natural science section of the
    free high school for spiritual science at the
    Goetheanum Dornach: Gaia-Sophia
    [*Jahrbuch der naturwissenschaftlichen
    Sektion der Freien Hochschule für Geisteswissen
    schaft am Goetheanum Dornach: Gäa Sophia*]
    (annual), 20, 43, 50, 94
yoga, Indian, 50

Zeeman effect, 41
zero-point, 33
zodiac, positions in the, 43

Paul-Eugen Schiller
Natural Scientist
b. 4.10.1900 Stuttgart-Bad Cannstatt (Germany)
d. 18.11.1992 Arlesheim (Switzerland)

Paul-Eugen Schiller since 1926, with a short break during world war II, was co-worker at the Goetheanum, most of the time in the Natural Science Section. Became known above all for his experiments with sound-sensitive flames. In the middle of his career the research into heat quality stands out. He pursued experimentally, *inter alia*, whether water that was heated in different ways (with gas or electricity [and wood?, Tr.]) showed differences in qualities, e.g. in their effects on plants. Further, he researched sensitive processes such as the reaction of fine metal spirals at various times of day and night; similarly with the behaviour of fluids.

Sadly, at the end of his life he confirmed that apart from the experiments with the flame the expected results failed to appear. This apparent lack of success became in any case a new fruitful approach to the etheric for his successors.

Paul-Eugen Schiller was born on 4 October 1900 in Stuttgart-Bad Cannstatt. He had a humble background, his parents worked with selfless devotion in order to enable their children to have a good education. Already as a child Paul-Eugen tended to shut himself off. The mother once asked the 8-year old why he was always so serious and not like other children who would happily play. *"Because something was always looking over my shoulder!"* (Quoted by Heertsch 1993). Paul-Eugen experienced this 'something' not as hostile but rather as a warning.

His school days were continually painful. At 14 years he left the *Realschule* [secondary school] and embarked on a period of learning in a machinery workshop. At last he was free! His teacher, a master craftsman, encouraged his technical abilities and strengthened his self-confidence. Discharged from military service he could in 1919 take part in 'emergency courses' for helping those who had suffered in the war, continue his maturation and conclude his studies for a diploma in engineering at the *Technischen Hochschule* [Technical High School] in Stuttgart. The offer of a place as an assistant in the Technical High School in Stuttgart, however, was rejected – the meeting with Anthroposophy lead to another decision.

Early in 1920 he heard three public lectures by Rudolf Steiner. A visit to the Goetheanum and more lectures decided him. The connection with Anthroposophy was at first not easy for Schiller. He explained how he listened to the lectures sitting behind a curtain because he could not bear the gaze of the speaker: *"everything went against the grain but he forced himself to listen because he was inwardly convinced that he had found the only way into the future."* Finally the decision was clear: he would dedicate his work to Rudolf Steiner and Anthroposophy. In 1923 he became an assistant at the research laboratory in Stuttgart and worked on a task set by Rudolf Steiner.

After the death of Rudolf Steiner, Guenther Wachsmuth, leader of the Natural Science Section called Schiller to Dornach. From the dissolved Stuttgart Institute he brought apparatus and set-up a simple Physics Laboratory in the *Heizhaus* [boiler house] at the Goetheanum. The strained financial position and the building of the second Goetheanum meant, of course, that the necessary money for research had to be earned. The numerous conferences, lectures and seminars, also the internal Society matters, took time and energy.

Among other things Schiller worked on the sound-sensitive gas flame. In this connection he developed the so-called super stroboscope that different firms produced. On one such journey in England he was surprised by the outbreak of world war II. He was interned and a few months later, together with 3,000 other internees was shipped to Australia. The ship was torpedoed and 1,500 people lost their lives. Schiller survived.

In Australia he lectured regularly on Anthroposophy. In 1946 Schiller could take up his work in Dornach again; at first in Wachsmuth's secretariat, with lecture courses held mainly in Switzerland. Continuous research was again hardly possible because of technical considerations and co-operation with Swiss firms to provide the necessary resources for the laboratory work. In connection with these activities he became acquainted with Marie Bourquin-Troesch, for whose firm he corresponded with the far east. A friendship developed and in 1951 they married. In the following years Schiller made longer lecture tours, including U.S.A., Canada, South America, New Zealand and Australia.

His natural-scientific questions, orientated to the tasks given by Rudolf Steiner to the Stuttgart laboratories, he accompanied with fundamental anthroposophical studies. As a result of this, for instance, is his writing about the *being* of heat. In later years he spoke about the anthroposophical Inner Path and later this theme was published.* His manner of speaking expressed care and responsibility, warmth and encouragement. He himself, towards the end of his life, declared that this 'Inner Path' had been too little taken into account and that it should not only complement but penetrate scientific research. He died at a great age on 18 November 1992.

Werke [Works]: *Naturwissenschaft und Geisteswissenschaft* [Natural Science and Spiritual Science], Dornach 1957; *Vom Wesen der Wärme* [On the Nature of Heat], Dornach, 1961; *Der anthroposophische Schulungsweg* [The Anthroposophical Path of Inner Schooling], Dornach, 1979; 2nd edition 1990; *Anregungen und Aufgabenstellungen von Rudolf Steiner für naturwissenschaftliche Forschungen* [Suggestions and the Setting Up of Tasks for Natural Scientific Research Given by Rudolf Steiner: The 'Schiller File'], in: *Beiträge zur Rudolf Steiner Gesamtausgabe* [Supplements to the Collected Edition of Rudolf Steiner], Nr. 122, Dornach 2000; Übersetzungen ins Englische, Italienische, Spanische und Russische erschienen; zahlreiche Beiträge in *Was in der Anthroposophischen Gesellschaft vorgeht*, weitere in *Das Goetheanum* und Fachzeitschriften [Translations into English, Italian, Spanish and Russian appeared; numerous contributions in *What is happening in the Anthroposophical Society* and in *The Goetheanum* and technical periodicals].

Literature [Literature]: Hagemann, E.: *Bibliographie der Arbeiten der Schüler Dr. Steiners* [Bibliography of the Work of the Pupils of Dr. Steiner], o.O. [no place (of publication)] 1970; Heertsch, A.: Paul Eugen Schiller, in: *Was in der Anthroposophischen Gesellschaft vorgeht* [What is happening in the Anthroposophical Society] 1993, Nr. 7.

BIOGRAPHY by Johannes Kühl translated from: '*Anthroposophie im 20. Jahrhundert: Ein Kulturimpuls in biografischen Porträts* [Anthroposophy in the 20th Century: A Cultural Impulse in Biographical Portraits],' Edited by Bodo von Plato, Verlag am Goetheanum, Dornach, 2003, S. 703-704.

---

* Schiller, Paul Eugen, 'Rudolf Steiner and Initiation: The Anthroposophical Path of Inner Schooling – A Survey,' The Anthroposophic Press, Spring Valley, N.Y., 1990.

www.ingramcontent.com/pod-product-compliance
Lightning Source LLC
Chambersburg PA
CBHW061135030426
42334CB00003B/41